Crisis and Commitment

Crisis and Commitment

The Life History of a French
Social Movement

Alexander Alland Jr.

Columbia University, New York, USA

with

Sonia Alland

harwood academic publishers
Australia • Canada • France • Germany • India • Japan
Luxembourg • Malaysia • The Netherlands • Russia
Singapore • Switzerland

Copyright © 2001 OPA (Overseas Publishers Association) N.V. Published by license under the Harwood Academic Publishers imprint, part of The Gordon and Breach Publishing Group.

Amsteldijk 166
1st Floor
1079 LH Amsterdam
The Netherlands

British Library Cataloguing in Publication Data

A catalogue record for this book is available from the British Library.

ISBN 90-5823-199-2 (softcover)

The last several years have seen a spate of anthropological books treating violence in culture. These are good and important works. To this date, however, anthropology has ignored an equally important and opposing aspect of culture, active nonviolence. This book is written to help fill the gap. It is dedicated to the memory of Guy Tarlier, a major actor in a ten-year nonviolent struggle against state power in France and the pre-eminent figure of the post-struggle community. Guy died of cancer on May 7, 1992.

Contents

At an opening of *Ecomusée* Exhibit from left to right: Jacques Lang, then Minister of Culture; Guy Tarlier; Pierre Bonnefous. Credit: *GLL*.

Preface

The reader will note the use of both "I" and "we" throughout this book. This is an artifact of how it was researched and written. The fieldwork on which it is based was in every sense a joint venture, and references to "we" in the text reflect this. Although Sonia Alland was concerned with every aspect of the work—fieldwork, the interpretation of data, and a great deal of editing in the final version—the use of the first-person pronoun reflects the fact that the book's overall structure, its theoretical orientation and the major portion of the writing are mine. Furthermore, it was Sonia's choice to have her name under "with" rather than as a coauthor. This book could not have been researched and written without her full-time participation in the research and editing processes.

Real names of informants and actors are used in this book. The Larzac is well known in France and the actors involved have been named frequently and cited in the press during and after the struggle. Some of the data presented, particularly the interviews, were judged by us or our informants to be delicate enough to require anonymity. The reader should in no case be led to believe that because a name is left out, the individual concerned is less important than persons named.

In some cases negative opinions of others or of Larzac activities are attributed to specific individuals. In these cases we feel that the status in the community of the person concerned will not be affected (he or she has left the community and is no longer involved in plateau activities or the situation described is not considered damaging) and/or we have the understanding that the names of individuals providing such data can be used.

To guide the reader through the many associations, a list of acronyms and their translations will be found after the Introduction.

All speeches and documents—unless otherwise specified—are our translations.

This work could not have come to fruition without the extraordinarily kind help of three individuals—Florence Filaski, Jane Lamplighter and Kerri Lubell Nelson—who gave generously of themselves to my aging parents. Each contributed, in different ways, to making sure that my father and mother were properly cared for during our absence from this country. There is no way to thank them adequately for their selfless devotion.

We also wish to express our appreciation to the following colleagues who took the time to read this book in draft and make helpful suggestions: Professors Elaine Combes-Schilling, David Koester, Robert Murphy and Susan Carol Rogers; Drs. Robin Nagel and Joel Wallman. Our thanks go, as well, to Chantal de Crisenoy for a careful reading of the manuscript and her useful commentary. As the principal author of the work, I take full responsibility for any errors it might contain.

Alexander Alland, Jr.

Acknowledgments

We thank the following individuals for their help in bringing this project to completion. Many of them provided us with one or more interviews. (A date after a name signals that the individual was interviewed, as well as the month and year of that interview.)

Didier Adnet, January 1989; Dominique Aldon, August 1984; Michel Alla, June 1987; Alain Alla, June 1987; Françoise Alla, January 1988; Lucien Alla, January 1988; Odette Alla, January 1988; Odile Alla, September 1988; Chantal Alméras; Michel Alméras; Chantal Alvergnas, July 1986; Jean Andrieu, Mayor of La Cavalerie, June 1988; Georges Artières, May 1989; Albert Austruy, January 1988; Claude Baillon, December 1988; Elizabeth Baillon, July 1984; Jean-Luc Bernard, July 1984; Nicole Bernard; François Boé, March 1989; Catherine Boé, March 1989; Pierre Bonnefous, July 1984, 1987, 1988; Daniel Boscheron, July 1986; Jeanine Boubal, August 1989; José Bové, July 1984; Cathy Burguière, August 1987; Sylvie Burguière, August 1987; Christiane Burguière, July 1986; Jean-Marie Burguière, September 1987; Janine Burguière, June 1985; Léon Burguière, December 1987; Marie-Hélène Burguière-Bascoule, November 1988; Pierre Burguière, July 1984, 1988; Alain Cabanes, February 1988; Brigitte Cadot, April 1989.

Elizabeth Calazel, April 1988; Robert Calazel, April 1988; Jean-Michel Caron, June 1988; Maryse Caron, June 1988; Joëlle Chancenotte, December 1988; Jean Chesneaux, July 1985; Marcel Chinonis, February 1988; Didier Coppin, July 1986; Aline Coppin, July 1986; Jean-Louis Coulon, December 1988; Michel Courtin, November 1988, Ghislaine Dambrin, April 1988; Eric Darley, July 1986; Daniel Darras, July 1984; Nobué Darras, July 1984; Elie Depardon, June 1988; Marie Depardon, June 1988; Gérard Deruy, Mayor of Millau, May 1988; Pierre-Yves de Boissieu, October 1987; Chantal de Crisenoy, July 1986; Alain Desjardin, July 1985; Mario Digirolamo, September 1987; Danièle Domeyne, July 1987; Christian Dumas, July 1986; Jacques Dupont, Mayor of La Couvertoirade, May 1988; Susie Emmick; Philippe Fauchot, April 1988; Gilbert Fenestraz, January 1988; Martine Flahault, July 1986; Alain Flottard, October 1987; Gabriel Flottard; Yves Frémion, December 1988; Marie Gaillard, October 1987; Gerard Galtier, July 1986, January 1988; Jean-Claude Galtier, July 1985; Renaud Galtier, February 1988; Isabelle Gastal, July 1987; Robert Gastal, July 1984.

Francine Gellot, August 1984; Jean-Louis Geniez, Mayor of Ste. Eulalie du Cernon, December 1988; François Giacobbi, December 1988; Patrick Goujon, February 1988; Anne Greslou, February 1988; Auguste Guiraud, April 1988; Dominique Guiraud, September 1988; Jean-Yves Guiraud,

September 1988; Marie-Rose Guiraud, April 1988; Philippe Guiraud, September 1988; Laurence Hingre; Louis Joinet; Elie Jonquet; Jeanne Jonquet, August 1987; Madame Jordy (of Pierrefiche), July 1985; Benjamin Knopff, July 1986; Pierre Laur, June 1988; Raymond Laval, October 1988; Michel Lefeuvre, July 1984; Nicole Lefeuvre, July 1984; Elizabeth Lepetitcolin, November 1988; Blandine Léonard; Dominique Léonard; Patrick Lescure, September 1988; Léon (Pépé) Maillé, July 1985; Jeanne (Mémé) Maillé, July 1985; Léon Maillé, July 1985; Osla Maillé, July 1985; Richard Maillé, September 1987; Paul Maistre, April 1988; Pierre Marcilhac, January 1988; Pierrette Marcilhac, January 1988; Michel Marguerite, October 1987; François Mathey, July 1985; Marie-Jo Mathey, July 1985; Elise Mauron, August 1984; Jean Mauron, August 1984.

Monique Mauron; Robert Mazeran, February 1988; Marie-Catherine Menozzi; Marie Möller, October 1987; Alice Monier, July 1984, 1987; Suzanne Morain, June 1985; Pierre Morain, June 1985; Francis Moreau, June 1985; Roger Moreau, August 1984; Alain Moulin, December 1987; Danièle Moulin; Maryse Moulin, December 1987; Sophie Munoz, January 1989; Brigette Muret, October 1988; Eric Muret, October 1988; Hervé Ott, July 1984; André Parenti, January 1988; Bernard Parsy, July 1987; Ginette Parsy, July 1987; Joseph Pineau, December 1987; Christiane Pinet, July 1985; François Pingaud, January 1988; Robert Pirault, February 1988; Christine Poutout, December 1988; Simonne Proner, July 1984; Jean Rabier, Mayor of La Roque Ste. Marguerite, June 1988; Marie-Laure Reyes, October 1988; Serge Riausset; Gilbert Rieu; Dominique Robin, June 1988; Christian Roqueirol, February 1988; Francis Roux, May 1988; François Roux, October 1988; Maryse Roux, May 1988; Jean-Claude Sanchez, August 1984; Jean-Emile Sanchez, July 1986; Robert Siméon, April 1989; Guy Tarlier, July 1984, 1988; Marizette Tarlier, July 1984; Benoit Thélen, July 1985; Christine Thélen, July 1985; Volker Tönnatt, September 1988; Hélène Trichereau, October 1987; Michel Trichereau, October 1987; Claudine Vaillant; Auguste Valette, January 1988; François Vérier; Jean-Marc Vignolet, October 1988; Michèle Vincent, October 1987; Claude Voron, July 1986; Pierre Vuarin.

Introduction to the Second Edition

Since the first edition of this book was published in 1994, the Larzac community has proved its staying power as a movement for progressive change in French society. It is now nineteen years since the victory in 1981, and social action remains the force that binds the plateau's militants together.

TRADITIONS, INVENTED AND OTHERWISE

In the first edition I borrowed the concept of 'invented tradition' to describe how the people involved in the Larzac struggle created a charter for resistance against state power. This set the stage for the extension of their concerns from saving their own farms from expropriation towards action on national and international issues. 'Invented tradition' means the creation in the present of a past, the existence of which may, in reality, lie more in the realm of fiction than in fact. What matters in an invented tradition is not its truth value but its ability to mobilize a sense of common identity in a social group, culture, nation, or state. The major element of the past was the adoption of the word 'peasant' to describe the farmers of the plateau. However, while the word was borrowed from the past, its connotation was radically changed to serve the present. Previously, the term had come to represent an 'other,' a living anachronism, ignorant of the wave of modernization that swept France in the years beginning with the close of the Second World War. 'Peasants,' if they existed at all, were seen as remnants of backwardness among small-scale rural agriculturists: people who clung to ancient farming practices in marginal areas of remote parts of the countryside. Those Larzac informants who were native to the plateau and who, during the struggle, became known as 'purs porcs' told us how they were considered outcasts by their neighbors in the city of Millau. They bitterly resented the fact that in the city's schools, their urban neighbors' children would tease those from the plateau saying they "smelled of animal manure." The Larzac movement changed all that. 'Peasant' was adopted as a term of pride and resistance.

This 'invented tradition' was different from a construction based purely on a real or imagined past. It had a dynamic of its own. This is the reason why, borrowing from the art critic Harold Rosenberg, I called the Larzac's constructed ideology a 'tradition of the new.' Let me now clarify why I feel that this distinction is so important. The change of the word 'peasant' into a term of pride was accompanied by major changes in ideology, stimulated, in part, by recent arrivals to the plateau who, in the 1950s and 60s, bought or rented large farms in the west, by the more politically radical squatters who flocked to the area, by summer volunteers who participated in the building of an illegal *bergerie*, and by members of support groups (the Larzac committees), who joined the struggle soon after it began. These groups contributed to the radicalization of the indigenous Larzac population by challenging the acceptance of what had been considered immutable truths. The reader of this book in its first edition will remember Marie-Rose Guiraud relating how traditional Larzac farmers had previously held unquestioning faith in the words and deeds of local authorities—the prefect, the gendarmes, and the priests. In the new context the term 'peasant' represented, first and foremost, prior and inherent rights to the land in the face of the State's claim to eminent domain. Thus, if the adoption of 'peasant' was a symbolic return to the past, the past became a legitimation of defiance against those very authorities to whom peasants in past had submitted without qustion.

In his excellent book, *Memories Cast in Stone*, a study of the Greek island of Kalymnos (Oxford and New York: Berg, 1998), the anthropologist, David E. Sutton, offers the following criticisms of the concept of 'the invention of tradition' as it was used to analyze the development of a nationalist conciousness:

> First, excessive emphasis was placed on the construction of the past from above: its creation was viewed as an elite project controlled by intellectuals and national leaders, who then disseminated the results to the masses...such a view tends to deny agency to the people who, seemingly, passively accept such inventions.
>
> When we look at modern Greece in these terms we must perform a difficult balancing act in order to capture the interplay of forces. We must recognize the interconnectedness of social processes across national borders and cultures—the shaping influences of Western European projections on modern Greek consciousness—while at the same time not reducing local historical consciousness to a reflection of, or resistance to, Western impositions (Sutton, 1996:6)

The 'tradition of the new' on the Larzac represents a case in which a diverse group of militants developed a powerful set of symbols used to challenge, rather than support, French nationalism and the highly centralized French state. In this case the new 'tradition' was designed specifically to counter the historically strong and centralized nationalism of France.

It is important to note as well, that the Larzac 'peasants' did not invent their tradition in a vacuum. As I have already pointed out in the introduction to the first edition, the entire Larzac struggle and its ideology must be placed in the historical context of the events of 1968 and their aftermath, which saw a major challenge to French state authority, a challenge that struck directly at the center of power in Paris. If the use of the term 'peasant' and later 'pur porc' by Larzac farmers was, in part, their *own* response to the State, it owes some of its resonance on the left to the elevation of peasants to saintly stature in China, then under Maoist ideology. The Maoists who arrived in the 1970 were the first left-radicals to support what was then a nascent struggle. Although they never establisled a power base on the plateau, French Maoists, following Mao's ideas of peasant revolution, seized upon the camp extension as a political cause even perhaps as the prelude to revolution! Informants who experienced this phase of the protest were unanimous in telling us that, although the Maoists were seen as strange outsiders they played an early role in raising the consciousness of the local population to the injustice of the extension.

The reader of this edition will discover that the legitimacy of a nationally powerful post-struggle leader, José Bové, is in full conformity with the ideas presented in the first edition concerning the central importance of the 'new peasantry' in the original struggle. During the course of the *lutte* Bové, a nonviolent radical with intellectual and urban roots, squatted on a farm in Montredon, the more radical part of the Larzac in the 1970s, where he came to be accepted as a Larzac 'peasant'. After the camp extension was annulled, Bové continued and intensified his militant actions. In the immediate post-struggle years he was influential in the establishment of an innovative long-term leasing program which attracted young farmers to the plateau, allowing them to rent farms on land that had been expropriated by the army. In the years that followed, continuing to use his base as a small farmer on the Larzac, Bové became a prominent farm union organizer and, more recently, leader of a series of popular protests against globalization both in France and internationally.

Pierre Burguière, one of the original figures of the *lutte* and a 'Pur Porc,' recently reaffirmed José Bové's 'peasant' status in an interview we conducted in the winter of 1999–2000 and have published in the last chapter of this edition. In that interwiew he compared himself to José, by saying: "I was a peasant who, by force of circumstance, became a militant and José began as a militant but, by force of circumstance during the struggle, became a peasant." He went on to say that José's attachment to the land was real and profound. In saying these things about Bové, Pierre was not down playing José's intellect and strategic insight, but rather emphasizing that his legitimacy as a leader among his peers (beyond his evident talents) rests squarely on his acquired identity as a 'peasant'.

DISCORDS

In the first edition I noted my lack of neutrality in regard to the Larzac struggle. In all my ethnographic work I have always felt a commitment to the people I choose to study and live among. This leads me to make a distinction between objectivity and impartiality. In my analyses of the Larzac I have attempted to remain objective, treating the data as best I can honestly and as completely as possible but, at the same time, I wish to reiterate that I have been and remain today a supporter of the Larzac and much of what it stands for. In this sense I am far from a neutral observer. This does not mean, however, that I agree with everything plateau militants decide to do nor with everything they believe. For example, while not all Larzac militants are anarchists, (this would be far from the truth), most of them adhere to an ideology which fosters suspicion of and, in some cases, a rejection of *anything* official; anything coming from the established center of power. In the case of the Larzac, as the events testify, this can be a healthy attitude, but it can also lead to a non-reflective approach in domains that go beyond the circumstances of a specific case. If I may be granted a generalization about culture, I would say that a feature of human symbolic life is to build persistent systems of thought that display a high degree of internal consistency, even if they contradict a set of relative and easily available facts. It is the persistence of systems that reinforces and perpetuates ideology.

To return to the Larzac as an example, a large number of plateau inhabitants reject modern medical theory and uncritically accept various forms of alternative medicine. (From a comparative perspective this appears to be equally true in the United States, particularly among those on the far-left and far-right of the political spectrum who, like the Larzac, reject the dominant political system.) Homeopathy is particularly popular among Larzac inhabitants along with herbal medicine. While I admit that some herbal medicines may be effective, I remain unconvinced of the efficacy of homeopathy. It is based on a belief system that anthropologists refer to as 'sympathetic magic', in which a chemical that causes symptoms similar to those produced by a particular disease agent is given to a patient in very low doses. The assumption behind this system is that, in popular terms, cure comes from a 'bit of hair of the dog that bit you' or, in this case, *something like* the hair of the dog that bit you. In fact, the majority of homeopathic medicines are made up of a succession of weak dilutions of the purported curative agent, to the point where they lack even a single molecule of it. To counter the objection that the agent is no longer present in the water, the defenders of homeopathic theory claim that the chemically simple water molecule has a memory. No scientific evidence exists to support homeopathy. In conversations with Larzac friends I have attempted, with a significant lack of success, to explain why I am unconvinced.

Cognate to their support for homeopathy is the Larzac's almost unanimous rejection of, and active opposition to *any* transgenic modification of plants and animals. They are horrified by the idea that a gene from a fish that produces resistance to freezing has been inserted into the genome of strawberries, considering this a violation of natural law. They are apparently unaware that natural transgenics has occurred as part of natural selection since the beginning of life forms. For example, the 'engines' that run the cellular metabolic processes the mitochondria, were long ago injected into animal cells, via the action of invading viruses. An article published in the January 2000 issue of the semi-popular science journal, *La Recherche*, by Andrew Chesson and Philip James, draws a useful distinction between what they refer to as 'risk' versus 'danger'. This is an important point because, while it is logically impossible to eliminate all potential danger from a new product, it is possible to estimate its risk. In their judgement:

> ...the problem posed by genetically modified plants remains hypotheti-cal: no death or disease has been observed that can be attributed with any certainty to the consummation of food containing genetically modified plants. In Great Britain...the debate is so biased that any coherent discussion has become practically impossible. For the estab-lishment, all accusations of danger from food containing genetically products is considered as a nonscientific manipulation of the facts, stimulated by an almost religious fervor against all genetic manipula-tion. On the other side all discussion related to the possibility and potential interest of biotechnologies leads to a suspicion that its author is in the pay of Monsanto or some other agribusiness or government agency.
>
> First, let us distinguish between danger and risk. This may be illustrated by an experiment conducted recently in the U.S. on the Monarch butterfly which has a reputation for its beauty. Caterpillars of this butterfly were fed with corn leaves artificially covered with the pollen from plants rendered resistant to a parasite by the introduction into its genome of a gene producing an insecticide. These caterpillars turned out to have a slower growth than normal and a higher frequency of mortality than a control group fed on pollen from non genetically modified plants. The experiment thus demonstrated the 'danger' to which the butterfly was exposed. But one should not confuse this with the 'risk' that this danger will occur. In other words the danger is real, but when one knows that the caterpillar of the Monarch normally feeds on the leaves of milkweed, a weed that normally grows on the borders of corn fields, and does not touch the corn itself one is led to the conclusion that the risk is low. Besides, corn pollen is rarely deposited in the border areas of cornfields and corn plants do not pollinate at the same time as the development of the caterpillar (Chesson and James: 2000: 27–28, translation mine).

The 'attack' on McDonald's

When the French government recently refused to accept the importation of hormonally treated beef from the United States, the latter brought a complaint before the World Trade Organization demanding retaliatory tariffs on a wide range of French products. The U.S. won a partial (and mostly symbolic) victory when the WTO decided to punish the French with 100% tariffs on a limited number of luxury goods including *foie gras*, Roquefort cheese, and Dijon mustard. The Larzac along with the left wing farmer's union, *The Confédération Paysanne*, opposed both the beef imports and any retaliatory tariffs. Larzac militants were particularly enraged when their own local product, Roquefort cheese, was placed on the list. The *Confédération Paysanne*, led by one of their key members, José Bové, decided to confront the issue by attacking a local McDonald's under construction in the city of Millau. McDonald's was chosen as a symbol of the imposition by multi-national (American run) companies to swamp the world with low quality, standardized food products. After a British scientist claimed that transgenic potatoes were dangerous (which was later shown to be false), Europeans opposed to genetic modification began to call any such products 'Frankenstein foods' and McDonald's was accused of using such genetically modified potatoes for their fries. As a counter example to McDonald's, and in opposition to all transgenic products, the *Confédération* vaunted the quality of local French products and, particularly, Roquefort cheese, which was taken as a key symbol of high quality, locally made food. While the anti-McDonald's demonstration in Millau will be discussed at length in the last chapter I wish here to voice my feelings of discomfort concerning the issue.

I have no particular liking for fast food and am not a defender of McDonald's. However, I was somewhat disturbed that it was signaled out as a target and am also unhappy with the propaganda against McDonald's, accepted, in my opinion, uncritically, by the *Confédération* and its Larzac allies. In addition to the general charge that the company's food was at best the bland product of standardization, which is certainly true, it was accused of running unsanitary establishments, of underpaying their workers, and of having connections to the Church of Scientology. I know that, what ever the quality of its food, McDonald's has almost obsessive concerns about cleanliness. Many years ago the first McDonald's restaurant in Paris lost its franchise when the corporation found it wanting in hygienic practices. It soon reopened under franchise from a French company, known as 'Quick' which now has a large number of outlets around the country. The quality of 'quick' food, I must add, is at least as low as any other fast-food chain. As young part-time workers, McDonald's employees are certainly low paid.

But this is as common a feature of part-time work in France as it is in the U.S. Many large French companies are as susceptible to this charge as McDonald's. As for the charge that links exist between McDonald's and the Church of Scientology, it is possible that a few of the individual McDonald's franchises in France and elsewhere have some sort of tie to Scientology. It seems unlikely that the company itself would risk its reputation by having any association with such an organization, particularly in France where public hostility to the Church (perhaps with good reason) verges on hysteria. Many French, who do not understand the United States' position on freedom of religion and its tolerance towards many sects, believe that the U.S. actively favors Scientology!

Prejudiced reporting in the U.S. press

On the other side of this issue, I feel obliged to emphasize that the press reports in the United States concerning the McDonald's action in Millau placed too much emphasis on the 'violence' and anti-American flavor of the protest. The December 6th 1999 issue of *Time Magazine* carried an article concerning the McDonald's action in Millau, under the headline, 'Super Fries Saboteur.' José Bové, with whom I don't always agree, is a thoughtful and intelligent person thoroughly committed to nonviolence. In the article he was referred to as "The French rabble rouser" (p.74). *Newsweek*, for Sept 13, 1999, said of the McDonald's action: "Don't look for the Southern French town of Montredon on your globe. It isn't even on local road maps, perhaps because it only has 20 inhabitants. But one of them, a Parisian intellectual [José Bové is from Bordeaux; not Paris] turned activist-farmer, named José Bové, may change all that. He's the leader of the mobs of farmers who trashed several McDonald's in France lately" (p.33). While it is true that some of the actions in France against McDonald's were much more violent then the Millau incident, involving attacks on functioning restaurants rather than one under construction, the responsibility for these belongs to members of the conservative union and rival to the *Confédération Paysanne*, the FNSEA.

Even the *New York Times*, in a relatively objective article by Susan Daley (October 12, 1999) pointing out that José Bové had become something of a national hero in France after the McDonald's protest, also could not resist saying that Bové had, "...organized the destruction of the McDonald's in nearby Millau—using tractors to tear down half the roof—to highlight what he sees as the United States' decision to levy high tariffs on Roquefort cheese, *pâte de foie gras* and other luxury imported food (p.A4). Two errors here: neither tractors or anything else were used to "tear down half the roof" of the restaurant in question. In fact, as the reader will see later, only minor damage was done, and this to the inside of the unfinished building by a few unruly youths. The other error is a minor point but speaks the *Times* reporter's ignorance of French products. There is a vast difference in quality and price between the untariffed *pâte de foie gras* and the expensive luxury product *foie gras* (the entire liver) that *was* taxed 100%!

Protesting the WTO meetings in Seattle

Larzac militants joining with a coalition of American protesters, including union members, ecologists, church groups, and other opponents of globalization, sent delegations to Seattle to protest against the meeting of the World Trade Organization in the fall of 1999. The Larzac contingent was led by José Bové who speaks English well and is highly articulate. Bové arrived in Seattle with 50 kilograms of Roquefort cheese (tariff-exempt because it was to be used for gifts for protesters as well as natives of Seattle).

Concerning these demonstrations my disagreement is more with the reporting in the American press than with the actions of the protesters, the vast majority of whom were committed to nonviolence. In fact, many were the victims of a police riot, tear gassed, pepper sprayed, arrested, and, in many cases, held for long hours handcuffed in busses or holding pens in local jails. These protests were described in the majority media as violent riots with little attention to the role played by local and State police. Readers will later see how impressed the Larzac militants were by the dignified and nonviolent actions of young American people in the face of police provocation.

We find another kind of reporting in the reliable, militantly nonviolent and pacifist Fellowship of Reconciliation's magazine for March–April 2000, *Fellowship*, which describes the events as follows:

> Police don't know how to deal with nonviolence; they don't know how to deal with disciplined nonviolence. Most protesters were not provoked by police actions I suspect were planned to allow—or even spark—violent reactions. Part of the police response was to use chemical sprays on nonviolent protesters in hopes of breaking the barricades. Chemicals inflicted real pain, but the barricades held. Meanwhile, those who engaged in property destruction had planned well in advance not to abide by nonviolence guidelines. By design or default, the police created conditions that allowed the property destruction to happen.
>
> The acts of destruction committed by a few—perhaps no more than fifty protesters—were used to justify a declaration of emergency and the suspension of the Constitution by creating a no-protest zone in down-town Seattle.
>
> The media, of course, kept an obsessive focus on the property destruction. They also distorted the protesters' knowledge of the issues.

Many reporters attributed ignorance or vagueness to the demonstrators. Not one reported the exchange I heard between a young man and a delegate from the European Union, one of hundreds that took place that day.

During a thirty-minute conversation, the protester offered well-reasoned arguments supported by statistics and analysis. Similar scenes were repeated throughout the day (Chris Nye: 2000: 9).

NEW INTERVIEWS IN THIS EDITION

The last chapter of this edition ends with a series of interviews taken in the winter of 1999–2000 concerning a range of specific issues with which Sonia and I are personally familiar. We believe that the information contained in these interviews, which come from a number of militant Larzac inhabitants, provides important insights from within the community about contemporary activities including one recent major internal dispute, that have occurred since this book was first published.

Introduction

The Larzac and Invented Tradition

On March 7, 1989, the left-wing, Paris-based newspaper *Libération* reported on a growing protest led by local ecologists against dam construction along the Loire River. The article began: "An impression of *déjà vu*. Like the birth of the Larzac. . . ." The word *Larzac* also appeared in articles published by local papers in the region of the proposed dam sites. One headline made reference to the protests as, "Larzac on the Loire." When a group of Spanish peasants organized to oppose the extension of a military camp over their land, page twenty-six of the July 26, 1989 edition of *Libération* carried the following subhead: "The army had chosen this isolated site in La Mancha as a bombing range. But for the past year the villagers have mobilized against the project. A Spanish Larzac. . . ." The question begged here, of course, is "What is the Larzac?" Geographically, it is a relatively poor farming region in southern France. This 100,000 hectare limestone plateau (1 hectare equals 2.471 acres) in the department of the Aveyron, along with other agriculturally poor regions in southern France, has suffered from a depopulation trend based on growing economic marginality that began just after World War I. The Larzac's modern notoriety began suddenly in 1971, when it came to the attention of the French public as a center of a popular protest against governmental authority. What was at stake was a proposed extension of a military camp in the northern sector of the plateau from 3,000 hectares to 17,000 hectares.

Only a few years earlier, many farmers in this area had been begging the army to buy their land. The government was, therefore, taken by surprise when the extension plan rapidly became a *cause célèbre* on the local and national levels. In the Aveyron itself a wide spectrum of the public, including many religious and secular leaders, Occitan separatists and all political parties from right to left (except the Gaullists, who had proposed the extension), opposed the plan. Nationally, the opposition came from the left of the political spectrum, consisting primarily of pacifists, ecologists, left-Catholics and small parties more radical than the Communists. What made it possible for these varying groups, often at odds politically, to work together was their acceptance of nonviolence. This tactic was imposed by the Larzac farmers, who had themselves been converted early in the struggle[1] by Lanza del Vasto, the charismatic leader of the nearby pacifist community of The Arc (*L'Arche*). For ten years this unnatural alliance fought to maintain a stalemate between itself and the government in the hope that the left would eventually come to power. Victory finally came in 1981 when François Mitterrand, the newly elected president of France, kept a promise he had made to the Larzac in 1974 to annul the extension project.

The 1970s were a turbulent period in French history. The aftermath of the 1968 student rebellions in Paris led to a series of local movements against central power, which were fueled by a return to the land by left-wing activists, so-called "marginals," ecologists and regional separatists. Among the most publicized of these movements were the Lip watch manufacture in Besançon, where—for a short time—workers took over their factory, and Plogoff in Brittany, where violent protests against the construction of a nuclear power plant led to its annulment (but only after Mitterrand's election). Of these and other protests like them, the Larzac was both the longest in duration and the most successful. The ten-year-long struggle, the ultimate victory and the determination of its militants to continue to press for goals that had developed during its course made the Larzac an enduring symbol for both the left and right in French politics.

Today while the left-wing press in France treats the Larzac with reverence, the counterpart media on the right—when they mention it at all—do so pejoratively. For the latter, the Larzac has become the central symbol of a fossilized vestige of the 1968 rebellion: A not-to-be-taken-seriously but nonetheless irritating remnant of the years when, in the view of the right, a collection of left-wing *groupuscules* and, worse, "hippies" posed a major threat to middle-class values and political stability. Even today when the very word *Larzac* is pronounced in public, it is capable of stirring passions in France on both the left and right of the political spectrum.

How could this small, isolated and sparsely populated region succeed so well where other movements had failed or played themselves out after victory? How could the Larzac come to play so important a role in the recent history of French politics and, in the context of contemporary France, come to symbolize social justice and pride for some and an anarchic menace for others? This book will attempt to answer these questions by analyzing the events of the 1971–1981 period, as well as its aftermath through 1992.

Although the Larzac protest was little known in the United States (members of the Fellowship of Reconciliation, a pacifist group, did hold a demonstration against the camp extension in New York in 1975), my wife, Sonia, and I were never strangers to it. We have had a long romance with France that began in 1957 during our first trip there together. Ten years later, in 1967, we bought a house in a small Midi village just to the south of the Larzac. Since 1968 we have spent every summer and four sabbatical years there—1980–81, 1987–89 and 1991–92. It is from this village, Soubès, that we have followed French culture and politics and, since fieldwork began in 1984, the activities of the Larzac community. The plateau is only a brisk fifty-minute hike upward through pine forests from Soubès; it is ten minutes by car. Life on the Larzac, however, is quite different from life in our village. Although the communal land of Soubès extends upward to the southern fringe of the plateau, the village is typical of the Midi with fields of grape vines and fruit trees. When we began our research we had to learn about a region that might as well have been hundreds of miles away rather than in our own backyard. The fact that we have had a house nearby for twenty-five years, however, stood us in good stead with the people of the Larzac, who saw us as distant neighbors as well as foreigners and Americans.

We were horrified when we heard about the camp extension even though it was planned—at least, at the time of the announcement—only for the northern half of the plateau. Rumors of further extensions were rampant from the beginning, and our concern for the peacefulness of the entire Larzac and of even our own valley mounted with the years. The idea of studying the Larzac movement did occur to us in the 1970s, but fieldwork did not begin immediately. Nonetheless, we did keep abreast of the struggle and attended some important demonstrations against the extension. In 1973 we were present in Paris when a Larzac tractor cortege arrived in the city. We were also at the huge demonstration held on the plateau in August 1974. During a sabbatical year in 1980, we attended the public meeting in Millau, where François Roux, the movement's lawyer, announced the court decision annulling a major portion of the expropriations for technical reasons. In the same year, we were in Paris when Larzac militants occupied the Champs de Mars. Later we ran into a group of them distributing flyers in the Forum des Halles, where they demonstrated after being expelled from their improvised campgrounds. Finally, we attended the victory celebration held on the Larzac in the summer of 1981.

In spite of these sporadic contacts during the years of the struggle, most of our time was spent on other projects. It was only in 1981 that we began to think seriously about research on the Larzac movement. From the beginning we felt that the focus of the study would be on the contemporary community rather than the struggle itself. We realized, of course, that in order to understand the contemporary community,[2] we would have to find out as much as possible about the period from 1971 to 1981 as well. We have used this information in the historical part of this book (chapters one through five).

It has been said that what makes humans so different from all other species is the fact that we are both the subjects and objects of history. This double place in the order of things renders all the social sciences—in particular anthropology, in which the major tool of research is personal experience— most problematic. No matter how careful their data collecting, anthropologists are bound to interpret what they (think they) see in terms of past training and a whole series of cultural prejudices they bring with them to the field.

This fact raises legitimate questions about how, as prisoners of our own cultures, we could ever describe and interpret other cultures. Additionally, as they enter into a community's life as "participant observers," anthropologists are bound to effect, in greater or lesser degrees, the outcomes of daily experiences for themselves as well as for those they have come to study. Furthermore, in this "postmodern" period many in and out of the profession have become sensitized to the problems associated with our "privileged" position as the putative recorders and interpreters of other people's lives. For this reason, the very possibility of producing an objective account of such lives—as well as whatever right anthropologists *think* they might have to describe, to interpret and sometimes even to speak for others—is called into question. Recent debates concerning these issues within anthropology have, needless to say, not left me indifferent (cf. Clifford 1983, 1988; Clifford and Marcus 1986; Crapanzano 1977; Dwyer 1977; Geertz 1988; Lurie 1989; Marcus 1980; Marcus and Fischer 1986; Polier and Roseberry 1989; Rabinow 1977, 1986; Said 1983; Tedlock 1979).

Nevertheless, this book *does* contain both description and interpretation. It is *our* view of how the Larzac community came to be, what it is and why its members—in spite of their current and past differences—have managed (rather successfully) to remain united socially and politically after victory. The purpose of this book is *not* to present both sides of the Larzac struggle: we do not claim to speak for the people of the Larzac, nor do we speak for or against their adversaries. Rather, its purpose is to document and analyze how those opposed to the camp extension—those individuals who now make up what we choose to call the Larzac community—won their battle with state power and how they changed in the process.

Long-term fieldwork is very special in that what begins as an "objective" outside view of a community is slowly transformed into "subjective" experience lived and felt almost, but never quite completely, as a member of that community. What follows is a very personal account. However, it is not a *reflexive* ethnography in which the heartaches and joys of fieldwork are foregrounded against the background of an "alien" culture. Still, we must say that over the years we have come to identify in many ways with the Larzac community, developing ever-deepening friendships with a good number of its inhabitants. Since our work began in 1984, we have shared the Larzac's successes and failures, its moments of joy, as well as the profound sadness that came with the premature death of a newly cherished friend. We were depressed when major conflicts erupted on the plateau that appeared to signal the destruction of a fragile social order, and elated when these conflicts were finally resolved.

We do not wish to hide our prejudices from the reader. Although we do not agree with all the actions taken by the Larzac community, we do sympathize with many of its goals and methods. We *were* opposed to the camp extension and found the arguments against it more convincing than those that came from supporters. There is, for example, evidence that land speculation played a role for some who were close to people in the government favoring the extension. It is also the case that experts within the French military were *not* unanimous in supporting the project. We readily admit, however, to having no competence to judge the validity of the arguments for the extension made by military authorities: we are not experts in matters of defense. Concerning pro-camp individuals in the local community, we *do* understand why commercial interests and members of the municipal council in La Cavalerie (the town serving the Larzac camp) favored the extension, but we cannot sympathize with their generally aggressive attitude toward their neighbors who stood to lose their farms. While the businesses of La Cavalerie would surely have profited from the extension, its annulment did not portend failure for them. Additionally, even if it is a reflection of our own prejudices, we were negatively impressed by the often vulgar public response of local pro-camp groups. One example was in their reaction to the behavior of some Larzac militants. In a tract entitled a "Call to Population," they exhorted people to "chase away the hippies who dishonor our tombs and our churches. Say no to free love in cemeteries and churches." Also, we admit our *a priori* distaste for any action in France that is, as was the camp extension, wholeheartedly supported by the Front National, the French neo-fascist party.

Furthermore, information on the pro-extension position was rather hard to come by. Except for newspaper clippings and a few government tracts, we know of little published material on their point of view. We were able to interview the present mayor of La Cavalerie. During the struggle, he was a pro-extension member of the municipal council, but his moderate views have led to a rapprochement with the post-struggle anti-camp community. Business people who favored the extension remain bitter, however, and refuse to talk to outsiders.

For us, at least, empathy with the people one has decided to study is a requirement of good fieldwork. The exclusive focus on the protest community to be found in this book is thus the result of a personal as well as pragmatic choice. But it must also be made clear that while what follows is an *inside* view of the Larzac, it is far from being *exclusively* an insider's view. Our integration into the community was never complete; at best, we attained the status of trusted confidants—outsiders, still, but welcomed inside the Larzac world because of the relationships we had formed.

While being seen as *outsiders* (which remained obvious throughout our comings and goings on the plateau) could be useful, it also had its special hazards. We had access to a great deal of information precisely because we were defined, at least in part, as individuals who would take the message of the Larzac community to American readers, but this perceived role opened us to the danger of being used as a sounding board, being told only what the community wanted us to hear. This problem was abrogated to a great extent, however, by our diligent observation of Larzac social and political life through attendance of social events and our presence at almost all the meetings of nearly every Larzac association over a twenty-six-month period. If our presence had inhibited normal, and often painful, confrontation, the Larzac community would have been paralyzed for over two years, unable to pursue its various social and political goals. Obviously, it was not so handicapped. In fact, rather quickly, our informants came to expect us at all their events and, it appeared, were not affected by us as observers.

Yet it was, at times, precisely our status as *outsiders* that provided unusual opportunities to gain access to sensitive data. We were, for example, asked to serve as nonvoting members of a committee of inquiry that was charged to deal with a major and deeply felt dispute that threatened the fabric of plateau social life and the dissolution of a key plateau association. The data gathered by this committee, through interviews and existing documents, provided access to information that we could never have obtained otherwise. Thus, the people of the Larzac confided in us with a certain freedom because we *were* outsiders—not actors in the plateau's dramas—but, at the same time, they could talk and act in our presence as if we were part of the "inside," one of "theirs."

This relationship with the Larzac community contrasts with the experience I had several years ago when doing fieldwork with a New York theater group in the process of making a play. I attended all rehearsals from the beginning of casting through opening night. A few months into the research, I was attacked by the actors for "ripping off their work" for my book. I had to explain that they had their work and I mine, and that the book resulting from my research would contain not the raw material of their rehearsals but rather my analysis of the play-making process. I had no such problem with the Larzac people. There was no question that after they got to know us, they wanted us there and were looking forward to reading our analysis of research in which they were the "raw material."

The reader will find very little theory in this book. Our purpose is *ethnographic*, that is, to present an analytic description of a particular people's way of life. I will readily admit that I am wary of what passes for theory in the discipline of anthropology. Since completing graduate work over thirty years ago, I have seen the rise of a host of theoretical frameworks that promised to unlock the secrets of human behavior, only later to be proven exaggerated or false. A partial list of these would include culture and personality, componential analysis, ethnoscience, neoevolutionism, human ecology, cultural ecology, cultural materialism, structuralism and post-structuralism. Among the great figures of social science, Freud and Marx have left their mark on the discipline, but Freudian and Marxist anthropologists are a contentious lot, often differing among themselves as much as with those who ply the trade outside of these schools. The current postmodern trend, if one can generalize about it at all, takes an interpretive stance, often equating anthropological data and published material with literature, to be explicated and criticized as such. They find generalizations about cultural and historical processes distasteful. The best of this perspective certainly has a place in the discipline, providing important correctives to the hubris displayed by so many "scientific" anthropologists. However, postmodernism should be recognized for what it is: meta-anthropology, not anthropology *tout court*. It is my opinion that good anthropological work must still be grounded in fieldwork. What is left after the debris of theory has fallen away is the descriptive ethnographic core, to be used and interpreted by new generations of scholars, whatever their theoretical orientation.

Ethnographic discourse, since it began in earnest in the 1920s, has provided a solid framework for understanding how individual cultures and societies work. It is this framework rather than bits of theory that have guided our data collection and analysis. Although ethnography used to have an anti-historical bias, in the last two or three decades anthropologists have been taught to look at both culture (systems that guide belief and practice) and society (networks of significant social groups) in relation to specific historical conditions as they affect the lives of individuals.

In this book the data have been organized according to these principles as they apply in the specific case of the Larzac. The interpretation has been further guided by the work of a small number of contemporary social scientists. Among these are philosophers concerned with the role of individuals in the "making" of history (Popper 1957; Danto 1985; Aron 1989) and scholars who study the processes through which social groups establish their identity in the face of state power (Hobsbawm and Ranger 1983; Cohen 1980). I have also been guided by studies of the means by which people construct mythology to fit their own interests (Sahlins 1981).

The historical and ethnographic description in this book covers twenty-one years: the ten years of the struggle (1971–81) and the subsequent years of change and consolidation, up to the time of its writing (1990–92). The analysis will consider the reasons behind the spectacular success of the Larzac movement as well as its particular failures, conflicts and contradictions. During the struggle years, it was necessary for those active within the movement to bury disagreements over ideology and strategy. The existence of a common enemy made this relatively easy. After victory, however, differences came to the surface, producing considerable dissension—not all of which could be easily managed. We were witness to several conflicts that occurred after 1981, which festered on the plateau for a rather long time. They were severe enough to threaten the economic, social and political goals set by the new Larzac community. So necessary had these goals become, however, that major efforts were made to resolve the dissension. An important feature of the ethnographic analysis to follow will be the description and analysis of these conflicts—what factors, both structural and personal, produced them in the first place, and what were the different means used to bring them to resolution.

The Larzac case brings to the forefront fundamental issues in anthropology. In this book we document an instance in which farming people of a local region prevailed against the highly centralized power of France. The Larzac struggle was a process in which a local population and its allies used symbols, actions and myth to build a movement and, after 1981, to consolidate their victory. Indigenous resistance to coercive power has been important in anthropology in recent years (e.g., Comaroff 1985). Most studies have focused on "non-western" indigenous peoples resisting "western" colonialism. The Larzac is distinctive since it provides an instance of resistance to centralized power taking place within a western democratic nation, itself.

Equally important, the Larzac struggle provides an example of culture and collectivity in consolidation and thus adds to the work of Hobsbawm and Ranger (1983). These authors note that one means social groups use to establish and justify their separate identities is to create traditions that they claim are old but that are actually recent or even invented. To these, Hobsbawm and Ranger give the name "invented traditions."

> "Invented tradition" is taken to mean a set of practices, normally governed by overtly or tacitly accepted rules and of a ritual or symbolic nature, which seek to inculcate certain values and norms of behavior by repetition, which automatically implies continuity with the past. In fact, where possible, they normally attempt to establish continuity with a suitable historic past. (1983:1)

Hobsbawm himself goes on to point out that such invented traditions are responses to "novel situations which take the form of reference to old situations. . ." (Hobsbawm and Ranger 1983:2). From the beginning of the struggle, the Larzac community attempted to establish its legitimacy through its claim to ancient peasant status and all that this implies in French culture (see chapters one and seven). Internally, this constructed identity functioned to provide cohesion among socially disparate elements on the Larzac and, externally, to establish the local population's right to keep their farms in the face of what was claimed to be the national interest. Thus, the people of the Larzac consciously reversed the process of making the peasants of rural France into Frenchmen that began in the last quarter of the nineteenth century and was complete by 1914 (cf. Weber 1976), remaking Frenchmen into peasants.

But if the "peasant" status of the Larzac farmers was a major facet of an "invented tradition," the Larzac community also developed what the art critic Harold Rosenberg has called "the tradition of the new." Of this Rosenberg says the following:

> Whoever undertakes to create soon finds himself engaged in creating himself. Self-transformation and transformation of others have constituted the radical interest of our century, whether in painting, psychiatry *or political action*. Quite ordinary people have been tempted to assume the risk of deciding whether to continue to be what they have been or exchange themselves to fit a more intriguing role; *others have had self-substitution forced upon them*. (1961:10, italics mine)

The re-creation of peasanthood on the Larzac involved the "rediscovery" of an age-old identification with the land, but also a new identification with Third World peasants. The same peasanthood brought a renewed a appreciation of traditional small-scale farming, but also an appreciation of the emerging ideas of a left-oriented, modern ecology movement. In addition, the new Larzac "peasant," contrary to peasants in the past, empathized with the struggles of the militant, if non-Communist, part of the working class. Finally, the new Larzac peasant discovered nonviolence, making it the central dogma of a self-constructed ideology. The Larzac community also displayed a new penchant for innovation by developing a large number of task-specific voluntary associations during and after the struggle. After victory, the Larzac movement shifted gears, focusing its attention on revitalizing its farms. With the cooperation of the government, the Larzac community created a way of providing land at low rent to young farmers. By giving young people a means of livelihood on the plateau, the community was able to reverse the depopulation trend that had begun after World War I. In addition, a more traditional method of easing access to land, in the form of corporate land-holding associations (GFAs), was used innovatively on the plateau. These successes put the Larzac in the forefront of experimentation in land tenure at a sensitive moment in the development of a global agricultural policy for the European Community.

In reality, the Larzac has never been a peasant movement. In spite of a certain degree of regionalism that was manifested by Occitan separatists the

Larzac is not a case of "traditional" local people with a long-standing, distinctive identity, resisting central power. The people of the Larzac and their allies had no intrinsic ties uniting them, only the goal of keeping the land out of the hands of the military and in those of local farmers. The movement included so-called "traditionalists"—people with their roots deep in the land—as well as outsiders—leftists, intellectuals and counterculturists. This potpourri of folk, ideologies and cultures was brought together by the common desire to maintain the land for farming and the necessity of mobilizing a popular political movement in order to do so. This study attempts to trace the process of consolidation as these people of vastly different socioeconomic, cultural and political backgrounds came together through shared concerns, events and actions, forming an effective whole while retaining their differences. Each affected the other—the traditional farmer, the conservative populist, the leftist ideologue, the counterculturist—and each in turn was affected by the common events and cultivated understandings that came to mark them all. An examination of the Larzac struggle is an examination of culture, ideology and community in construction.

This book focuses on the historical context, as well as the historical experiences, interpretations, innovations and myth-making that resulted from the struggle and continue to unite the newly formed collectivity. Chapters one through five based on interviews, published material and the Larzac archives, are largely historical. Chapters six through ten, while using the same kind of materials as the preceding chapters, are more heavily based on our extended fieldwork, which began in the summer of 1984 and continued through two sabbatical years 1987–89. Further field research was pursued during winter breaks in 1990 and 1991, as well as the two summers of these years. Follow-up continued during a further sabbatical year in 1991–92, as well as the winter break of 1992–93.

Chapter one provides a geographic, ecological and historical background to the Larzac and the larger region in which it is imbedded. It also describes the growth and development of the movement in its early days. Chapters two through four follow the struggle to victory in 1981. These chapters present data on how specific individuals contributed to the development of local and national strategies to counter the government's efforts to expropriate their land. They also describe the growing number of locally created associations, each of which played a particular role in the struggle. These associations were a major feature of the Larzac movement and contributed to its success. While some disappeared after the 1981 victory, others continue to play an important role in the contemporary life of the plateau. Still others have been created since 1981 and fulfill new goals and activities. The existence of so many voluntary associations provides a flexible structure for the pursuit of

Larzac-oriented activities and allows individuals to choose issues that interest them, as well as the people with whom they can work most compatibly.

Chapter five discusses the immediate aftereffects of the victory, the formulation of plans for the future of the plateau and the further evolution of the structures and associations necessary to make these plans functional. It also introduces a note of criticism through the voice of an important militant. This person felt, even in the early post-struggle period, that the ideals developed during the struggle were too quickly shunted aside by the more conservative farmers, who—in his opinion—took control of the major association in the spring of 1981.

Chapter six contains an analysis of this criticism as it pertains to the economic realities following the relegalization of the Larzac farms. This chapter also compares the utopic plans formulated in 1981 against the unfolding reality of life on the plateau in the immediate post-struggle period.

Chapter seven analyzes how the Larzac militants created an effective symbolic system that they used to bring their struggle before the French public, countering the propaganda machine of the national government. The chapter is guided by the notion that much of the power inherent in symbols comes from their multivocality—their multiple linkages to significant ideas and associated feelings (Turner 1975)—and takes a close look at the means by which political action was guided by and, itself, guided a changing cultural framework. Chapter seven and, to some extent, the chapters that follow it, in Abner Cohen's words:

> . . . explore the dramatic processes underlying the rituals, ceremonies and other types of symbolic activities that pervade social life. With this approach the study of sociocultural causation and change becomes the analysis of the creation of transformation of dramatic forms, their production, direction, authentication, the techniques they employ; and the transformation they bring about in the relations between the men and women they involve. (1980:65)

A major feature of chapter seven is an analysis of the process by which the leaders of the Larzac struggle manipulated historical facts to their advantage and eventually transformed them into a charter myth which was to guide the community after victory. As Arthur Danto (1985) has pointed out, history is—in a real sense—something that is made only after the fact. To use Danto's example: "The Hundred Years' War began in 1337" is a statement that could only have been made at the end of that war. So it is with all historical processes in which post-facto interpretations locate "causation" in earlier events. History, at least formal history, belongs to historians, not the people who live through events. To put it another way, individuals may think that they are making history at any particular moment in time (a thought which may or may not be true), but they cannot know *what* history they are *actually* making.

Myth, when compared to the flow of historical events and their post-facto interpretations, assumes a different generative and time-bound stance. Myth self-consciously and straightforwardly adopts the supposition that the past—the mythic past, that is—should be used to shape the future, and that conception of the past allows the myth to construct its version of reality. A charter myth is a justification and a guide for action to be taken along the path of future history. When, at the end of the struggle, Larzac militants took a real and crucial ten-year period and integrated the potpourri of events into a more coherent and purposeful form, they converted the ten-year struggle into a myth. In myth-making they were attempting, consciously or not, to take history into their own hands and guarantee the future of their movement.

Chapters eight and nine deal with contradictions and conflict on the plateau. The first of these chapters takes its material largely from interviews with present and past militants and explores the various cultural and political divisions that were, and are still, manifest on the Larzac. It shows how the seeds of dissension were sowed on the basis of personal and structural differences among those living on the plateau, as well as by the necessity during the struggle to make quick decisions, often in a semi-secret and undemocratic fashion.

Chapter nine deals with two major conflicts (both finally resolved after much effort) that broke out in the post-victory period, but which had their roots deep in the differences that existed from the beginning among community members. These conflicts were each played out in the context of different institutional structures, and with a slightly different cast of characters. This comparison allows me to tease out how diverse forms of organization foster or impede conflict resolution on the Larzac. In chapter nine, I also attempt to show how differences in both ideology and social status played roles in the creation and the resolution of conflict.

In these chapters, I draw a distinction between those I call *affectives* and those I call *politicals* among the members of the contemporary Larzac community. Affectives are individuals who, in the context of conflict, hold personal relations to be most important. Politicals, on the other hand, put their long-range goals above personal feelings. While these two terms do not describe absolute differences among individuals on the Larzac, I believe they are useful in helping the reader to understand the dynamics of conflict and its resolution as it developed in the post-struggle period. I also believe that one can generalize from this material beyond the Larzac case to other popular protest movements.

The final chapter summarizes the cultural and social situation of the contemporary Larzac community. Twenty-one years of Larzac history furnish material with which to judge the ongoing debate among historians and philosophers concerning what has come to be known as "historicism" (Popper 1957). In broad terms some historians, especially Marxist historians, claim that history is controlled by social forces, particularly the class struggle. In contrast, Popperians claim that a close look at history will show that it is made exclusively by individuals, whose many acts, often performed anonymously, are the only source of change. The chapter attempts to answer the questions, "How important are specific individuals in the social process?" and "How, if at all, does the social process contain and direct change?" I take an intermediate position between Popper and the Marxists, close to that of Raymond Aron (1989). Aron has noted that individuals make history but only within an institutional framework. Such a conclusion, it seems to me, is logical and in no way startling, but it does, nonetheless, need confirmation through empirical data. This study provides this data and shows that the Larzac struggle *was* shaped by specific, documentable individuals, whose actions, although innovative, were guided by the community's place in the structural, historical and cultural particularities of the Larzac. The analysis clearly shows that none of the means used by Larzac militants were completely original. Rather, most were borrowed from the past history of mass movements in France and elsewhere. These were, however, used with great skill under the guidance of a series of individuals, each of whom played a different key role in the struggle.

Seen in their own terms, if not in their own language, the history of the Larzac protest is the history of the lifting of the veil of false consciousness from the ideology of a group. Up until the announcement of the camp extension, the farmers of the Larzac had been sincere believers in law and order and followed the secular and religious authorities of their conservative region. Although the initial motivation of the protest was clearly to save the land from expropriation, a new ideology of nonviolence—brought by a charismatic leader (who himself questioned legal and political authority)— took root and developed its own charismatic authority over the Larzac farmers and their supporters.

A final word before I turn to an examination of our research methods. The term *peasant* appears frequently in this book. Yet, there have been no peasants in France since at least the end of the nineteenth century. I have already noted that the concept of "peasantness" presented in this study is a part of the *invented tradition* of the Larzac community. Therefore, one should not consider this book a study of peasants. Nor, strictly speaking, is it about farmers either, except insofar as farmers were the local actors in the development of a successful social movement that grew to be national in scope. It is, rather, an analysis of a movement whose nature stands as an example for marginal farming areas in France and perhaps elsewhere in the coming years of the new European Community.

Most anthropological studies have concentrated on established communities of long-standing, so-called traditional societies. Modern communities have been studied as well. This text concerns a community *in formation*—an artificial, historically conjunctural coming together of people who were forced to negotiate a common identity in order to survive. Faced with displacement, the Larzac community rapidly developed its own set of self-definitions, values, actions—in short, a basis for cultural continuity.

In the process, each individual involved had to negotiate his or her own identity in relation to the social field that was defined from within and without the community. The established Larzac farmers, large and small, became "peasants," easily. Squatters, who lived under precarious conditions during the struggle, had to wait until victory to achieve the same status. Shepherds and farmworkers either left the Larzac or were assimilated as full partners in corporations organized to run the larger farms. They too became "peasants."

Younger farmers who came to the Larzac after the struggle are still negotiating their identities. Although only a few are politically active, they have already gained the respect of the wider community through their willingness to engage in hard work—a traditional criterion for acceptance that remains important in the small world of the Aveyron, even on the Larzac plateau.

Research Methods

As I have already noted, this study is both historical and ethnographic, based on bibliographic and archival research as well as on extensive fieldwork. It is the result of a long-term project that began in 1984 and continues as of this writing.

Our original entry into the community was facilitated by a bit of luck. One of my books, *La Dimension Humaine*—a translation of *The Human Imperative*—was in the library of Le Cun, a center for nonviolence on the plateau. The presence of the book helped identify us as people in whom one might have confidence. It was at Le Cun that we began our work by interviewing one of its founders, Hervé Ott, who later served as an intermediary for us with other militants. Later that summer, he invited us to meetings of the *bureau*, which represented the various associations and geographic subdivisions of the Larzac community. At that point, the *bureau* met every two weeks. We did not attend board meetings of any other Larzac associations in the summer of 1984, but we did complete fourteen interviews.

Interviews continued throughout fieldwork. Each potential interviewee was phoned by Sonia, who set up our appointments. Most people were cooperative from the beginning. By the end of the study, we had interviewed more than 150 people and had only been refused by 3 individuals. Three others did not wish to have their interviews recorded on tape. In these cases, Sonia and I discussed the interviews immediately after they were completed and recorded our impressions of them. Sonia handled most of the questioning during the interviews that lasted, on the average, about one hour. Questions were open-ended, and we let each interview take its course in an informal way. We did, however, pose a set of standard questions concerning age, origins (region, class, and educational background), the size and type of interviewee's farm, knowledge of the struggle, extent of participation in it, present economic situation on the plateau, and personal opinions of disputes and /or projects current at the time of the interview.

These interviews were not transcribed. Instead I typed copious notes from the tapes as I reviewed them, including quotes that might be cited in the body of our text. During the writing stage, I relistened to tapes when necessary. All quotes from interviews have been cleaned up grammatically in minor ways and some sentences have been rearranged to flow better. The purpose was not to alter content or emotion but rather to clarify it by accommodating the act of speech to the demands of the written word. To transcribe something that was spoken into a written text is already to alter it; through careful re-editing, one can minimize the distortions caused by transcription. Unless one is performing a strict discourse analysis, where it is absolutely necessary to transcribe all the words, hesitations and grammatical mistakes of informants, an edited version of an interview is often more faithful to the content than a literal transcription. Provided that the interviewer edits carefully and *only* after familiarity with the interviewee and the culture has been established,[3] editing serves to convey both the informant's meaning and feelings about an issue.

Looking back on the experience, I don't think we could have proceeded with our work as quickly as we did if we had not begun the study with these interviews. They were useful not only as an information source but also as a means to become acquainted with the dispersed inhabitants of the plateau. The private tête-à-tête was an occasion for people to satisfy their curiosity about us and our intentions as well—the first step in establishing the trust necessary for our work. To avoid putting yet more kilometers on our aging car and as a way of seeing our Larzac population in as many contexts as possible, we arranged for stays of a week or so in several hamlets and farms, including Les Truels, Montredon, Les Baumes and La Salvetat. These visits allowed us to schedule interviews more closely together. We could also spend the intervening hours stopping in at various farms for casual conversation, which almost invariably took us further along in our understanding of prevailing attitudes. Naturally, the shared meals—and, on occasion, work, as well—and the evenings of conversation helped cement relationships with our hosts. As our research progressed, people began to recognize our ancient, orange Renault 4 on the many small roads that cross the plateau. Soon, we exchanged horn toots and waves with Larzac residents as we passed them on our way to various appointments. Our frequent presence appeared to increase our informants' confidence in the seriousness of our purpose. By the end of the study, we had put over 40,000 kilometers on our car.

The people of the Larzac are used to being interviewed and are not shy when talking about their experiences. They have a flair for expressing themselves, which is what one might expect in their highly verbal culture. They are also anxious that their views be conveyed to a larger, national and international community. After we got to know the Larzac well, we were amused by the disclaimer so many of the plateau's official orators made at the beginning of their public speeches. Essentially, they began with variations on the cliché, "Unaccustomed as I am to public speaking. . . "

Even those who obviously did not feel comfortable in the public arena or even in association meetings appeared to be quite at ease during our private interviews. In fact, most of our informants seemed to enjoy talking about their experiences in the past as well as their present situations, and many were quite eloquent as they described the struggle—a high point in their lives, which has left vivid memories. In order to return their hospitality and to maintain and strengthen the personal relations we had begun to establish, we invited many informants to dinner at our house, where, around the table, we could discuss Larzac events without the formality of an interview. Before the end of the study period, we counted a significant number of plateau residents as our friends.

In the summer of 1985 we were introduced to the board of directors of the principal Larzac association, the Association for the Development of the Larzac (APAL), and the board allowed us to attend its monthly meetings. But it was not until we began continuous fieldwork in June of 1987 that we asked for and received permission to attend the board meetings of all the Larzac associations. From then on, however, we were present at almost every meeting. Sonia and I both took copious notes at all meetings—she in French and I in English. While writing this book, we were able to consult both sets for accuracy and to discuss any discrepancies. It was sometimes important to see what people had said in French to get the correct tone of a conversation or debate. After a while, our ubiquitous presence led us to be seen—if we were noticed at all—as "flies on the wall." Before long, people were comfortable enough to argue with one another, sometimes passionately, in our presence. During the entire course of fieldwork, we were excluded from only one meeting (of the APAL board in which finances were to be discussed) and that was only at the very beginning of our long stay in 1987–89. Most of our informants were so embarrassed by our exclusion on that occasion that they fell over one another to describe to us what had transpired. Evidently, they were concerned about the accuracy of their reporting, as well. The various versions of that meeting that were related to us were both detailed and consistent. As people got to know us, our advice was solicited with increasing frequency, and when the situations did not involve disputes, we gave it freely. Our presence became so usual that a standing joke developed around the scheduling of special association meetings: when such events had to be arranged, we were always consulted for the best date—one that did not conflict with some other plateau event. It was soon appreciated (with both seriousness and humor) that we were the ones with the most complete Larzac appointment calendar! Attendance at association meetings was crucial for this study since it provided direct information on how the Larzac community's major form of social structure actually functioned in a series of different situations.

In addition to attending meetings and conducting interviews, we made ourselves as helpful as possible to the community. In 1985 we began to volunteer at the Larzac ecological museum, spending several days each summer at the ticket desk, selling admissions, books and posters, and arts and crafts made on the plateau. We soon became familiar enough with the Larzac and the history of the struggle to answer questions and offer advice to passing tourists concerning sites they might want to see and places where they could stay during their visit to the plateau. We also became members of SCI-CUN, a group that supports building projects at Le Cun and, later, joined other Larzac associations. In the fall of 1987, we bought one share of stock in a cooperative land-management company (GFA), which was founded during the struggle, to ensure that we could attend what we knew would be a divisive shareholders' meeting that coming summer.

In the spring of 1988, we made our first trip to the house of a former Larzac militant, Robert Pirault, where the Larzac archives were then located. In exchange for allowing us access to these papers, we helped him classify the tons of material that militants had been sending him over the years. We spent about ten full days, dispersed over several visits, working on this project. Between visits, Robert kindly let us take sections of the archives home, where they could be consulted at leisure.

In the winter of 1988, I was invited by a former militant, who was an advisor to then Prime Minister Michel Rocard, to visit Paris in order to consult documents relating to the years of protest, conditions in the region at the end of the struggle and cabinet recommendations concerning economic and social plans for the Larzac region in the post-struggle period.

In addition to these valuable sources, I was also able to consult all the issues of the Larzac newspaper, *GLL*, thanks to the *GLL* board's generous gift of an entire set.

In this book I have avoided the standard technique used in writing anthropology of placing people and events alike in a static "ethnographic present." I agree with Fabian (1983) that the use of this essentially literary device serves to distance both ethnographers and their readers from the subjects of ethnography; these subjects become "others"—historically decontextualized and automatically relegated to a distant, inferior and unchanging world.

In rejecting the ethnographic present, I have chosen to document the historical flow of events that characterize the Larzac movement and to analyze these events as part of an overall process of change. The data and analysis in this book are therefore linked to specific dates up to the end of 1992. (What comes after that date is the subject of another study, but the reader can be sure that life on the Larzac will continue to evolve.) Since this study, based as it is on both fieldwork and archival research, covers twenty-one years of rapidly changing history the use of the ethnographic present in it would have been patently absurd.

This work is conceived of as a joint effort of two ethnographers—Sonia and myself—and the people of the Larzac who suffered our presence over the course of so many years. An earlier version of this text (the introduction and conclusion have since been modified) was read by five Larzac militants, José Bové, Chantal de Crisenoy, Suzie Emmick, Catherine and François Boé. However, the final choice of what is included and what is excluded, which voices are heard and which not, is my responsibility, seconded by Sonia's careful reading of the text. I have attempted to meet this responsibility by providing the reader with what I hope is a fair sample of the many voices that made up the Larzac before and during our presence. The data is consciously presented as multivocalic. I take full responsibility for the interpretations and analyses it contains. In the division of labor that is ethnography, it is the informant who informs the anthropologist but it is the trained anthropologist who uses his or her expertise to present and analyze the data.

We were on the side of the Larzac cause from the beginning, and at first we wanted their community to fit our preconceived ideal picture of it. We were cautioned against taking this view by many of our informants, who insisted that the Larzac was not a paradise and that it would only be harmful to present it as such.

Though Sonia and I are still passionately attracted to the idealism of the Larzac community and identify strongly with many of its past and present goals, we do not feel that our subjectivity in this respect has blinded us to the very real and omnipresent conflicts and contradictions that are a part of the living praxis of the Larzac community. We hope that our intense involvement has, upon reflection, allowed us to see clearly how day-to-day reality, economic problems and individual conflicts interact with the ever-present idealism to produce a constantly evolving, always interesting, but less than perfect utopia.

Notes

1. In this book the word *struggle* is used throughout as a translation of the French word *lutte*. *Lutte* can also mean *fight* or *battle*, but in the context of the Larzac movement, *struggle* is the more appropriate translation.

2. A standard use of the word *community* is not appropriate for this work. The population of the northern half of the Larzac at the beginning of the struggle was approximately 1,700, including those living in La Cavalerie. The group indigenous to the plateau that opposed the extension numbered just above 500 (including children). They were joined first by local militants in Millau, the urban center to the north of the plateau. During the struggle, several dozen squatters installed themselves on various farms that the government had bought or had planned to buy. In the post-struggle period, many of them established legal residences as subtenants on government-expropriated farms now rented to a Larzac association. In 1991, approximately 160 individuals—farmers native to the Larzac, as well as ex-squatters and post-struggle newcomers—made up the core of the militant community dedicated to at least some of the Larzac struggle's new economic, political and social goals. It is to these individuals that the term *community* is applied in this book.

3. See Malcom (1990) for an interesting discussion of this problem from a journalistic point of view.

Acronyms

APAL 1973–1981: Association pour la Promotion de l'Agriculture sur le Larzac (Association for the Promotion of Agriculture on the Larzac); From 1981: Association pour l'Aménagement du Larzac (Association for the Development of the Larzac)

CDJA Centre Départemental des Jeunes Agriculteurs (Departmental Center for Young Farmers)

CFDT Confédération Française Démocratique du Travail (French Democratic Confederation of Workers)

CFPPA Centre de Formation Professionnelle et de Promotion Agricole (Center for Professional Training and Agricultural Promotion)

CGT Confédération Générale du Travail (General Confederation of Workers)

CIE Centre d'Initiatives à l'Environnement (Center for Environmental Projects)

CIR Centre d'Initiatives Rurales (Center for Rural, Cultural and Educational Projects)

CMR Chrétiens en Milieu Rural (Christians in the Rural World)

CNJA Centre National des Jeunes Agriculteurs (National Center for Young Farmers)

CNRS Centre National de la Recherche Scientifique (National Center for Scientific Research)

CREA Centre de Rencontres, d'Échanges et d'Animation (Social and Cultural Center of Millau)

CUMA Coopérative d'Utilisation de Matériel Agricole (Agricultural Equipment Cooperative)

EC   European Community

FDSEA   Fédération Départementale de Syndicats d'Exploitants
          Agricoles (Departmental Federation of Farmers' Unions)

FLNKS   Front de Libération Nationaliste Kanaky Socialiste (The
          Kanaky Socialist National Liberation Front)

FNSEA   Fédération National de Syndicats d'Exploitants Agricoles
          (National Federation of Farmers' Unions)

FRCIVAM   Fédération Régionale des Centres d'Information et de
          Vulgarisation pour l'Agriculture et le Milieu Rural (Regional
          Confederation of Centers for the Diffusion of Information on
          Agriculture and the Rural World)

GAEC   Groupement Agricole d'Exploitation en Commun (Partner-
          ship for Farm Management)

GFA   Groupement Foncier Agricole (Agricultural Land-holding
          Corporation)

GIE   Groupement d'Intérêts Économiques (Association of Related
          Commercial Activities)

GLL   *Gardarem Lo Larzac* (We Shall Keep the Larzac)

INRA   Institut National de Recherche Agricole (National Agricul-
          tural Research Institute)

JAC   Jeunes Agriculteurs Catholiques (Association of Young
          Catholic Farmers)

MAN   Mouvement pour un Alternatif Non-Violent (Movement for a
          Nonviolent Alternative)

MDPL   Mouvement pour le Désarmement, la Paix et la Liberté
          (Movement for Disarmament, Peace and Freedom)

MPOL   Mouvement pour l'Ordre et la Liberté (Movement for Order
          and Freedom)

PSU   Parti Socialiste Unifié (Unified Socialist Party)

RPCR   Rassemblement pour la Calédonie dans la République
           (Association for a French New Caledonia)

SAFALT   Société d'Aménagement Foncier Aveyron-Lot-Tarn (Office of
           Land Management in the Departments of the Aveyron, Lot
           and Tarn)

SAFER   Société d'Aménagement Foncier (National Office of Land
           Management)

SCTL   Société Civile des Terres du Larzac (Larzac Land Manage-
           ment Association)

SEB   Syndicat des Éleveurs de Brebis (Union of Sheep Farmers)

SPLB   Syndicat des Producteurs du Lait de Brebis (Union of Sheep
           Milk Producers)

TP   Confédération Nationale des Syndicats de Travailleurs
(CNSTP)   Paysans (National Confederation of Worker-Peasant Unions)

UDF   Union pour la Démocratie Française (Union for French
           Democracy)

UDR   1968–1971: Union pour la Défense de la République (Union
           for the Defense of the Republic); 1971–1976: Union des
           Démocrates pour la République (Union of Democrats for the
           Republic)

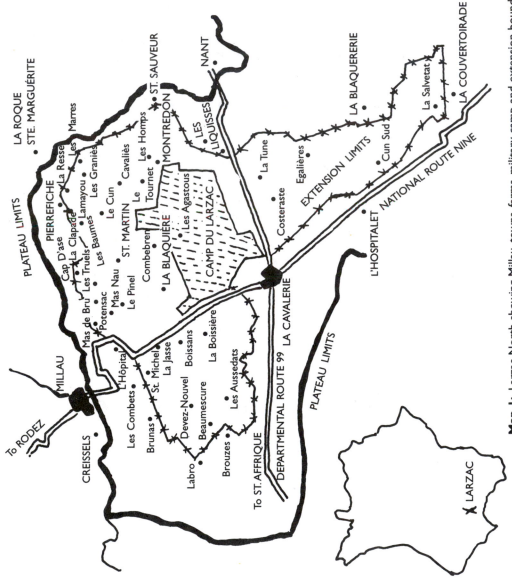

Map I: Larzac North showing Millau, towns, farms, military camp and extension boundaries

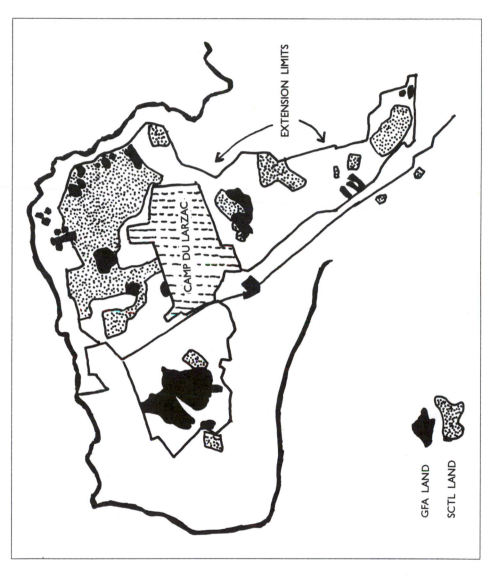

EXTENSION LIMITS

CAMP DU LARZAC

GFA LAND

SCTL LAND

Map 2: GFA and SCTL land in 1992

Part One
The Community Forms

CHAPTER ONE
Background

Wind-raked! Soaked in the fall and winter by rains carried inland by the sea wind (*marin*) that gathers its strength in the Mediterranean, burnt dry in the summer by the sun and fierce north wind, the Larzac is a region of climatic extremes. It is the southernmost of five great limestone plateaus, or *causses*, and is located in the department of the Aveyron, less than seventy kilometers from the sea. Like its siblings, it is composed of the sedimented remains of uncountable microscopic animals deposited in an ocean that once overflowed the land between the two most southern mountain chains of the *massif central*. Ranging from 560 to 950 meters above sea level and 1,000 square kilometers in area, the Larzac brings the cold winters of the *massif central* within sight of the clement south, the Midi. The natives of the Larzac see themselves as the stubborn inhabitants of a harsh and stingy land on which thin soils and unpredictable weather make pastoralism the only possible way of life. They are fully aware, and sometimes proud, of the contrast between "their" plateau and the valley floors on which a long and stable growing season favors the cultivation of peach, apricot, almond and olive orchards, as well as wine and table grapes. It is not uncommon to hear Larzac farmers refer to this other world, which in reality is only a few kilometers away, as if the distance were multiplied by hundreds. They are also proud of their ability to live and work in such an ungrateful environment. As Pierre Burguière, one of the protagonists in this book and a typical inhabitant of the plateau, has said of the Larzac: "As for me, the Larzac — I love it as if it were a handicapped child. The more it makes you suffer, the more you become attached to it." Auguste Guiraud, whose roots are deep in the Larzac, expressed the same sentiment in different words: "The peasant is married to the land. Of course, here the bride is pretty skinny and her dowry's not big either. But then, we are here to fatten her up."

The Larzac also represents an area of "wide open spaces" — a Far West (it is actually referred to by some as *le far-ouest*) in miniature that, until recently, was uncluttered and uninclosed by fences. François Boé, an outside militant during the struggle against the

3

extension of the military camp, remembers the first time he saw the Larzac as a child: "My grandmother was a grape farmer on the plain near Beziers [a city in the nearby department of the Hérault]. Every fall she would drive up to the Larzac in her truck to hire local people to harvest her crop. Although I was very young at the time the extraordinary beauty and breadth of the landscape stuck in my mind. For example, as long as I live I will never forget my impression of a spectacular golden sunset glowing against the cliffs of Le Caylar."

To the casual traveler on National Highway Nine (the road that splits the Larzac from north to south) the plateau can appear arid and deserted. Michelin's tourist guide for the immediate area, the Gorges du Tarn, describes the Larzac as rocky, sterile, deforested and monotonous. Yet, below this inhospitable surface — referred to by some as a "moonscape" — is a reservoir that feeds sixty streams and rivers! The torrential rainfall of autumn and winter (the Larzac equals Normandy in total annual rainfall) rapidly disappears from the surface to infiltrate the spongy limestone where it forms the subterranean streams that surface in the river valleys below the *causse*. But, in most years, enough humidity remains to nourish the plant cover and provide at least the minimum amount of water necessary to support the rural population with its flocks of sheep. There are no water courses on the plateau, but the usually abundant rainfall is captured from house and barn roofs and stored in cisterns or, in the fields, in stone-lined depressions (*lavognes*), where sheep come to drink when they are out to pasture.

Although the rain- and wind-tortured — but often breathtaking — rock formations *are* the most visible features of the plateau, the expressions "desertlike" and "moonscape" are best applied elsewhere. The Larzac is actually one of the most varied floral areas in Europe. Crossing the plateau at a hundred kilometers per hour, or more, one's eyes — when they are not on the road — are naturally drawn to the dramatic, inorganic rock outcroppings. Unless the observer has a passion for open country, he or she will scarcely notice the slightly undulating surface on which grass, wild thyme, juniper, thorny scrub and boxwood grow. Only a very few farms are to be seen from the road, and these, at some distance. Flocks of sheep are rare. This monotonous scenery is deceptive. The majority of farms are far from the main highway, and the predominant wild vegetation — most apparent in the spring when there are few tourists (the annual migrations toward the beaches of the Mediterranean and Spain begin at the end of June and last for only two months) — consists of relatively hidden, low, seasonally flowering plants. Located between the Mediterranean and the Cévennes Mountains and on the divide between the Atlantic and Mediterranean drainages, the Larzac is host to about one-quarter of all wild plant species found in France. Plants typical of the Mediterranean region, the steppes and the Alps all flourish on various parts of the *causse*. Among its riches are wild narcissus, irises and a large number of orchid species. In late June, "Angel's Hair," a silvery-headed wild grass particular to the *causse*, undulates in the wind like a snow-white inland sea. Huge, flat thistles (*cardabelles*) hug the dry soil. As they mature in the fall, their centers turn into lemon-yellow suns surrounded by thorny, green spikes.

The oak and beech forests that once covered the Larzac are mostly gone, although their remnants can still be found on the northeast rim of the plateau that overlooks the river valley of the Dourbie. In the deforested areas the untrained eye will confuse the shaping force of human occupation, including in some places flora typical of overgrazing, with what appears to be an impoverished, if untamed, natural area. The surface of the plateau, wild-looking as it is, has been lived upon and worked by humans since Paleolithic times. What the traveler who cares to notice sees on the Larzac is not a virgin chaos of rocks with an unvarying plant cover but a rich, natural and cultural synthesis — the end product of centuries of human activity.

Here and there, clay and other soils deposited in low-lying areas of the *causse* trap humidity that otherwise would have rapidly found its way down to the underground rivers. These fertile *sotches* are cultivated to provide winter forage of various grains, hay and alfalfa for the flocks of sheep that graze in spring and summer on wild *parcours*, or uncultivated pastures. For the interested traveler who wishes to drive a few kilometers off the main road on one of the many local paved lanes that connect the hamlets and isolated farms of the Larzac, it becomes apparent that, in addition to the *sotches*, there are other areas sufficiently fertile for cultivation. These areas can be quite extensive, and where they are, permanent settlements have developed. They range from individual farms, small hamlets with a few houses to rather substantial villages. Indeed, the national highway itself bisects the largest fertile area on the Larzac where it also splits the two most populous communities, L'Hospitalet and La Cavalerie. The latter once had over 1,500 inhabitants and now boasts a permanent population of about 800.

La Cavalerie's population consists of farmers, shopkeepers and hoteliers, who offer their services to local farmers, passing tourists and the military camp that covers about 3,000 hectares of what was once largely communal land.

Today, as in the past, the primary resource of the Larzac is sheep, the majority of which are milked for the production of Roquefort cheese. The milk for this luxury product is collected on the Larzac, the rest of the Aveyron, and four surrounding departments. It is then taken to centrally located dairies where the cheesemaking process begins. In the dairy, the milk is curdled, the whey disposed of, and the solid matter pressed into large, round loaves that are inseminated with the mold *Penicillium roqueforti*. After a few days the loaves are transported west to the village of Roquefort-sur-Soulzon, just below the plateau. There, each loaf is made ready for aging. They are salted and pierced with long needles to allow air to circulate in the developing cheese. Thus prepared, the loaves are stored in deep natural caves that provide a unique environment for ripening before sale.

Eighty percent of Roquefort cheese is made by a single producer, Société de Roquefort, which is in turn owned by Besnier, a French producer of Camembert. The remaining 20 percent is made by five independent producers. The cheesemakers control the production of Roquefort through the activities of an association, the *Fédération des Industriels de Roquefort*. This association jealously guards its ancient monopoly over France's most expensive dairy product, which was granted by decree of the Parlement of Toulouse on August 31, 1666.

Milk producers for Roquefort are also grouped in an association, *La Fédération Régionale des Syndicats d'Eleveurs de Brebis* (SEB). The cheese producers' association and the SEB negotiate problems concerning production, milk quality and prices among themselves within yet another association, *La Confédération Générale des Producteurs de Lait de Brebis et des Industriels de Roquefort*. In general, the SEB is controlled by the larger milk producers, although they constitute a minority of farmers supplying milk to the Roquefort industry. In 1990 a group of small milk producers, inspired largely by Larzac militants, founded its own union, *Le Syndicat des Producteurs du Lait de Brebis* (SPLB), but so far it has not been allowed to participate in negotiations with the cheesemakers.

While the Larzac furnishes several of the smaller producers with the majority of their milk supply, it provides, overall, only about 3 percent of the milk used in the fabrication of Roquefort. Yet, the plateau — with its open space, unpolluted environment, and tradition of production by small peasants — remains the symbol of purity and rural wholesomeness that — the industrialists never cease to remind the buying public — is the *sine qua non* of their product. It is even claimed that the best quality Roquefort is made from the milk of Larzac sheep fed on grasses native to the *causses* (Develotte 1979).

The relationship between the masters of the cheesemaking industry and the regional peasants is more paternalistic than symbiotic. While it is true that Roquefort needs locally produced milk to maintain its image and pays a good price for it, the farmers are the dependent members of an unequal partnership. Their vulnerability, however, became evident only recently when increasing production (originally encouraged by the industry and the leading agricultural bank, the *Crédit Agricole*) led to large milk surpluses. In response, the cheese producers, acting through the *Confédération* and, therefore, with the apparent agreement of the SEB, imposed quotas (beginning in 1988) on the amount of milk that would be bought at top prices. These quotas differ from farm to farm according to a complicated formula based largely on past production. Beyond these quantities, milk is still bought, but at a much lower price — a price that frequently does not meet costs. Those who suffer most from the quotas are small-scale producers, especially young farmers in the process of building up their flocks who have borrowed heavily from the *Crédit Agricole* and who need to increase output in order to survive.

The reader will have noted by now that I have tended to use the terms *farmer* and *peasant* interchangeably when referring to agricultural activities in the region associated with Roquefort. The meaning of *farmer* should be clear enough but the same is not the case with the word *peasant*. For most anthropologists, this word is used specifically in reference to groups of people who are essentially subsistence farmers, more or less independent of the money-based economy of the nation in which they happen to live. Many also agree that peasants are distinct from farmworkers who, as members of an agricultural proletariat, are paid wages for labor. The term may also be applied — as it frequently is in Latin America — to poor tenant farmers who occupy the land of absentee landlords, paying their rents in cash or in kind.

Peasants are said to differ from the preliterate populations of the "Third World" — often studied by anthropologists — in that, unlike these populations, they do not have their own distinct culture or language. Rather, they make up a special, if underprivileged, enclave within a national entity. For this reason, peasants have been referred to as groups having "part cultures" — somewhat distinct, but not separate, from the culture of the larger society in which they are imbedded. Thus there can be *French* peasants or *Chinese* peasants defined as such within the context of a national culture. What peasants everywhere have in common (if indeed they have anything in common beyond their being poor farmers) is a set of negative characteristics, based on their exploitation by some other segment of the national culture, their isolation from the mainstream of that culture, or both.

In the French language the term *paysan* is fraught with semantic traps. Rogers notes that in France the term is "a highly charged and manipulable symbol" (1987:56). In some cases, it is used by writers on agriculture interchangeably with the term *agriculteur* to designate anyone who farms for a living. (The word *fermier*, however, refers unambiguously to farmers who rent their land.) In other cases, *paysan* is used to refer to small, traditional farmers in distinction to those who run large, modern enterprises.

In current usage, traditional farmers, native to a particular area, often use the term self-referentially to contrast themselves with newly installed farmers, whatever the size of the newcomer's farm. One Larzac native, for example, on looking with us through a book about the history of the struggle against the military camp extension, made a point of distinguishing *paysans*, those whose roots were in the immediate area and whose families had been farmers for generations, from the more recently installed farming population on the plateau. Most of the latter come from outside the Aveyron. For our informant these were, most emphatically, not *paysans* and he considered it dishonest to label them as such.

Turning now to the anthropological treatment of peasants that I will apply in this study,[1] I would first argue that, until the beginning of the 1950s, the majority of farmers in the Roquefort basin shared many, if not all, of the characteristics attributed in the literature to peasants. Indeed many, if a reduced number, still maintained these characteristics at the beginning of the 1970s. In the 1950s the typical farm was minuscule and extremely poor. Farming methods were backward, little changed from those used over the course of previous centuries, when farmers led relatively autonomous, if miserably poor, lives. Production figures from this period indicate that even those farmers who were lucky enough to sell their milk to Roquefort were barely able to live above subsistence levels. Flocks rarely exceeded sixty animals and each sheep yielded only fifty to sixty liters of milk per year — far from the present day average of 150 to 200 liters (Pilleboue et al. 1972:458).

Second, when looking at the ideology of the movement, it needs to be stressed that the Larzac struggle began in the context of the immediate post-1968 period, which coincided with the first blush of the ecology movement. In this context the term *peasant*, which up to then had pejorative connotations for some, began to be used as a term of positive affirmation. Small farmers, who, before 1968, had preferred the term *agriculteur*, seized upon *paysan* as a badge of honor — a claim to a special and strategic place in French society.

Third, and still within the realm of ideology, the term *peasant* was consciously chosen as a form of self-reference by the farmers of the Larzac from the very inception of their ten-year struggle against the extension of the military camp. It served as a cover for real cultural and economic differences among them, facilitating their presentation to the outside as a united and homogeneous force. Yet, on the Larzac itself, while all peasants were equal *some* were clearly more equal than others.

Shortly after the struggle began, natives of the plateau developed a new term of self-reference, *pur porc*, to distinguish themselves from the pioneer settlers of the immediate pre-struggle period. But even the *purs porcs* were not a homogeneous group. Three large, economically successful farms in the northwest of the plateau were occupied by *purs porcs*. In the northeast, in contrast, several *pur porc* farmers were more traditional, small-scale agriculturalists. The same was true for a number of farmers in and around La Cavalerie, the site of the military camp, but two of them, Robert Gastal and Louis Massebiau, were partners in a large modern farm. Like *peasant* the term *pur porc* as a reflection of rootedness was an invention of the struggle and does not indicate class membership or real common interests other than a certain emotional approach to human relations that can be seen in the division, to be discussed in chapter nine, between *affectives* (mostly *purs porcs*) and *politicals* (mostly pioneers and new settlers). In reality, as shall be demonstrated below, the "peasants" of the Larzac were a varied group of geographically distinct, small and large farmers (natives, pioneers and, as the struggle developed, squatters), as well as assorted agricultural laborers, including a significant group of underpaid shepherds.

Without the Roquefort industry, the plateau (except for some secondary residences) would have become largely depopulated in the last hundred years. In fact, in spite of Roquefort, a slow process of depopulation began just before the First World War, becoming more accentuated after that conflict which took a terrible toll upon the youth of the Midi. In general, farms in the isolated mountain zones of the Aveyron, with their poor soils and difficult weather conditions, stand as disadvantaged competitors with those in the more fertile and more temperate zones of the nearby valleys and the rich farmlands of the north. In 1979, for example, 5,046 or 37 percent of farmers in the entire Aveyron were classed as small peasants as measured by economic units equivalent to twenty hectares or less of land producing wheat and yielding a maximum yearly income of 84,000 francs (approximately $14,000) (Jegouzo 1984:205).

In the mountainous regions of the Aveyron, and particularly on the *causse*, much of the land is uncultivable, rocky pasture and forest. Few farmers have more than a small percentage of land planted in forage crops. This means that farming for profit — which, here, means animal husbandry — has to be extensive rather than intensive. Farmers must take full advantage of available wild pastureland. Many of those not fortunate enough to produce for Roquefort must quit the area. Even the number of those who do sell to Roquefort has declined in the past several years. Between 1975 and 1985, the sum total of Aveyron producers dropped from 3,007 to 2,178 (*Patre* 1986:56). In 1969, in the five departments of the Roquefort basin, 4,526 farms or 79 percent produced between zero and one hundred hectoliters of milk for Roquefort. By 1986, testifying to the necessity of a minimum production level vital to the existence of a farm, the number of small producers had dropped to 574 or only 19 percent (*Patre* 1986:57).[2] In 1969 no farms produced more than 600 hectoliters, and in 1986 the majority (70 percent) still produced only 400 hectoliters or less, just a bit higher than the minimum necessary to support one family. Thus, when a farm is taken over by an elder son, younger brothers are often forced to leave the rural area. It is no wonder that the number of Aveyronnais living and working in Paris is astonishing only to those unfamiliar with the poverty of a large proportion of southern French farmers, which has produced the shifting demography of the rural population.

Although Millau is located within minutes of the plateau and is the place where the Larzac peasants who live on the northern half of the *causse* do their shopping, life in this city of 22,000 and life on the Larzac are worlds apart. In spite of its decline, Millau remains a center of industry and commerce. The majority of its population (not counting a rising number of retired people) are members of the urban working class. As one might expect, the city dwellers and the peasants of the plateau hold diametrically opposed images of the Larzac that are based on the vastly different ways each group uses the *causse*. For the Millavois, the plateau is their recreational backyard — a source of fresh air to be used on weekends for hiking, picnicking, hunting and mushrooming. For the peasants — as much as they might love and take pride in its spectacular natural beauty — the Larzac is an ungrateful land on which, in order to survive, one is forced to wring out a precarious living through long hours of difficult labor. Before the struggle, the notion of recreation was foreign to the traditional Larzac peasant, except for occasional Sunday hunts in the fall and a once-yearly seasonal village fête. To this day, many of the older farmers have never taken a single vacation.

Thus, even with their guaranteed source of income from Roquefort, life for the peasant of the Larzac has never been easy. Even into the 1970s, milk, with only a few exceptions, was produced on small, ill-equipped farms. Flocks barely supported a family and its shepherd who often lived as a family member, eating at the family table, sleeping in the barn or in a small room in the farmer's house and working long hours for very low wages. Where there were no shepherds, the peasant's wife tended the sheep. In addition to her daily house work, it was she who was responsible for the production of the *basse-cour* (the farm yard with its chickens and a few pigs), as well as the vegetable garden. She also helped in the lambing season. If the forage harvest was large enough to require outside helpers, she prepared lunches and dinners for temporary workers or neighbors who brought in the hay and cereal crops. In many cases, peasant wives also did piecework for the glove industry (using lambskins from the Larzac) that flourished in Millau until the 1960s.

During periodic labor troubles, especially an epic six-month-long strike in 1935, these women provided scab labor at home — a fact that alienated the working class of Millau from the peasants of the plateau. This alienation was amplified during the Second World War. The inhabitants of Millau, who suffered from severe food shortages, saw the peasants, at best, as stingy and, at worst, as profiteers. While it is true that farmers are generally better supplied with food during wartime than city dwellers, the stories of the Larzac peasants growing rich on the backs of their urban neighbors were surely exaggerated even if, in isolated cases, some farmers might have profited from scarcity in the urban market. Accusations of profiteering must be taken with a grain of salt. They reflect a mutual lack of trust between city dwellers and the inhabitants of rural areas — particularly between the urban working class and peasants. Farmers see workers as people who have access to the benefits of city life, work regular and relatively short hours, earn a guaranteed wage and, particularly in recent years, take ample vacations of legally established length. On the other hand, workers see peasants as enjoying the "good life" of the country and being rich enough to own the tools of their labor, as well as their land and houses. Workers resent the government subsidies they know are available to farmers and often characterize country dwellers as ungenerous even though well-off.

As I have suggested, the rural and urban populations of the Larzac-Millau area hold these misconceptions of each other even though the peasants (particularly those in the north of the plateau) and the workers of Millau live in close physical proximity. Real cultural differences serve as a basis for self-constructed ideologies, creating barriers to understanding that are difficult to surmount.

Conditions on the Larzac in the immediate postwar period were not unique to the plateau or even to the Aveyron. Into the 1960s, French agricultural production (except for a few favored areas in the northern half of the country) was concentrated in traditional farms that did not exceed a few hectares in size. Machinery was limited and primitive. Ploughing, for example, was more than likely done with hand ploughs. Horses or oxen were used for traction. Animal husbandry was limited to small herds or flocks of genetically inferior stock. Production did exceed the subsistence needs of farm families, and this surplus found its way into the local and national markets. However, profits rarely provided for more than the purchase of basic essentials. Conditions were particularly primitive in the mountainous backcountry of the Mediterranean littoral.

The plateau has shared the backwardness and poverty of other agriculturally marginal regions of France. Additionally, its somewhat unusual geopolitical structure has served to undermine its political power. With the exception of merchant-dominated La

Cavalerie, L'Hospitalet, and the small village of La Couvertoirade, with its population of artisans — the sparsely distributed farms and hamlets of the northern half of the plateau belong geographically and politically to nine separate, valley-centered communes. A good part of the northwestern rim of the plateau is subject to either the city of Millau or the nearby town of Creissels. In these two communes the population of merchants and workers vastly outnumbers farmers, and the interests of the urban center normally dominate political decisions. Although the other seven communes that contain separate parts of the Larzac are rural in nature, the population center of each is in a river-valley village. The majority of the inhabitants of these villages are active or retired farmers. However, they tend to vote as a local block, supporting the interests of their own village not those of the isolated and less numerous farmers living on the plateau. It can be easily demonstrated that this difference in political power has had major consequences in the lives of the rural peasants. One need only note that the valley villages received such amenities as paved roads, electricity, running water and telephones long before the farms and hamlets of the Larzac. In fact — except for electricity, which had been installed on most farms by the end of the 1950s — these same amenities were granted to the Larzac farmers on the northern half of the plateau only after the successful struggle against the camp extension when, for a brief period, the people of the Larzac could act as a political entity to put pressure on local politicians.

To fully understand the dynamics of the Larzac struggle and its aftermath, we need to examine yet another set of geographic divisions on the plateau. The planned extension of the military camp included only the northern half of the *causse*. Within this area, three internal, if unofficial, zones may be delineated. Each of these can be distinguished on the basis of economic and cultural factors that have had their effect on the history of the Larzac before, during and after the struggle. The first zone, located in the south of the extension area, includes the villages of La Couvertoirade, L'Hospitalet and La Cavalerie. Because La Cavalerie was the site of the military camp, its business people were the center of support for the extension. La Cavalerie, however, also had a significant proportion of relatively successful farmers. The first leaders against the camp extension came from among these farmers, some of whom were also members of the *Fédération Départementale des Syndicats d'Exploitants Agricoles* (FDSEA), the local branch of the national agricultural union, which took a stand against the extension from the very beginning.

The peasants of La Cavalerie who opposed the extension (and their children who attended the village school) were in the uncomfortable position of having to face the every day hostility of the camp's supporters — including the military personnel. The struggle against the camp extension created an air of crisis that reigned everywhere on the Larzac, but it was in La Cavalerie where the adversaries shared daily life. To oppose the camp under such circumstances must have been particularly stressful.

The second zone is located on the extreme northwest of the plateau, to the west of the national highway. There, one finds the largest, most modern and most successful farms on the Larzac. Two of these farms were developed by dynamic outsiders. One, Léon Burguière, who arrived in 1952, was native to the Aveyron. As an Aveyronnais, he was easily assimilated into the Larzac and during the struggle was accepted as a *pur porc*. His authority with the peasants increased as his farm grew in importance. This authority was enhanced not only by his reputation for absolute integrity but also by his active membership in several local associations and by his many years of service on the board of the regional *Crédit Agricole*, a position that gave him the status of a *notable*, or local dignitary. The other dynamic outsider was Guy Tarlier (known on the plateau as the "préfet du Larzac"), whose origins were in a northern French agricultural family. He came to the *causse* in the 1960s from Africa, where he had been a coffee planter for ten years.

These two individuals had the most to lose from the extension, at least in terms of capital and labor invested. Both had strong personalities, and each soon became an active leader in the struggle, eventually replacing a major figure from La Cavalerie who quit the battle early. Tarlier eventually became the towering figure of the struggle and the post-struggle community.

The third zone lies to the east of the national highway. It consists of small, isolated farms and a number of hamlets. The soils here tend to be the poorest on the northern half of the plateau. Many of the farms in this zone were unoccupied at the beginning of the struggle. Three hamlets — Pierrefiche, La Blaquière and St. Sauveur — were inhabited by small-scale, traditional farmers. Two other hamlets, Montredon and St. Martin, had become completely depopulated. Although several of the peasants in this area became important figures during the struggle, with much to say in and out of meetings, their contribution to it was more in the area of moral authority than in leadership in the planning of strategic actions.

Because so much of this zone had unoccupied farms and because it was strategically located in relation to the proposed extension, it became a center for squatters. Many of them settled on property that had already been bought by the army from absentee owners. These people composed the most radical opponents to the extension and often served as the movement's shock troops.

It should not surprise the reader that the squatters, along with the small farmers in the same zone, sometimes expressed a lack of confidence in the richer and more powerful farmers to their south and west, whom they suspected were ready to compromise with the army in order to save their own farms. Rumors of such compromises were rife during a good part of the ten-year history of the struggle. As Didier Martin has pointed out in his book *Le Larzac: Utopies et Réalités*, the three zones, with their different populations and special interests, provided a basis for internal conflict throughout the struggle. That such conflict was generally overcome, although sometimes with great difficulty, is a tribute to the strength and faith of those who fought to save their land from expropriation. When the struggle ended, however, the strains among the inhabitants of these three zones reemerged and, in certain conflicts, became acute.

The part of the Larzac affected by the extension of the camp can thus be usefully delineated into three socioeconomic zones. However, we must also define the specific geographic area affected by the extension. The existing camp has been located since 1902 just east of the village of La Cavalerie. It was to be extended from 3,000 to 17,000 hectares. The proposed extension would have covered most of the plateau to the north of La Cavalerie on both sides of National Highway Nine and, to the south, a relatively narrow strip along the east side of the road down almost as far as La Couvertoirade (a small, fortified and now largely restored village founded by the Knights Templars in the twelfth century). The extension spared the villages of L'Hospitalet, La Cavalerie and La Couvertoirade. The commercial well-being of the last, however, is based primarily on tourism — an industry that would have been severely damaged if the camp had been extended to just outside the village limits. Two hamlets near La Cavalerie — Les Liquisses and La Blaquererie — were also spared, but these settlements depend almost completely on agriculture. The extension would have put most of the resident farmers out of business.

This is not to say that all the land owners, or even all the peasants of the Larzac, were against the camp extension. A few absentee owners of large tracts sold early and made substantial profits on land that had been bought only a few years previously. These transactions led many opponents of the camp to claim that the extension plan was arranged by the government in Paris to favor friends who had bought land for speculative purposes. It is well known that a close friend of Michel Debré — the minister of defense who presented the extension plan to the nation — made a good deal of money from the sale of land that was included in the extension plan.

In order to understand the dynamics of resistance in 1971, we have to go back in history to the founding of the camp. We must also take another look at the state of Larzac farming when the extension was announced. In addition, we should take note of the way the government chose to make public its decision to extend the camp. Prospecting for the construction of a military camp in the Larzac area began in 1899. The local population, already suffering from economic hardships, welcomed the move. On September 10, 1899, the municipal council of La Cavalerie proposed that the village cede, at no cost to the military, a section of communal land for the construction of the camp. Between 1900 and 1902, the government went through the necessary expropriation process, which led to the ceding of 1,500 hectares by Millau, 1,400 hectares by La Cavalerie, and 150 hectares by the commune of Nant in the valley of the Dourbie to the east (Boyer et al. 1986:6). According to this reference, the army signed an agreement in 1927 with the communes of Millau, La Cavalerie, Nant and La Roque Ste. Marguérite, giving their inhabitants the right to pasture sheep within the confines of the camp when maneuvers were not taking place. In return, the army was given the right to install artillery batteries on the communes' land. In 1951, the government developed its first extension plan under which the camp was to be enlarged to 20,000 hectares. In 1963, acting on their own initiative, eight land owners, including an absentee Belgian, petitioned the government to extend the camp. Later the same year the mayors of Nant and La Roque Ste. Marguérite, as well as the first deputy mayor of Millau, made public statements in favor of the proposed extension. This decision was reinforced in 1965 when the mayors of St. Affrique, Millau,

L'Hospitalet and La Cavalerie all asked that the camp be permanently occupied by French or foreign troops. (English troops had been using the camp as a base, with the French army, for some time.) As might be expected there were rumors concerning the extension during this period, but the more they circulated, the less they were taken seriously. Finally in October of 1970, although no official position had been taken by the government, the secretary of state for defense — when questioned by a peasant at a local party meeting in La Cavalerie about the installation of water lines on the plateau — remarked in passing that such installations would be paid for by the army as part of the coming extension. On May 9, 1971, a group of leftists and pacifists in Millau mounted the first public demonstration against the camp, but the peasants did not join them. They were busy mobilizing their own opposition to the camp with the aid of local *notables* and union leaders.

Officials in Paris must have been surprised at the reaction of the local population to the extension plan. While it was welcomed by the business people of La Cavalerie, elsewhere in the Aveyron, it was met with immediate, wide-scale protest. Discussions concerning the proposition were opened in the city of Rodez between opponents of the camp and the local representative of the national government (the prefect of the Aveyron). Given the size and representativeness of the opposition, those against the camp felt confident that the project could be stopped, or at least modified, to satisfy local opinion. Then on October 28, 1971, Michel Debré announced on national television the definitive decision of the government to extend the camp to 17,000 hectares. The peasants and their allies were outraged. Their conservative ideals had led them to trust authority. As several of them put it in their interviews with us: "We considered ourselves apolitical. Only leftists are political! We believed in the total honesty of the clergy, the prefect and our elected officials." Even the current mayor of La Cavalerie, a supporter of the extension, told us that announcing the project on television, without any previous warning — either to local officials or the population at large — was a tremendous blunder. After the announcement, it looked as if the negotiations at Rodez were a cover for the unilateral imposition of what had so rapidly become an unpopular plan.

The explosion of populism, real as it was, cannot fully explain the massive turnabout in public opinion concerning the extension. Its rapidity and magnitude can only be understood in terms of a radical change in economic conditions in the agricultural sector that had occurred, almost unperceived, during the course of the 1950s and 1960s. By 1970, at least two partnerships had been established among the productive farms at La Cavalerie. In the northwest sector, two large farms (also partnerships) were developed by recent settlers, and even on the poorer soil of the eastern sector, several newer arrivals had joined together on the farm of Les Baumes to rework land that had been abandoned for many years. Thus an economically strong and dynamic minority of farmers had already proved that the Larzac could be a viable agricultural area.

The first major changes seen in agriculture on the Larzac involved the creation and modernization of large farms. As Pilleboue et al. (1972) point out, before the extension of the camp on the Larzac was announced, the demographic situation had left a good deal of land on the market. A few farsighted individuals took advantage of this opening. Advanced farming methods on the Larzac can be dated to 1952 with the arrival of Léon Burguière and his family. Born in Espalion, a town northwest of Millau, in the Aveyron, Léon Burguière worked for his grandparents on a small, rented farm. Two years after completing his military service, he married and began looking for a farm of his own. His wife was from the Millau region, and it was in that area that he began his search. Through the grapevine, he discovered that the large farm of L'Hôpital (named for the Millau hospital that owned it) was available. Arriving on the Larzac, he was immediately taken with its beauty and vast open space. He also realized that, with hard work and modern methods, L'Hôpital — which by then had become quite run-down — could be made profitable. He describes the situation on the Larzac at that time as follows:

> We had thirty cows and a few sheep, pigs and horses on the old farm. We bought the first tractor that was used on the plateau. We arrived at the end of September. My brother-in-law came to help me. Working alone, or sometimes with a few hired hands, we began on a small scale and increased production gradually over time. When we took over L'Hôpital, only a few hectares were cultivated. It was the tractor that made the difference. As for the rest of the plateau, at the time, there were certain areas that were completely abandoned. Conditions were very primitive. There were no roads, no electricity, no water; life was very difficult. Parents wanted their children to leave. If the army had decided to extend the camp during that period they would have had no problem. Progress in farming came with the use of modern machinery — particularly tractors and rock crushers — fertilizers, and increases in milk pro-

duction per sheep through better breeding methods, including the introduction of the Lacaune race of sheep. We began to get advice from agricultural technicians.

When the extension plan was announced Léon Burguière had just retired. He ceded his farm to his two sons, Pierre and Jean-Marie, who worked it in a partnership made official through the creation of a GAEC (*Groupement Agricole d'Exploitation en Commun*). By that time L'Hôpital extended over 750 hectares, of which 210 were planted with forage crops of various types. Its large flock of 750 high-production milking sheep was able to support two families.

Guy Tarlier, accompanied by his wife, Marizette, started farming on the Larzac in 1965. He told us about their decision to live on the plateau.

> We chose the Larzac for a number of different motives. My brother, who was an agricultural engineer, worked in Millau so we had heard of the area and knew that land was available. I first came here in 1960. A great deal of land was for sale and if the army had wanted to extend the camp at that time they would have had no difficulty. We also chose this area for aesthetic reasons. I was struck by the beauty of the Larzac from the very beginning, and although at first Marizette would have preferred to stay in Africa, she is now as taken by the *causse* as I am. When I bought the farm of Devez Nouvel [*devez* means *pasture* in Occitan], I had already seen the possibilities for expansion. At that point the farm had two oxen, one hundred sheep and a horse. There were four cultivated hectares.

Until his death in May 1992, Guy Tarlier was in a GAEC with three young farmers. The land of the GAEC consists of three farms: two were originally owned by Tarlier and one is rented from a GFA (*Groupement Foncier Agricole*). GFAs are organizations of shareholders that buy land and rent it to farmers. This particular GFA was founded by militants during the struggle in order to buy land that might otherwise have been sold to the army. The Tarlier GAEC is heavily mechanized. It consists of approximately 1,000 hectares, 200 of which are cultivated. Nine hundred fifty sheep are milked on a mechanical *rotolactor*, a rotating milking machine, developed by Tarlier himself. The GAEC is also a member of a CUMA (*Coopérative d'Utilisation du Matériel Agricole*), organized by a group of Larzac farmers occupying the northeast and northwest parts of the *causse*. The CUMA buys commonly used agricultural machinery and then rents it at cost to its members. In this way, equipment that is used only for a limited number of days per year can be shared, reducing expenses for everyone.

At present, with the European Community on the threshold of abolishing trade barriers among member countries, a great deal of attention is being focused on agricultural production. In the past several years, agricultural surpluses have threatened to be too large to be disposed of normally in the market place. In this context, France and its eleven partners in Europe have been working on plans to rationalize farming, balancing the needs of the various nations and, in the process, possibly imposing sacrifices.

The GATT treaty on international trade, pending in 1992–93, has complicated France's position in European agriculture. In spite of the high level of European production, France would like to see its own agriculture, particularly in cereals and oil-bearing seeds (such as corn, colza and sunflower) continue to maintain the trade surpluses that help counter the less impressive performance of French industry. The need to cut production in less successful farming areas will mean the disappearance of many small farms in France. In fact, the EC has already mandated the removal of many thousands of hectares from production in the coming years. Most of these are in southern Europe, especially the Mediterranean basin, where traditional farmers are still in the majority.

This policy has worried a number of concerned ecologists and those small farmers who, though aware of the economic situation, wish to continue a way of life that they value highly. They point out that peasants, using traditional farming methods, are the very people best-equipped to maintain the land in a state of semi-domestication — a condition that has positive value for the environment and society at large. While it has been adequately demonstrated that agrobusiness takes its toil on soil and water, it is argued that small-scale traditional farming protects natural areas in multiple ways — among them, keeping fields and woods in good order and reducing the risk of fires. By caring for the land as they do, small-scale farmers also serve ecologically oriented tourism by maintaining open country for hiking and other natural pleasures. Furthermore, taking vast, contiguous areas out of production puts more than farmers at risk. As we have seen during farm crises in the United States, when the family farm goes, schools, banks and businesses soon follow. The towns and small cities of rural areas, stripped of their *raison d'etre*, soon become deserted.

Two books recently published in France, *Les Champs du Départ* (Alphandern et al. 1989) and *La France en Friche* (Fottorino 1989) both warn of coming *désertification* in the mountain areas of France. This warning may be alarmist in overall terms, for there is evidence that many rural areas in France have been recovering population — but not farming population — in recent years (Kaiser 1988, pers. com.). However, it is certain that coming agricultural policy in Europe will strongly affect demographic patterns on the continent's southern fringe in the near future, in multiple ways. The post-struggle Larzac, for reasons both planned and accidental, can serve as an example for what might be accomplished with alternatives to current agricultural policies. Although depopulation on the plateau did in the beginning lead to larger, economically efficient farms, conditions specific to the struggle also gave rise to a considerable amount of experimentation on small-scale farms with low investment. Thus, today, one finds large, modern farms coexisting with small establishments. Some of the latter offer innovative and high-quality products to a market of discerning consumers. In addition, although the Larzac is no paradise and not everyone is satisfied with what has happened since the victory, the social and agricultural life of those farmers who care to participate in one or more of the many associations that have developed in the last twenty-one years has been enriched and broadened by the concerns of these organizations that often reach beyond the confines of the plateau. The young and varied population that has been attracted to its farms and hamlets also contributes to a more fulfilling social life for all the inhabitants. It is for these reasons that the post-struggle Larzac stands as a model for alternate forms of development in less favored rural zones in France and elsewhere.

NOTES

1. For a sample of anthropological writings on peasants see Archetti and Aass (1978); Ennew, Hirst and Tribe (1977); Mintz (1973); Roseberry (1983); Shanin (1980, 1983, 1987); Silverman (1979); Weber (1976); Wolf (1955, 1966).
2. Rather spectacular increases in milk yields per sheep are due to recently introduced scientifically controlled feed and genetic selection for better milk production. The introduction of the Lacaune breed in the 1960s, which has now replaced the more rustic Larzac strain, is a major factor in increased yields.

Chapter Two
The Struggle Begins

"... I salute your struggle for justice, liberty and peace, the most beautiful struggle of our twentieth century."

Jean-Paul Sartre, Letter to the peasants of the Larzac
October 28, 1978

I am an anthropologist, not a historian. My purpose in this book is to describe and analyze a contemporary community, but one whose gestation occurred during the long struggle against the extension of the camp du Larzac. To do so, therefore, without paying attention to the "heroic period," the years of conflict with the government, would be improper. The post-struggle Larzac community, as it exists today, is the direct outcome of events that occurred between 1970 and June 3, 1981, the date on which the camp extension was annulled.[1] Although the success of the Larzac struggle was undoubtedly the result of a highly creative set of internal responses to an immediate external threat, it would be equally improper to analyze the post-struggle community while ignoring long-range economic, historic and cultural factors — intrinsic and extrinsic to the Larzac — that also impinged on the emergent community and its constituent individuals. In addition, as Didier Martin (1987) has pointed out, the Larzac, both during and after the struggle, can only be understood in terms of a complex set of relationships that developed in the period of 1971 to 1981 between the peasants and their outside supporters. Of particular interest in this respect is the fragile local alliance between a segment of the Millau working class and the peasants, an alliance that did not survive the victory in 1981. In sum, what follows is an historically oriented description and analysis of those complex factors that, I believe, provided the legacy for the post-struggle community.

By the 1960s, the city of Millau had entered an economic crisis. The leather and glove industries were in severe decline. Layoffs and factory closings had begun and would continue for the rest of the decade and beyond. In 1966, Georges (Jo-Jo) Artières, a glove cutter, discovered that his factory was on the brink of failure.

23

Owning a farm property just outside of Millau and below the Larzac, on the plateau side of the Dourbie, he decided to try his luck at chicken farming. This, however, required that he build a chicken coop. Consequently, Artières filed for a construction permit with the local authorities. To his surprise, his request was denied. When he protested, he was told that a plan to extend the camp du Larzac had frozen all construction on the northern half of the plateau and the contiguous valley floor. On his request, he was shown a map of the area with the outlines of the extension drawn over it in grease crayon. Artières, an antimilitarist, immediately went up to the *causse* to warn two farmers he knew, Léon (Pépé) Maillé and Léon Burguière, that their farms were included in the proposal. Both men were incredulous and told Artières he was crazy.

As noted earlier, the secretary of state for defense, André Fanton, had alluded to the proposed extension at a Gaullist party meeting at La Cavalerie on October 11, 1970. His reference to an extension did lead to the organization of a broad-based regional association (*Association de Sauvegarde du Larzac*, the Association for the Protection of the Larzac), which was presided over by a group of *notables* and included among its members several well-known peasants. However, Fanton's comment did not lead directly to any public demonstrations. This lack of response at the base may have been due to skepticism on the part of the Larzac population, which had since the 1950s become accustomed to hearing rumors about the camp. In addition, the peasants were as yet not a coherent group united by shared interests and a common enemy.

As far as the urban population of Millau was concerned, the lives of their peasant neighbors were of little importance. There were a few people, however, who were disturbed by the rumors. One of these was Robert Siméon, who — like his friend Jo-Jo Artières — combined a love of the Larzac's natural beauty with active antimilitarism. On a spring morning in 1971, Siméon quit his position as the shepherd for the GAEC of Les Baumes on the northeast Larzac. Needing to make a call concerning a new job in Millau, he went to the nearby farm of Lasmayou, where the only public telephone in the area was located. While there, he exchanged the usual small talk with the inhabitants of the farm and was told, in passing, that several gendarmes had been by that morning to inspect the area as part of a study preparative to an extension of the camp. Siméon had spent a year in jail as a conscientious objector during the Algerian War. In the late sixties, he was also a member of the PSU, a small left-wing party. He was not about to ignore what he had heard that morning at Lasmayou.

Returning to Millau in the evening, Siméon phoned a number of his friends and colleagues, including Jo-Jo Artières, to plan a public reaction to the extension. On May 9 a group of leftists, pacifists and environmental activists from Millau, along with the MDPL (*Mouvement pour le Désarmement, La Paix et La Liberté*) of Montpellier — a total of about 1,500 people — met in Millau. After a series of speeches, they marched to the camp headquarters at La Cavalerie. Although no peasants took part in this demonstration, Artières told us that he had seen Guy Tarlier lingering in the background, quietly watching. In addition, he said that Louis (Loulou) Massebiau, a partner in a GAEC in La Cavalerie and a union militant, had agreed to let them store food supplies for an evening picnic on a patch of his land at the edge of the village. This demonstration soon gave birth, in Millau, to the first off-plateau committee of support for the Larzac. The second was organized in Rodez in 1972. By the end of the struggle there were a hundred such groups, scattered all over France.

Aside from the Millau committee, which had the constant ear of the peasants, the most important group was in Paris. It was organized by Alain Cabanes, a leftist militant, and several of his friends and colleagues. Cabanes' description of the founding of the Paris committee and its operation conveys the improvisational, yet efficient, nature of the Larzac movement in all its parts.

> The Association for the Protection of the Larzac had a press conference in Paris at the end of 1971. They organized the "Open Farms," [see below] which I heard about from the Occitanists [regional separatists] in Paris. I'm from the Hérault and my wife is from the Sorgue. We know the region and its spirit well. We decided to go down to the Larzac and see for ourselves what was happening. The movement at the time was headed by Loulou Massebiau. During visits to the open farms we met people from all over France. Someone had the idea of setting up support groups. Right away about ten people from Paris agreed to organize a committee to introduce the Larzac to Paris. We decided on the spot to have a demonstration at the Mutualité [a traditional location for indoor demonstrations in Paris]. When I went back to Paris, I got a group together. I was a militant at the time in the PSU and the Occitanist movement. We managed to organize the whole demonstration in fifteen days! Our principle was that, while we supported the Larzac, we wanted people from the plateau to speak for themselves. Loulou Massebiau, Pierre Bonnefous, Guy Tarlier and Pierre Burguiere came. It was all very improvised and I was worried that

we wouldn't have enough people there to fill the hall. But the Mutualité was completely full! We were very surprised and felt overcome by the events. The work of the committee developed empirically and very fast. Each time something happened on the plateau, we tried to organize something in Paris. We would also go down to the Larzac on a regular basis.

In the summer of 1971, a group of Maoists from Toulouse got wind of the extension and decided to mount an attack on the French government via the Larzac, which they saw as an ideal opening battleground for the "coming revolution." With Jo-Jo Artières' permission, they set up camp on his property and spent the summer on a "long march," going from farm to farm, offering free labor and propagandizing against the extension. The peasants were wary of the Maoists. Rural France had been almost unanimous in condemning the May 1968 demonstrations in Paris. The students involved were viewed as dangerous leftists and hippies. The Maoists were quickly identified with the worst of the *soixantehuitards*. Their dress and comportment — particularly their sexual mores, which they displayed freely — scandalized the local people, who also found their long-winded political discourse both foreign and difficult to bear. In spite of these negative feelings, the Maoists did have an impact on the then-latent militancy of the Larzac peasants. Every inhabitant of the *causse* we interviewed who remembered them said the Maoists were a pain in the neck, or worse, but also one source of the growing political awareness that was still to reach maturity on the plateau.

Tensions were mounting. On September 23, a group of peasants demonstrated at La Cavalerie by dumping stones and manure on the mayor's doorstep. Not much more was needed to set off an explosion. The final spark came with official announcement of the extension by Michel Debré on October 28, 1971. The government had promised the Association for the Protection of the Larzac that it would consult with the local people concerned by the extension before any final decision was made. Instead, it acted unilaterally. The mounting opposition to the camp was now ready to counterattack, but the peasants of the Larzac had not yet emerged as an internally organized group. The first organized reaction came from the FDSEA. On November 6, 1971, the union called a mass demonstration in Millau, which was attended by 6,000 people — the majority of whom were peasants. Loulou Massebiau was one of the principal speakers at that rally. His militant discourse was a far cry from the nonviolent message that was to mark the next phase of the struggle. More than once in his speech Massebiau called explicitly for violent action against the extension. A look at his language also shows that the term *peasant* had not yet come to be used as a label on the Larzac. Massebiau consistently uses the word *agriculteur* rather than *paysan* when referring to his fellow farmers. In the fall of 1971, the ideology that would define a national movement had not yet taken form.

In spite of the violent tone of Massebiau's speech, negotiations between the members of the Association for the Protection of the Larzac and the prefect continued between November 1971 and April 1972. The Larzac's position in these discussions was explicit on at least one essential point: Not one farmer who wished to remain on the plateau should be forced to give up his land. The Larzac protest soon became a hot local issue. Very few people in the rural Aveyron were indifferent to it. The question of whether a locally supported protest against the national government could succeed on its own was soon raised. One person who felt it was imperative to get national attention for the movement was Pierre Laur, one of the leaders of the Roquefort producers' association. He sponsored the publication of a full-page advertisement protesting the extension in *Le Monde,* one of France's leading newspapers. In addition, he and Léon Burguière, who had just retired from L'Hôpital, began a national speaking tour against the extension plan, which was to last until the plan was annulled in 1981. Here were two local, widely respected, conservative individuals ready to speak out against the national government to any audience that cared to listen. Laur's conservative (actually, right-wing) credentials were perfect. Indeed, in 1988, he would back Jean-Marie Le Pen of the Front National for president of France. His active participation in the Larzac struggle is one of many examples that could be cited to show how broad the local coalition against the extension really was. As Pierre Burguière put it to us: "With a few exceptions, on the local level, the extension was opposed by the extreme right, the right, the center, the left and the extreme left." The broad-based nature of this opposition grew out of a strong populist strain that runs deep in the Aveyron and elsewhere in the backwaters of rural France.

Because it was a populist issue, one did not have to be a pacifist to be against the extension. Laur, for one, made his position very clear in his interview with us. He said that he had nothing against the army as such and, indeed, considered himself a patriot. In fact, he had served without regret as a volunteer during the Second World War, even though he was exempt for family reasons. His opposition to the extension came not only from his life-long attachment to the natural setting of the plateau but from his strong conviction that the extension was contrary to local interests and useless for the national defense. For him, the project was another flagrant case of Paris imposing its will on the provinces. Of course, it must not be forgotten that the proposed extension was also a real threat to Laur's own economic interests. As one of the smaller Roquefort producers, his share of production was heavily dependent upon the Larzac for milk.

The peasants of the Larzac were fortunate that their protest had such fertile soil in which to take root. In 1970 populism was not the only pathway to opposition. One need not search far to discover a totally different factor that was to favor the Larzac over the army. The recent events of 1968 had created a mass movement (what I should like to call a "cultural mode" because of its relatively ephemeral nature) that was anti-institutional, ecologically oriented and antimilitarist. For a brief time, a broad segment of the French public — at least, the left of the political spectrum — was more than ready to sympathize with the peasants of the Larzac. Traditionally preoccupied by working class demands, the left became responsive to the claims of both a growing ecology movement and a normally conservative rural population. Thus, by the end of February 1972, 300,000 people from all over France had signed a petition against the extension. At the same time, Laur and other leaders who had taken the movement to the nation realized that a wide base of support in the Larzac's own backyard was as important to the legitimation of the movement as its growth beyond the limits of the Aveyron. Consequently, as the struggle took shape on the national level, the attention of its leadership also turned to the inhabitants of Millau, who, in general, had been cool to the protest.

On February 12, 1972, huge fires were lit on the plateau above the city and the *tocsin*, the traditional means used to warn the population of disaster, was sounded by the church bells of Millau. (Pierre Laur claims — and there are others who support his claim — that this action chosen to sensitize Millau's population to the potential loss of their Larzac playground was his idea.) The response of the local population was almost immediate. This impressive spectacle awakened the people of Millau to the realization that "their" Larzac was in danger. From then on, increasing numbers of Millavois —what was soon to become a majority of the city's inhabitants —joined the opposition to the extension plan.

Ties with the working class of Millau were established in the spring of 1972, when workers at the SAMEX pants factory struck for higher wages, amelioration of working conditions and the right to unionize. This was one of the first strikes in France by women workers. According to Albert Austruy, a militant in the CFDT (the labor union, Catholic in origin, closely associated with the Socialist party), who was also active in the Larzac movement:

> The directors of SAMEX practiced repression. All they knew was work. They pushed the assembly line as fast as they could and continually raised production quotas. The CFDT decided that it would not help the workers until they requested it. Finally they did send us a delegation. We met with fifty women, and a strike as well as a factory occupation were agreed upon. At first, the president of the company refused to negotiate. There had never been a factory occupation in Millau before, but after forty-eight hours, management agreed to talks. The first talks lasted forty hours, day and night, with the participation of the mayor and the state work inspector. We went up to the Larzac and encouraged the peasants to send a delegation to the factory. The Burguières came and discussed the situation with the workers, but I felt that they could not really understand what conditions were like unless they saw the production line in operation. I asked the women to start it up at the rate of 500 pairs of pants per hour. The peasants were shocked. Léon Burguière said, "It's not possible! It's shameful!" He immediately asked to meet with the union officials. He said he would never want to see his children work under the same conditions. The peasants returned to the Larzac and the next day they came down with food for the workers. Later, when a Larzac exhibition concerning the struggle took place at La Jasse [the information center on National Highway Nine, later to become the Larzac ecological museum], the women of SAMEX offered part of their vacation time to act as hosts.

Yves Hardy and Emmanuel Gabey suggest in their book, *Dossier L . . . Comme Larzac,* that the interaction between the peasants and the SAMEX workers opened the way for the subsequent alliance between the Larzac and the workers of the Lip watch factory. In 1972, during a particularly difficult confrontation between union and management over an announced factory closing, the Lip workers occupied their factory and took over production and management. This action, an example of *autogestion* (worker self-rule), drew national attention. When the peasants and the Lip workers formed their alliance in 1973, the ties between the traditional left and the Larzac were considerably strengthened. The workers of Lip were featured participants in the August 1973 demonstration on the plateau, which was attended by 50,000 to 60,000 people. The relationship between the Larzac and labor was fragile, however, and never really took hold. The Lip protest fell apart in 1974, and increasing unemployment in Millau weakened the CFDT. No other alliances between the Larzac and labor were formed.

French history has frequently been punctuated by violent worker and peasant protests (cf. Tilly 1986). In this respect, the Larzac movement's commitment to nonviolence was an aberration that requires explanation. The Larzac protest, no doubt, gained part of its strength from the "revolutionary" climate of 1968. But 1968 was a *failed* revolution. What remained of it on the left in the 1970s was a continued hope for profound change in French society — a *spirit* of revolution that could be achieved for some through active experimentation with new lifestyles, for others, through support for local protest movements. The Larzac provided an ideal place — both real and imaginary — for the materialization of such a spirit. It became an experimental ground for the emergence of a new set of tactics designed to test the resolve of state authority by attacking its military establishment. What better way to do this than by facing "the force of arms" with the moral force of nonviolence?

Nonviolence was supported by some out of conviction, by others, as a tactic. We shall see below that pre-struggle personal histories and group meetings centered around Bible study prepared several important farmers for nonviolent political action. Ultimately, nonviolence worked because it united a disparate set of groups with disparate political and social aims, who could face off against the state together. The actions of this union resulted in a series of propaganda defeats for the government that kept the army on the defensive and solidified the Larzac farmers and their allies in their resolve to continue the struggle. The tactic of nonviolence also made it possible for local political authorities and *notables* in the Aveyron to safely legitimate their own claims to power over the central authorities in Paris.

The Aveyron in general and the Larzac in particular are profoundly Catholic. Shortly after the Second World War, a national farmers' organization (*Jeunes Agriculteurs Catholiques*, or JAC) was founded to encourage young rural people to participate in cultural activities, educate themselves and become involved in local and international issues in accordance with their religious convictions.

An offshoot of the JAC, *Chrétiens en Milieu Rural* (CMR), was created to allow small groups of farmers and local priests to discuss personal, national and international problems in relation to the Gospels, but outside of the organized Church and the Mass.

Both the JAC and the CMR were very influential in the Aveyron. The priest assigned to the Larzac CMR was Pierre Bonnefous, whose own roots lay in the Aveyron. He was one of ten children born to a poor peasant family that worked a minuscule, ten-hectare farm. Bonnefous, a highly intelligent and skilled moderator, organized twice-monthly meetings of his CMR. Among those attending were Robert Gastal, a peasant from La Cavalerie who had been disgusted by what he had seen as a young recruit during the Algerian War, and Elie Jonquet, who had been a worker-prisoner in Germany during the Second World War. This CMR group often discussed the horrors of war at its meetings. They were joined in their discussions by Auguste Guiraud of La Blaquière, Guy and Marizette Tarlier, several members of the Burguière family and others. These gatherings are recognized today as having played a role in preparing many Larzac peasants to accept the concept of nonviolence. The transformation of this essentially moral commitment into an active strategy came about only later through the influence of Lanza del Vasto, the charismatic founder of a local nonviolent community, *L'Arche* (The Ark).

When the Millau radicals, inspired by antimilitarism, decided to stage their march on La Cavalerie in May 1971, they appealed to *L'Arche* to join their ranks. The members of the community agreed to participate if the demonstration was strictly nonviolent and if they could be in charge of security to insure nonviolence. The Millau group accepted these conditions and *L'Arche* made its first appearance in the protest against the camp extension. Soon thereafter, Lanza del Vasto decided to commit himself personally to the Larzac cause. Lanza was convinced that a self-sacrificing, nonviolent but dramatic action on his part would be an effective means of opposing the camp extension and, at the same time, would move the peasants toward a pacific form of protest. He fasted at La Cavalerie for two weeks during the Easter season of 1972. Several peasants took turns joining the fast for one or two days at a time, and a larger public attended the sermons on nonviolence that Lanza gave each evening. The impact of the fast on public opinion was amplified when the bishops of Montpellier and Rodez gave it their support—even spending one day each at La Cavalerie fasting with Lanza. At the same time, an episcopal letter of support for the peasants was read from forty pulpits in the Aveyron. These actions by Church authorities galvanized the basically conservative peasants. Lanza del Vasto provided them with an ideology and a means of action that were in perfect accord with their religious beliefs.

The Larzac movement was off and running. Throughout the rest of the struggle, nonviolence was the only means acceptable to the peasants. Furthermore, it was this commitment that endowed the peasants with a sense of being guardians of a just cause, providing the moral strength needed to maintain local control even after the movement had become national. Throughout the ten-year struggle and beyond, the Larzac was able to resist co-optation from the outside. One either respected the rules of the game as dictated by the peasants, or one left the struggle. It was probably for this reason that, after a few tentative efforts in the very beginning of the movement, the local Communist party in Millau, as well as the CGT (the Communist-controlled labor union) soon refused to cooperate with it.

On March 28, 1972, inspired by Lanza del Vasto's fast, 103 of the 107 peasants threatened by expropriation (ranging from 5 to 100 percent of their land), representing families and employees totaling over 500 people, signed a solemn pledge that they would never sell to the army. This commitment became the charter of the Larzac movement — the concretization of the moral force created during Lanza's fast. On several occasions during the struggle, those in favor of the extension attempted to discredit the peasants by attacking the pledge, asserting that many signers had actually sold out to the government. By 1978, they could point out that the army had bought 8,697 hectares of the 14,000 included in the extension.

In the same year, the peasants responded by publishing a detailed analysis of these claims in a report called, Gardons le Larzac. According to this report, of the thirty-two people who had abandoned the pledge, three had died, one had left agriculture, twelve had retired, two had seen their land excluded from the proposed extension and two had refused to sign again — although neither had they sold to the army. Of the twelve others, eleven had indeed sold their land to the army. Seven had sold small parcels (the largest contained fifty hectares), and none of these sellers had been active in the struggle. One person sold 800 hectares of pasture land that the peasants claimed was of little interest to the army because of its location on the outer limits of the extension. Three other signers of the pledge had sold their entire farms, as had another nonsigner. At the time of the report, two of these three signers continued to occupy and farm their land as renters.

The report also belittled the apparent success of the army in purchasing 8,697 hectares. Most of the army's acquisitions had come either from buying communal land or from sales by nonresident owners. Furthermore, inflated sums were offered for land that the government itself had declared of little value. Throughout the struggle, rumors circulated that this or that owner had sold out. These rumors may have been sown by forces in favor of the extension in order to divide the peasants. Considering the outrageous prices offered and the suspicions that the rumors may have caused, tempting others to "sell out" as well, the tenacity displayed by the majority of the peasants is quite extraordinary.

Activity intensified in the spring and summer of 1972. The day Lanza del Vasto ended his fast, April 1, "Operation Open Farms" was begun. Its purpose was to allow outsiders to see for themselves that there was life on the Larzac. Over 3,000 people visited Larzac farms under this program. On July 2, two information centers were opened along National Highway Nine. That same summer, support came from the separatist Occitanists, who quickly adopted the Larzac as part of their "anticolonialist" cause. Although they continued to be a presence throughout the struggle, the Occitanists were soon overshadowed by the rapidly developing national scope of the movement.

On July 14, Bastille Day, a large group of peasants, in response to a request by the Larzac committee of Rodez, drove their tractors to Rodez, where they were met by 20,000 demonstrators. This action was organized by the *Comité Départemental de Sauvegarde du Larzac et de son Environnement* (Departmental Committee for the Protection of the Larzac and its Environment), a newly formed support group comprised of representatives from various local organizations. Among them were the presidents of the local chambers of agriculture, the FDSEA, the CDJA (*Centre Départemental des Jeunes Agriculteurs*) and SEB (the milk producers' association), a wide selection of nonagricultural unionists, as well as important local politicians.

The major speaker at the Rodez demonstration was Robert Gastal, a peasant from La Cavalerie who attended Pierre Bonnefous' CMR meetings. Although Bonnefous had helped him frame his discourse, Gastal's words came from the heart. Reticent at meetings, he was a convincing public speaker. In fact, Gastal was to become one of the important authentic voices of the Larzac. It was he who coined the term *pur porc* ("pure pork," the label of authenticity put on quality sausages in the Aveyron and elsewhere in France) to distinguish long-term natives of the Larzac from recent arrivals. As a *pur porc* himself, Gastal could speak with authority for the Larzac. Note his switch from the word *farmer* in the beginning to *peasant* throughout the rest of his speech:

I began to take care of a flock of sheep when I was only ten years old. Since then my professional life has not changed and I am not used to speaking in public. This has been a good year on the Larzac and I have never had a better harvest. This morning, like my friends on the *causse*, I brought the sheep back to the sheepfold and we took the route to Rodez with our tractors. I am not a special case. All the farmers of the Larzac are like me. If we have come here with our tractors, it is not to make folklore, but rather to prove our vigorous determination. The army wants to chase us away, to amputate us from our farms, with our families, our children; take away all that we have accomplished and all the investments we have made. What has taken place on the Larzac for the past two years is scandalous and inadmissible. We have a right to the truth. The decision to extend the camp was made by a single individual, Michel Debré. No deputy, no senator has given his opinion on the extension. It is an attack on democracy and the rights of man. . . .

One thing that makes us, the peasants of the Larzac, sick is when Debré and Sanguinetti [deputy from the Haute Garonne] accuse us of being bad Frenchmen. My good friends, you have only to stop in front of the monuments erected to the war dead on the Larzac . . . the lists are long. Mr. Debré, we do not need any lessons from you!

One of us, Elie Jonquet from La Blaquière is an eloquent witness. He lost his grandfather in the first expropriations for the Larzac camp in 1902. Then there was the War of 1914. He lost two of his uncles, and his father, who was gravely wounded, died two years after the war ended. In 1939 Elie began five years of exile in captivity [as a prisoner of war in Germany]. He has a right to respect rather than being insulted. . . .

In the name of the peasants of the Larzac, I thank you all: you women and young people who support us. You are from all over the area and you represent a range of different opinions: respect for democracy, for freedom, peace, disarmament, protection of the environment, etc. It is thanks to you that we have held on and will continue to hold on. . . .

As for us, the peasants of the Larzac, we are going to adopt a firm and clear attitude towards those who are trying to destroy us.

We will never accept being bought. . . . We will not leave the Larzac alive! . . . We are the guardians of the Larzac.

Today we will have driven 250 kilometers on our tractors and we will not hesitate to go all the way to Paris on them if Debré does not withdraw his decision. (Boyer et al. 1986:16–18)

The flavor of the pro-camp discourse, referred to by Robert Gastal in his speech, can be savored in the following letter by Alexander Sanguinetti, written to Max Bardet, a supporter of the movement, on June 16, 1972.

I fought the Nazis for five years. My reward for this was one year in the hospital and the amputation of my right leg, not to mention other wounds.

I received the Legion of Honor for my military service as well as the Military Medal and several other citations, including two from the army.

I will always remember the way France was crushed in 1940 and the consequences of this defeat under the occupation. I will do everything in my power to prevent this from happening again. The Larzac affair was cut out of whole cloth by leftists [*gauchistes*] and Marxists with the complicity of a Church that no longer believes in God but in Saint Marx.

The peasants of France have served as a patriotic example for centuries. It would seem that this era is now finished.

You are free to oppose an important national effort. I, as a representative of the people, will continue to do my duty even if it displeases you.

Undoubtedly to Alexander Sanguinetti's great chagrin, his brother, Admiral Antoine Sanguinetti, became an active partisan of the Larzac struggle on retiring from the navy. Another military personality, General Jacques Bollardière, a veteran of Indochina and Algeria, quit the army and turned to pacifism. He was a major speaker at the Larzac demonstration of 1973, attended by approximately 60,000 people. Beyond these defections from the military, the utility of the camp extension was questioned by even some highly placed officers on active duty. Thus, for example, Alain de

Boissieu, head of the army's general staff, said in 1974, "We have studied the expansion of the Larzac military camp and are not very enthusiastic because the terrain is very rocky and difficult to maneuver over" (*Gardons le Larzac* 1978).

Throughout 1972 the peasants continued their efforts to keep their protest in the news and turn public opinion against the extension. On October 25 of that year, sixty sheep were brought to Paris by truck and let loose under the Eiffel Tower. Three days later, 103 pine trees were planted along the national highway, across from the camp, to symbolize the determination of the peasants to remain on their land. The government was adamant, however. On December 12, 1972, Michel Debré announced to the French senate that the camp would definitely be extended, and on the twenty-sixth of the same month, as was required by law, the public utility of the project was declared officially by the prefect of the Aveyron.

The gauntlet had been thrown down. It was not long before it was picked up by the peasants. On January 7, 1973, twenty-six tractors left the Larzac for Paris. After several days on the road, they were stopped by the national police at Orléans with the excuse that their presence in the capitol would be a threat to the safety of Golda Meir, who was about to arrive as an official guest of the government. At this point Bernard Lambert — a peasant himself from the north of France, former member of the JAC, former deputy in the National Assembly and founder of the Peasant-Worker Union (*Les Paysans-Travailleurs*) — offered to continue the march to Paris on the tractors of his union members. The offer was accepted. The march continued, and Lambert's union became an important source of support for the movement. Alain Cabanes described the event from the point of view of the Paris committee.

> We were also involved when the tractors from the Larzac arrived in Paris. At the time the peasants were not very professional in their political actions and they really did not know what to do. We decided that everyone supporting the movement had to be ready to welcome the tractors. We called a meeting and found ourselves in a room with sixty-five different supporting groups, ranging from the Communists to the UDF [Gaullists]. We had to preside with no experience. I had nightmares about that week. We could not get these people to agree on anything and we could not call the Larzac for advice since the peasants were all on the way to Paris. The newspapers were full of stories of the tractor march. Finally Gastal came in by plane and the next day he went back to join the march. We got posters printed in support of the action and then it was blocked in Orléans. I met with Bernard Lambert, who phoned

around to get local farmers to lend their own tractors. It was decided that the tractors would stop at the edge of the city and that the demonstrators would proceed on foot to the Bourse du Travail [Labor Exchange]. There was a tremendous crowd at the Bourse. A few incidents occurred with the police, but in general it worked out very well. Afterwards the committee met regularly, once a week.

In the same month of January, the peasants formed the first major association on the plateau, the *Association pour la Promotion de l'Agriculture sur le Larzac* (APAL). Its function was to aid farmers in various projects, particularly in bringing water to farms and in constructing farm buildings. Both activities had been forbidden when the prefect had authorized the declaration of public utility. In fact, all construction was frozen within the boundaries of the future camp. APAL was able to appeal for funds, largely through the actions of outside supporters. Jean Desbois and Vincent Roussel, acting with the *Comité de Recherches et d'Action Nonviolente* (Committee for Nonviolent Action and Research), initiated a call to concerned individuals, asking them to withhold 3 percent of their income taxes — the equivalent percentage of tax money used for the military budget — and forward the sum to APAL. By 1975 over 2,000 people had joined this action. Yet, only months after the initial appeal, APAL had already accumulated enough money to begin a major project. This was to be the now famous *bergerie* (sheepfold) of La Blaquière.

La Blaquière is a small hamlet poised on the northern flank of the military camp. According to the army's plans, it was to disappear from the map. However, it was also home to two farming families: the Guirauds, and Elie Jonquet and his sister, Jeanne. Auguste Guiraud and Elie Jonquet were traditional peasants (*purs porcs*) and both were signers of the original Larzac pledge. By 1973, Guiraud's stone *bergerie* was in such bad condition that it could no longer be repaired. Nevertheless, according to law, he was forbidden to build a new one. Realizing that another dramatic action was needed to keep public attention focused on the plateau, APAL decided to begin construction of an illegal *bergerie* at La Blaquière. Plans were drawn up for a structure conforming to traditional Larzac architecture, and on June 10, 1973, a cortege of tractors laden with rocks wound its way up from Millau to the *causse* for the ceremonial laying of the cornerstone.

This project was one of the great successes of the Larzac movement and resulted in a monument so impressive that the government later offered to preserve it for visiting tourists, even if the camp were extended. However, it began without any clear organization or even hope of completion. It was done, as the French say, *au pif* — off-the-cuff, according to one's intuition. Robert Pirault, who at the time was a worker-priest from the city of Orléans, became the unofficial construction chief. He described the project to us as follows:

> We didn't know anything in the beginning. We did not even know how many workers we would have at the site, 30 or 300. I had brought my things from Orléans. There was nothing there; no idea of organization. An architectural drawing of the site existed but we did not have it. We finally did see the plan and followed it as best we could but we never did meet with the architect. A professional contractor helped us when we had to do something really technical like building the arches that support the roof. We also had specialists do the roof itself. With the wind on the Larzac, I would not have dared to do it on my own. People came from everywhere. There were students on vacation, the unemployed, hippies. APAL, of course, paid for building materials, but at first we were given nothing for food. The peasants did not seem to realize that we had to be fed each day. We began with big sacks of whole rice and that's all. We never knew how many people would come. We might have food for three and six would show up. I went to Millau each day to buy my own bread. There were undoubtedly items of food stolen in Millau. When we had sausages, they must have been stolen. There were no plates or forks. We found these things in the garbage. APAL finally allowed us five francs a day [about one dollar] for food. The peasants never realized what the conditions were like. We ate outside. The peasants never wanted us in their houses. I had one shower at the Jonquet house during the entire time we worked on the *bergerie*. They did appreciate the work, however. Some joined us for a day at a time. We had to tell them what to do on the site, and when they left we did not see them again for a week, a month or three months. The peasants were afraid of the people there and did not want to interact with them. There were exceptions. For example, Ti-Clo [Galtier], the Burguières and Léon Maillé did come and they learned a great deal. Many of the volunteers were students. They, too, had to learn how to work. In the beginning they did not know what to do. One day, for example, someone mixed plaster into the cement. There were things that had to be torn down and rebuilt. The architect had oriented the building to the south, into the marine wind, which is dominant on the *causse*. We turned the whole thing around and built it the other way. There is no reason at all for that project to have succeeded. It was total anarchy. But everyone believed in it and everyone wanted it to succeed. One person decided to build the silo and he did it. Afterwards he became a mason! There was no real budget. Towards the end of the project there were salaries for four or five permanent workers. Some people took care

of the canteen and did nothing else. I remember one day: there was a person building the wall of the milking room and he forgot to put in a window. He did not know how to read the plans. Every morning there were endless discussions; the Maoists present felt constrained to give their usual discourses on *autogestion*. I remember one saying: "I am a wheel in the capitalist system." All this would begin at six in the morning. I would leave them and go to work on my own. The talk just went on and on. Many of the workers viewed me as just a dirty priest — a fascist — because I told people who had not worked in the morning that they had no right to join us for lunch.

Auguste Guiraud, whose house is located just yards from the *bergerie* that now houses his flock, told us about the construction.

> I don't know how all those people managed to live here. We set up a canteen to feed some of them. They ate here by groups of twenty. They camped in the woods, in ruins around the village. When a piece of the *bergerie* was badly built, Pirault had it destroyed and started again. May of these people had never seen a rock or cement.

Jeanne Jonquet, one of the few inhabitants of La Blaquière, was stunned by the outpouring of goodwill among the volunteers but also expressed somewhat ambivalent feelings about them.

> They descended on us! It was extraordinary. I never thought there could be such support from outside the plateau. Those who came here were so far from our milieu that it was very difficult to accept them. There were those who just wanted to talk with us for half a day, and we did not have the time. Sometimes I would spend an hour talking even when I was very tired from my own work. They were very nice, however. Most of the work took place during vacations in the summer. By the end of the project, we got along very well.

The peasants did indeed find the young people "difficult to accept." They were shocked by their comportment, particularly by their sexual mores and their rather primitive hygiene. As an example of this, a peasant related the following:

> One day I came out of Jonquet's house in the early morning, and there was this couple making love at the bottom of the steps! I asked them if they could move a little bit since they were in the way!

Some of the volunteers who worked on the *bergerie* have unpleasant memories of their treatment at the hands of the peasants. Several told us they were shocked that they had never been invited to eat in a peasant's house. One pointed out, in contrast, that Robert Pirault — because he was a priest — received special treatment: "He ate at -----'s house every Wednesday." Another told us that, while the men were finally paid five francs a day for food, the women were never considered members of the construction crew and were, therefore, never paid at all.

Clearly, the two worlds that existed side by side for almost three years at La Blaquière were very different. Many of the volunteers were convinced that the peasants held them in contempt, in spite of the work they were doing. The peasants, though happy that the *bergerie* was getting built, felt put upon and invaded by a mass of people whose behavior was unacceptable to them. By the end of the project, however, at least some of the workers had gained the peasants' respect for their good humor, their generosity and their proven ability to work under very trying conditions. A famous story from that period, told by many on the plateau, concerns a certain "Paco" who came to work at the site in the very beginning and stayed until the end. He had nothing. His pants were in shreds; his shoes were tattered espadrilles. One day someone gave him a decent pair of shoes. Paco immediately gave them away to someone worse off than he. It was gestures like this that transformed the original culture shock felt by the peasants into bemused respect.

On February 3, 1974, the first sheep took up residence in the new *bergerie*, which was completed in 1975.

NOTES

1. Material for chapters two through six was drawn from interviews with Larzac militants, on and off the plateau, and the mayors of five local communes (Millau, La Roque Ste. Marguérite, Ste. Eulalie de Cernon, La Couvertoirade and La Cavalerie); the Larzac archives now in the library in Millau; *GLL*, the Larzac militant newspaper; and published sources.

CHAPTER THREE
The Struggle Continues

It was the acceptance of nonviolence, as both ideology and practice, that provided the Larzac peasants with an unbeatable riposte to national power. As one of them put it at the end of the struggle, "We won because we were the weakest." As the conflict developed, the peasants and their allies exploited the concept of nonviolence, making it encompass a set of powerfully successful symbolic oppositions between themselves and the state. In their terms, the Larzac was life-giving; the army represented death and destruction. The Larzac movement embodied small-scale, grassroots democracy; the army, as an arm of the state, embodied central power and, therefore, repression. The Larzac was the protector of a local archeological, architectural and natural heritage; the army would destroy that heritage.

The peasants engaged in a series of practical and dramatic actions that left the army with a choice between two equally bad alternatives. For example, when pro-Larzac squatters occupied farms bought by the army and immediately put them into production, the government had a choice between expelling the inhabitants and appearing harsh and repressive or ignoring the occupations and thereby displaying its own weakness. Similarly, when the army sent troops to occupy expropriated farms in order to impede squatters, the peasants responded by planting crops on the land of these farms (destined to be a gift for the Third World). The army could either ignore the illegal action, again risking a loss of face, or plow under the crops before they could be harvested, wasting the fruit of the land.

On April 28, 1973, the peasants took the first step toward active nonviolence when sixty of them sent their military papers back to the government with letters refusing to serve in the armed forces. (All Frenchmen who have been in the military are required to keep their papers in case of a national emergency.) This action — a punishable offense in France — put the peasants in a position of solidarity with those conscientious objectors who faced prison terms for refusing to perform alternate service, which, they felt, served the purposes of the army. Indeed, later in the struggle the peasants were to support objectors more directly by welcoming them to the plateau, appearing as witnesses at their trials and providing financial support for legal expenses. These actions brought a bright, young lawyer, François Roux, to the Larzac.

Roux comes from a Protestant family rooted in the Cévennes Mountains, the last stronghold of Protestantism in France left after the Wars of Religion. The people of this region have a reputation for fierce independence and commitment to human rights. We interviewed François Roux in October of 1988.

In 1975 I was the lawyer for a conscientious objector. A year later I worked on the case of another objector at Rodez, which brought me closer to the Larzac. De Felice [a well-known human-rights lawyer] and I became experts on the Universal Declaration of Human Rights [designed to serve as a reference in courts of law throughout the EC] and were the first to use it in pleading cases for objectors. I next became engaged with the expropriation cases and turned into something of an expert on land law, which I had originally known nothing about. I had to find a tie between the judicial problems of the Larzac and the ideology of the peasants because they were very reticent to demand reparations for their land. I had to convince them that legal problems were very important. If they lost in court, they would lose everything; therefore, it was necessary that they play the legal game.

The struggle was waged on two fronts. Civil disobedience puts people on the margins of the law. The peasants had never had any experience with the possible legal effects of their actions. I had to explain to them what the consequences would be. They would say, "If the government expropriates our land, we will stay anyway." I had to convince them that it could not be done that way. We finally decided that we would ask for compensation of 103,000,000 francs for each farm, to match the 103 who had signed the pledge. The sum was both too small — no one wanted money — and ridiculously large, so that there was no doubt about its symbolic nature. Thus, we played the government's game without really playing it. The expropriations were held up to the very end of the struggle, which was a lucky thing. If the government had won in the courts it would have been very difficult for Mitterrand to cancel the extension in 1981.

In August of 1973, the first great demonstration on the plateau was held at the Rajal del Gorp (Spring of the Raven, in Occitan). This demonstration was organized by the peasants in cooperation with the national Larzac committees and Bernard Lambert's left-wing farmers' union, the *Paysans-Travailleurs*. Sixty thousand people attended. Among the many organizations represented was a workers' committee from the Lip watch factory. The demonstration was billed as "apolitical" — participation by organized political parties was not welcome. This was to be the line taken by the peasants for the rest of the struggle.

As the protest movement gathered steam, the government attempted again and again to counterattack. A major argument offered to the public, besides the claim that the extension was crucial for national defense, was that the Larzac is a rocky desert, sparsely inhabited by a few old peasants ready for retirement. Michel Debré said of the *causse*, "The choice of the Larzac for the extension was self-imposed. The plateau is an austere place — the wind and the snow leave little chance for it to support any kind of productive activity" (Bouffanet and Kuligowski 1973:7). This was the image created for government-controlled television in a report presented during the first summer after the announcement of the extension.

The peasants expressed outrage over this documentary's biased reporting. However, they also chuckled over the clumsiness of the government propaganda machine responsible for the editing. Although the program was supposed to have been made in the month of August, the Larzac was shown covered with snow! As harsh as the Larzac climate is, it does not snow in the summer months.

The argument concerning the Larzac's demography and its economic viability was a constant one in the propaganda war between the peasants and the army (see chapter seven). Already in 1972 the Association for the Protection of the Larzac had published a white paper pointing out that the mean age of Larzac farmers was actually lower than the rest of the Aveyron and that the number of GAECs and CUMAs on the Larzac was superior to the national average as well.

Publishing these facts was not enough for the peasants, however. They felt that the truth needed to be dramatized in concrete actions as well. The genius and originality of the Larzac protest lay in the ability of the peasants and their allies to create an unending series of highly visible actions that drew public opinion to their side and kept the army on the defensive. It was, therefore, not long before the government's claim of demographic decrepitude on the *causse* was proved false in a most tangible way — the new Larzac elementary school.

When the struggle began, the last elementary school in the northern sector of the plateau at St. Martin had already closed. Young children from this area went to school either in Nant, if they lived in the east, or in Millau, if they lived in the west. Because there was only one morning school bus, children from the west had to get up as early as five A.M. to take the same bus that drove their older siblings to the high school in Millau. The parents of those children who went to school in Nant were forced to drive them down into the valley each school morning and pick them up each evening.

In 1973, the parents in these two zones got together and petitioned the mayor of Millau to reopen the school at St. Martin, which had been conveniently located for both the western and the eastern sectors. At first the request was refused, but the parents persisted in their demand. They threatened that if an elementary school were not provided for their children, they would demonstrate for one in Millau. Furthermore, they would keep their children out of the classroom altogether if their needs were not met.

The municipal council of Millau was prudent enough not to stand in their way but felt that rebuilding the school in St. Martin would be too expensive. A compromise was struck. During the summer of 1973, a prefabricated building was put together on land belonging to the farm of L'Hôpital, just to the west of the national highway and on the rim of the plateau. It was opened on October 4, 1973, and thus began one of two new schools on the Larzac. (The other, a nursery school, was built and organized by parents in the southern zone in La Blaquererie after the struggle.)

The heritage of the Larzac protest is present in the new school's stress on human rights. In a series of interviews with plateau children carried out by Larzac resident Nicole Lefeuvre in 1989, one can see the effects of both school and home in the children's sensitivity to the rights of the underprivileged and in their frank, unembarrassed remarks concerning relationships with racial and religious minorities.

The pupils' interest in other cultures is also sparked by their parents' political activities. This focus is reinforced by the teachers who are quick to develop projects that will inform their pupils' curiosity. When the issues of New Caledonian independence became a Larzac cause, for example, the children studied the native culture of the island. They also met representatives of the independence movement in their homes and at community gatherings.

One can observe the opening to foreign cultures in the school itself. Among the forty-four students in 1989, there were two foster children from minority populations in Millau, as well as two adopted children from El Salvador. In the interviews cited above, the children speak candidly about these new arrivals, showing understanding of their problems and special needs.

The Larzac proved that its population was not dying but, rather, young and expanding when it successfully obtained the new school. At the same time, the peasants forged ahead with a variety of protest tactics. For example, in order to make it difficult for the army to purchase land, the peasants began to sell mini-plots to interested militants for 1,000 francs each. This action would also impede the required title searches in the event of expropriation proceedings. One of these plots was bought by the national satirical weekly paper, *Le Canard Enchainé* (*The Chained Duck*). The sale stimulated militants all over France to buy similar plots. It was also the beginning of a close relationship between the paper's staff and the peasants.

It was soon realized, however, that something more had to be done to counter the government's growing success in buying land from those owners who had not signed the pledge. Desperate to buy, the army had begun to offer unheard-of prices for the rocky land of the Larzac. It was Guy Tarlier who found the solution.

Previous to the struggle, there was a general rise in the price of farm land. In response, the government had begun to encourage the development of GFAs as a means of helping young farmers establish themselves on land that they could not afford to purchase. GFAs are private companies, supported by the sale of shares. Funds generated by these shares are used to buy land, which is then rented to farmers. The law establishing the GFAs requires that interested farmers put a certain amount of their own land into the corporation before shares can be sold to the public.

Guy Tarlier had already set up a private GFA on his own farm and realized that the same mechanism could be used to buy farms on the Larzac from owners who needed to sell but who did not want to cede to the army. The first of four Larzac GFAs was established on December 12, 1973. Within a few years, two more GFAs had been created and enough shares had been sold to buy several strategically located plots of land and four complete farms within the extension area: La Tune and Costeraste to the south, Jassenove to the northeast and Boissans to the northwest. The extension was hemmed in on all four sides.

The summer of 1974 saw the biggest demonstration of the entire struggle. We were at that rally. Over 100,000 people jammed the Rajal for two days while grain, sown earlier in preparation for the event, was being harvested on a field owned by the army. Many of the participants camped out on the property of L'Hôpital surrounding the site. As in the 1973 demonstration and other rallies of that period, the program was a mixture of music and speeches given primarily by representatives of nonparliamentary leftist parties, ecologists, various separatist groups and, of course, the peasants themselves. Organized by the Larzac committees, it ran its course without serious incident, except for a brief moment of violence when François Mitterrand (then a candidate for the presidency) was attacked by a small group of leftists who resented his presence at what was supposed to be a nonpartisan rally. Quite shaken by this encounter, Mitterrand was whisked off to the house of Auguste and Marie-Rose Guiraud in La Blaquière, where his relatively minor scratches were treated. Later he continued to Montpellier by back roads, fearing another attack — but this time by pro-camp demonstrators at La Cavalerie. He was to remember the impressive number of people who had gathered for the demonstration, the awesome beauty of the land and, especially, the warm and protective treatment he received at the hands of the Larzac peasants.

After Lanza's fast, the presence of L'Arche continued on the plateau in the person of Roger Moreau, who worked out of La Cavalerie as the secretary and coordinator for the various groups involved in the struggle. The possibility of a dramatic, nonviolent action by a group from L'Arche was discussed among its members, and it was decided that the Moreaus (Roger, his wife Susana and their two children), along with another family — Claude and Marie-Claire Voron and their three children — and several others would move to the hamlet of Les Truels, which had just been bought by the army.

Nonviolent action was not new to Claude Voron. During the war in Algeria (he was writing his thesis in astrophysics at the time) he was imprisoned for twenty-seven months — for a while, sharing his cell with Robert Siméon — for refusing to serve in the army. Later, he and his wife became members of L'Arche and lived in the community for nine years. By 1973, they had moved to an urban branch in Grenoble. There, they heard of L'Arche's participation in the Larzac struggle. Soon after, they decided to join the action at Les Truels. This first squat in October of 1974 required a considerable amount of planning and courage. Claude described the event to us:

At the time, we had three small children — nine, seven and four years of age. We arrived at Les Truels on October 5, when the army was already in place. They had arrived the night before; it was evident that someone had told them about us. There were paratroopers in the only habitable house on the farm, and they also had control of the only working cistern, so we had no water. We decided to occupy the site anyway and while a group distracted the soldiers at their house, we moved into another. We began work on the house immediately with the help of about a hundred people who had come along with us. The two families involved took over a small house at the entrance of the hamlet. We had to keep a lookout for the arrival of the police, who we expected would expel us. During the first week, we occupied all the houses we could. Lanza del Vasto was there with us on the first day but did not stay the night. We tried to make contact with the soldiers. In the beginning, it was possible for us to have interesting conversations with them, but then an order came from headquarters not to fraternize with us. From then on the soldiers were changed each day so that they could not be "polluted" by our ideas. We put posters up all over the hamlet and arranged press conferences. A representative from the department of the Aveyron came up to see us when the television reporters were there. In front of the cameras we asked to see the commandant to tell him that our cow was thirsty and that it was the army's fault. The representative pointed out to the soldiers that it was not up to them to maintain order [that was the role of the police] and that they should not prevent us from getting water.

We organized a large construction project right away. There were workers who were on strike at the moment so it was a time of great solidarity. We roofed the house right under the eyes of the soldiers. We put a baby in a cradle at the foot of the army's sentinel. In the morning the soldiers did their exercises, and we passed with our cow. Unfortunately, during the first days of the occupation, there was a postal strike and so we had some difficulties with national publicity. But the occupation was very well covered in the local press. Although the army had sent parachutists in at first, we were worried because we knew that they would be followed by the Foreign Legion, which has a reputation for toughness. We wondered how long we would be able to stay but began immediately to work on the farm. It was very cold in Les Truels. At night the temperature often dropped to seven below [centigrade]. Several of the peasants came to help. Robert Pirault kept watch for us. We had to be particularly careful at night since we felt that the police would come in the dark when the press was not present. There was one false alarm and the soldiers were very surprised to see how fast our supporters got here. Finally, in the morning, at the end of a week, the soldiers began to pack up. We were very surprised and thought that it might be a trick. We hesitated for some hours and then forced our way into the house that had been occupied by the army. It was no trick. The army had had orders from Paris to leave. The next day the legionnaires came but they did not have an order to occupy the farm. They just came to look us over and we had good contact with them. Their commandant told us how impressed he was with our action and, at the same time, made it clear to us that if the occupation had taken place under the Legion, things would have been different. Later a gendarme came up to Les Truels in order to note that we had taken up residence there, and that was that! We continued with our work and began to improve our lifestyle. Later there was an expulsion trial, but the judge declared himself incompetent because he was a civil judge and it was, in his opinion, a military affair. Periodic threats of expulsion continued, but we did not have to worry during the winter months when such action is illegal. We mounted a permanent guard and put up heavy chains around the entrance to the village. Lanza visited frequently and slept over to make his presence felt. We set up a small flock of sheep and began to sell our cheeses in Millau. We had to play the game and show that there was real life here. Finally we began to get mail, and a phone was installed. Apparently the minister of defense was furious with the minister of communications. All the telephones within the perimeter of the extension were blocked — they even took down the line poles they had put up for us — and we had to set up a pirate telephone system.

During the remainder of the conflict, five more sites were squatted by militants: the farm of Le Cun in the south (1975), the hamlets of St. Martin in the north (1974) and Montredon (1976) in the northeast, and the farms of Les Homps (1975) and Cavaliès (1976) in the northeast. The squatters at Le Cun, who had set up a center for nonviolence, were expelled by the police on October 25, 1976. On July 23, 1977, work began on the new "Le Cun," located on land belonging to Jassenove, a farm owned by a Larzac GFA. No permit had been issued for this building, and the police stopped construction almost immediately. Though the action was not supported unanimously by the peasant militants, the squatters of Le Cun later built a house made of straw bales covered with stucco, managing to complete the major work in one night. The authorities never asked the residents of Le Cun to take down this building.

As for Cavaliès, the army had the squatters expelled three days after the occupation in October of 1976, but the peasants immediately set them up with a flock of sheep on private land adjacent to the farm. Later, militants built a sheepfold on this site with funds supplied by APAL. Meanwhile, afraid of further action by squatters, the army was taking over houses on land they had bought at

Le Tournet, Le Cun, La Salvetat and, later, in 1977, at Le Pinel. Le Pinel was bought from one of the few peasants who reneged on the no-sell pledge. On July 17, 1976, the army destroyed the cistern of the farm it had recently purchased at Cap D'Ase, rendering the place uninhabitable.

As has already been noted, a number of Larzac farms had no running water. On January 4, 1975, a group of peasants staged a commando operation on National Highway Nine in order to install a pipeline across the road to bring water to the nearby farm of Potensac. They had managed to dig a trench across half of the highway when the national police arrived and removed them — an action that the local press described as a brutal intervention in response to a nonviolent action. Although served with a desist order, the peasants staged another raid on January 25, attempting to install pipes in the second half of the roadway. When the police arrived the peasants "sat-in" peacefully and were removed. Four hundred people, including several *notables*, were arrested. In the summer of the same year, another attempt was made to complete the water line. This time, the peasants were joined by a delegation of eighty workers from the Lip watch factory, including their leader, Mr. Piaget. To the astonishment of all concerned, the police stood by and let the work proceed. The public support and media exposure of each attempt to install the water line had apparently tipped the balance. Another intervention could only have tarnished the image of the police further and, it seemed, would not have discouraged the peasants from achieving their goal.

Meanwhile, the government continued the process that would, it hoped, lead smoothly to expropriation of the land necessary for the extension. Legal protocol required an investigation of the precise location and value of each land parcel. Such work would normally be done by a special judge at the town hall of each commune concerned. However, the municipal councils of all the communes involved in the extension, except La Cavalerie, had passed resolutions condemning the expropriation searches. The peasants took these resolutions as a justification for direct action.

A group of women, feeling that they had not had the chance to express their opposition to the extension, decided to organize a commando raid against the expropriation procedures. On February 21, 1975, groups composed mainly of women invaded the town halls concerned and proceeded to tear up condemnation files. The raids were synchronized to occur at the same time, and the surprise was so general that only a few people were arrested (three as participants and two as accomplices). The story of this action was featured in the press the next day. It was another well-planned event that brought the struggle — in this case, the expropriation process—to the attention of the public.

The year 1975 was also marked by the foundation of two new and important Larzac institutions, *Larzac Universités* and the peasant-run newspaper, *Gardarem lo Larzac* (*We Shall Keep the Larzac,* in Occitan). *Larzac Universités* was founded on May 19, 1975 by an assembly of interested peasants, scholars and militants. Its purpose was to serve as a forum for new ideas and reinforce the participation in the movement of people outside of the Larzac. It also began a cooperative veterinary service, stressing preventive medicine, that continues to operate today. According to Jean Chesneaux, one of the founders of *Larzac U.* (as it came to be known), it created a great deal of interest among university professors in Paris.[1]

> *Larzac Universités* bought a building in Montredon. It thus became the only legally occupied structure in that hamlet, which had already been squatted. Its presence helped to insure that the squatters would not be expelled by the army. *Larzac U.* was in a strategic place and it became an important organization, serving, as it did, as an institution of resistance. During the struggle, I conducted several workshops on history there. We also organized discussion groups, where we considered such things as how the peasants experienced the Second World War. It was a work "with" [the peasants] rather than a work "on" [a subject].

From the very beginning, the Larzac struggle was covered in local and national newspapers, as well as on radio and television. Between 1971 and 1975, a group of militants collected press articles, and copied and bound them into small brochures with the title, *Larzac Informations.* The suggestion that the Larzac found its own newspaper came from a writer on the *Canard Enchaîné.* Michel Courtin, who came to the Larzac from St. Tropez and who at the time was a member of the GAEC of Les Baumes, was a founding member of *Gardarem lo Larzac.* He remembered the paper's beginnings:

> He [the journalist] had learned about the struggle from the Occitanists. My wife became the secretary of *GLL.* Roger [Moreau] worked with us. In the beginning we published what people sent in plus an editorial, which we cleared with the peasants as well as the

Larzac committees. This, as you might imagine, was very difficult. We set up an editorial committee that met every month to write a common text. There were articles that arrived that were too long and needed to be cut. Roger and I did most of the work, but that posed problems and many people complained. Actually, we did not reject many articles, but there were some that just could not be published. On the other hand, we had trouble filling the issues at first so we published almost everything. We wanted a text from a peasant in every issue. Léon [Maillé] began to write for *GLL* very early but he did not work for it until later. [Although neither Courtin nor Maillé remembers it that way, the latter is listed on the masthead of the first issue, dated June 6, 1975, as "editor."] In the beginning Léon had to rewrite his pieces. His spelling was very poor. His articles struck Roger and me as a bit too "peasant" in flavor. Léon frequently asked us to help him and we did. There are certain people here who discovered who they really were in the struggle and Léon is one of them.

Léon Maillé confirms Courtin's description of his first days at *GLL*:

The idea was in the air. When our articles were published in the local press they were often distorted. The journalists from the *Canard* suggested that we begin our own newspaper. Michel Courtin worked on it from the beginning and I was a member of the team along with Roger Moreau. I had never written before. I was a poor speller besides. The first articles I wrote were corrected by Roger or Michel. I found out that I like to write. Now I realize that I would not have minded being a functionary of some sort and paid for that kind of work. I don't express myself well in public meetings, but when I have ideas I write them down. I wrote an open letter to the prefect after the first action at Rodez [the first hunger strike]. I was inspired by something I heard on the radio or read in the newspaper.

Within a few months after its founding, Léon Maillé was writing articles on his own and functioning as the real rather than titular editor of *GLL*, a post he was to occupy until 1987. After a few issues, he began a monthly column, "Les Echos de Léontou," which continues today. He comments, often satirically, on various events of local or national importance.

The first issue of *GLL* contains a particularly interesting article, entitled "Larzac Terre D'Accueil?" ("Larzac Land of Welcome?"). It presents a set of interviews with a group of volunteer workers at the *bergerie* of La Blaquière, reflecting the difficult relationship that existed between volunteers at the site and the peasants. One interviewee described his reasons for coming to the Larzac:

After three years at the university I came to the Larzac because another wind is blowing here. I came because I am a conscientious objector and wished to do civil service here rather than for the National Office of Water and Forests. I came to fight at the side of the peasants, but also through the Larzac, to live in accord with my ideas. I thought I would find a community of men whose struggle would permit the liberation of each individual.

When asked what his relations with the peasants actually were, he replied:

They are limited to certain exchanges in relation to the building of the *bergerie*. This is normal when you consider that we have a life totally different from theirs. We don't see the shepherds [he is referring here to farmworkers, not peasants] since they work all day, seven days a week. To them, we are just builders. I would like to have better rapport with the peasants. I feel that I know Auguste [Guiraud], even though he is a man of few words. I know Jean-Marie [Burguière] a little. That leaves 101 others. Do they want to know me? We have all tried to get to know the shepherds. They also exist and have a right to speak out. The land is their tool, even if it belongs to the peasants. The shepherds are men like us, with their own worries and aspirations. I feel that the peasants are, at the same time, astonishing and deceiving, open and egotistical — with revolutionary attitudes based on a reactionary foundation. The peasants of the Larzac are the only people we see, but there are lots of other people who live on the plateau — the women, for example. I'm sure they have many interesting ideas to present concerning everyday life. It's too bad that they don't affirm their own personalities more often, instead of expressing themselves through their husbands. The battle of the Larzac and the economic life of the area appear to be a problem for the men and a few privileged individuals.

He was asked if his way of life proves anything.

Our way of life does not depend on the fact that we live at La Blaquière. We lived like this before and will live this way afterwards. We have made a choice to live with little, to consume less and to be free to participate in political and volunteer actions. But, in my opinion, we have not put aside the usual rules one finds between workers and bosses. We have a foreman here, for example. The women volunteers are not paid for their work, nor are they recognized as the equals of the men. Perhaps this is due to the peasants' mentality. In any case, it's the result of our patriarchal society.

Speaking of his political engagement:

For me the Larzac struggle is a way of fighting against the military, one of the pillars of society that needs to be opposed. The *bergerie* is a concrete manifestation of our ideals and thus represents more than just words. My hope is for a more permissive society, with a minimum of racism and repression, in which everyone can express his or her own individuality. The Larzac struggle has allowed us to concretize our ideas.

The four-page supplement to the first issue of *GLL* contains a speech give by Jeanne Jonquet after Lanza del Vasto's fast. Jeanne Jonquet has lived in La Blaquière all her life helping — at least up to her recent retirement — to run the family farm. Until the Larzac protest, she had little contact with the outside world, except through the eyes of her brother, Elie (who, as noted previously, had spent five years in Germany during the Second World War as a prisoner-worker). Her words show how profoundly some of the peasants were affected by nonviolence and the opening of the Larzac to the outer world.

Lanza del Vasto fasted in order to demonstrate his solidarity with the peasants of the Larzac. His fast took place at La Cavalerie in the presence of a changing group of peasants and sympathizers. Friends, Millavois and peasants from the area fasted with Lanza on a rotating basis. The goal of the fast, of course, was to influence the government, but it also brought us closer together and strengthened our ties to one another. In addition, Lanza taught us how to relate the Gospels to our daily lives and live them in the context of the Larzac struggle. Of course, we became more committed to nonviolence. In fact, we discovered that it was our weakness that gave us our power. Little by little we came to realize that it is correct to refuse to obey an unjust law, in this case one that would have us expelled from our homes. The fast marked us profoundly. It led us to reflect deeply on ourselves, and as a result we have become more tolerant. Now, after these years of struggle, we are better equipped to accept different ways of life, even those that are quite foreign to us. We have learned this so well that when I talk with certain outsiders, I get the impression that they are twenty years behind the times. We need Larzacs everywhere to wake up the people. The struggle has led me to feel concerned by problems that are not really my own. I am concerned by unemployment; by the fact that many workers have no job guarantees; by the type of life they are forced to live in big cities, while here, on the Larzac, we have the time to watch the days pass, to look at the sun and to organize the rhythm of our own work.

During the construction of the *bergerie*, Jeanne Jonquet and her neighbors rubbed shoulders with militants from all social classes and many geographic areas of France and Germany, as well as with people of a wide range of ages. Among those with whom

Jeanne became friendly was a cultured but strident individual who did not mince words in her criticisms. She was a gadfly, certainly, to the army but also to the peasants, who never came quite up to her expectations. She was also a pipe smoker and, true or not, considered by many to be a lesbian. The fact that this extraordinary individual enjoyed respect as well as affection from Jeanne Jonquet, among others, attests to the tolerance that was promoted in this normally conservative population by the many and varied contacts that were part of the daily scene during the conflict.

NOTES

1. Another major figure in the founding of *Larzac Universités* was Raymond Guglielmo, professor of geography at the University of Paris VIII. Professor Guglielmo and his students also did a study of the extension plan and mapped out the most strategic farms for GFA purchase.

CHAPTER FOUR
Victory

The night of March 10, 1975 was a black one for the peasants of the Larzac. At 3:00 A.M., a powerful bomb exploded in the house of Auguste Guiraud while he and his family, including seven children, and their shepherd slept. For the peasants it was a miracle that the vault supporting the roof held so that, although the building was destroyed, no one was hurt. Jeanne Jonquet — who, with her brother Elie, was asleep in their house a hundred yards from the Guirauds' when the explosion occurred — describes that night as follows:

> It is difficult to talk about the bombing. We were awakened at about three in the morning. I thought it was thunder. A neighbor came over and told us that something had happened at the Guirauds'. I thought that perhaps something that the shepherd had left in the house had exploded and that it was an accident. I did not think it possible that anyone could bomb the house. Everything was broken. It was a total mess. We had to find help and Elie got out his car to go to L'Hôpital where there was a phone. I was trembling with fear, afraid that another house would go up. I did not want Elie to go alone so I went and a young person from the village came along. As we drove out of the village, three tires blew. Someone had put nails across the road. We continued anyway. When we got to L'Hôpital, Jean-Marie [Burguière] was asleep and did not answer the door. Finally he did come, but their phone was out of order. We left for Millau to get the gendarmes. They were asleep too, and we had to bang on their door for some time. With the dawn, help came.

Pierre Burguière told us that when he went to La Blaquière the next day, he heard an expert say to one of the gendarmes present that the explosive used in the blast was military in origin. According to him, when they saw that he was within earshot, they stopped talking. The local newspapers reported that the investigators felt the explosive was of a type commonly used in quarries and was, therefore, accessible to terrorists. The guilty party was never found.

Several witnesses said that when the police arrived, they took a few of the young Guiraud children aside and asked them such questions as, "Why did your father blow up his own house?" The

55

Burguières were so traumatized by the event that for years afterwards both Pierre and his brother, Jean-Marie, would look out the window every morning to see whether or not someone had left a suspicious package on their doorstep. The Burguières also received a series of threatening phone calls. When Auguste Guiraud attended an anti-extension demonstration at La Cavalerie, he was threatened by pro-camp people in the crowd.

Informants tell us that if anyone had been killed in the blast at the Guirauds', the struggle would have been over. The peasants would have given in to the army because their nonviolent opposition would have ultimately spawned more violence and death. However, because there were no deaths, the event was seen by many as a sign to continue. When the struggle was over, Marie-Rose Guiraud told the Abbé Mazeran (a local priest and supporter of the peasants) that even if they had lost in the end, the struggle would have been worth the trouble. Before it, she said, the peasants walked with their heads bent down like sheep and could see nothing. The experience of meeting so many different kinds of helpful people who had given of themselves so generously had opened their eyes. Now they walked heads up, in pride.

By the end of 1975, the various organizations and campaigns associated with the protest were in place: APAL, tax protesters, GFAs, the Larzac elementary school, *Larzac U.*, *GLL*, the national Larzac committees, the campaign to send back military papers and legal support for objectors. The legal battles against the government's condemnations of farms and the attempts to hold the line against the army buying farms continued until the extension was annulled, as did sporadic negotiations between the peasants' representatives and the government. During this period, the peasants persevered in a daily life that was far from calm. Indeed, a war of nerves raged between them and the army. The road twisting through the eastern sector of the plateau became a proving ground. As they drove their children to school each day, parents were likely to encounter military vehicles careening around curves at top speed. This resulted in frequent accidents, particularly on a very bad curve near La Blaquière. Over the years *GLL* published several photographs of military vehicles overturned in the fields below the road. No children were hurt in these incidents, but their parents were forced to lodge complaints constantly with the police in attempts to end the careless driving.

There were, of course, other provocations. Troops frequently tested the mettle of the Larzac militants by maneuvering outside the camp's boundaries, particularly in the east near St. Sauveur, Montredon and, further to the west, in La Blaquière. Deprived of telephones, the peasants in this sector installed a pirate line between farms so that they could call one another during emergencies. Whenever the military breached the confines of the camp, a call went out for aid. Convoys soon found themselves surrounded by angry peasants and, frequently, by flocks of sheep or goats. Once immobilized, the soldiers were at the mercy of the peasants, forced to stand by as the air was let out of their truck tires and slogans against the extension were swiftly painted on the sides of their vehicles. Forbidden by law to arrest civilians, the military had no recourse but to call the police to intervene on their behalf, though they were themselves in the wrong for having violated the camp's boundaries.

From time to time, soldiers, supposedly acting on their own, physically attacked peasants or their property. There was one particularly violent incident at Cavaliès in which Pierre Burguière was badly hurt. When he pressed charges against the soldiers involved, we were told, the case was quashed by the military authorities. On another occasion, a group of soldiers cut down trees across the road between Les Truels and the route to Millau and put sugar in the gas tanks of all the cars in the area. This could have had very serious consequences since, at the time, one of the women of Les Truels was near the end of her pregnancy and at any moment might have had to leave for the hospital in Millau.

Robert Pirault, who frequently found himself on the "front lines" confronting invasive movements by the military, describes both the maneuvers and the attacks as follows:

> French soldiers have no initiative of their own! They wait for orders. This must be the way they are trained. A single person can take advantage of this and stop a whole regiment. The soldiers never thought up the idea of maneuvering against us, i.e., using us as the enemy. We were, therefore, able to stop them without any trouble. They could not crush us with their tanks; after all, we are French!

> One day I heard gunfire near La Blaquière. I drove out with my car and saw six tanks approaching the village. I parked just in front of the first one and said to the driver. "Now the attack is over." I told them that they were on private property and that if they did not leave, I would press charges against them. They turned around and left. We took the initiative all the time. One time José [Bové] jumped right onto a tank and the army had to stop. What else could

they do? Every time they attacked Cavaliès [beating up several peasants], the soldiers involved were punished because their action was taken individually and against orders. [The army was willing to discipline its soldiers. However, it would not accept that a civilian — like Pierre Burguière — had the right to hold it to account.] Whenever individual soldiers acted on their own they were replaced. At Les Truels this is exactly what happened. The commandos came on a snowy night, and the next day we were able to follow their tracks back to Le Pinel [a farm occupied by the army] and prove that the military had carried out the attack. If they had had any sense, they would not have done it that way.

Francis Moreau participated as a Larzac militant at La Blaquière and at St. Martin. He was raised in the Vendée (a very traditional and Catholic area of France below Brittany) and became a monk at the age of sixteen. After his compulsory military service he quit his order and lived for a time with *L'Arche*. Subsequently, he joined the Larzac protest, frequently assisting Robert Pirault in various militant projects. Moreau confirms Pirault's reflections on the comportment of the military during the struggle:

Our struggle with the army was territorial. Every time the army put a foot outside the camp, they had to be chased back within its borders. There were many types of confrontation — on the roads, for example, where convoys drove at top speed, risking the lives of civilian drivers. When I was at St. Martin, I saw a convoy of jeeps on the road. We took our 2CV [a low-priced, low-powered Citroen automobile], blocked the path and began to talk with the soldiers. They had been instructed not to be violent and were willing to discuss the struggle with us. Léon [Maillé] arrived later with his camera and we let them go on their way. Whenever they marched over an area outside of the camp, we chased them away. When they maneuvered at Montredon, we chased them away with a large group of militants. Now and then, the police would be called to give us summons but, with one exception, these were never pursued. One time in Montredon, I let my sheep go into a group of soldiers. They were in the process of maneuvering as if there was no enemy present. I never understood the attitude of the army. Sometimes the peasants would slash the tires of military trucks, although the people of Les Truels were against this kind of action. There were convoys blocked by mothers because the army trucks were dangerous for school buses. Once I was all alone at La Blaquière when a troop of soldiers arrived. I called for help and Marie-Rose [Guiraud] came. I think that if she had not come, I would have been beaten up. The peasants from Pierrefiche were by no means nonviolent, and the army stayed away from that zone.

On June 28, 1976, twenty-two militants (peasants and non-peasants) occupied the office of the military camp and in a well-planned action destroyed 800 kilograms (nearly 1,800 pounds) of documents, photographing those deemed interesting for the struggle. Among the latter was a map showing proposed lines of cannon fire from the extended camp to the *causse* on the other side of Millau, going straight over the city! The day after the raid, local papers published the map. As one could predict, the consternation of the local population was general.

The idea for this raid is claimed by Michel Courtin, whom we have already met as one of the founders of *GLL*. Courtin had done his military service before the struggle at the Larzac camp and was familiar with the layout of the building to be occupied. He said that the action was rejected at first by the majority of peasants and that, even when it was finally approved, some were afraid to participate for fear of prison terms or violence. Other informants told us that they had opposed the action because they felt that it was a violent act and therefore in contradiction with the philosophy of the movement.

When the occupation was finally approved, Courtin insisted that if it was to take place, the majority of those involved had to be peasants. Otherwise, he felt, it would be interpreted by the government and the media as a move by outside agitators. The judge handling the trials of those arrested in the occupation proved Courtin's suspicions to be correct. In sentencing the members of the commando, he gave harsher punishments to those who were not peasants. (A few of them — including Marizette Tarlier — spent several weeks in jail.) He even moderated his judgements to the degree that the *purs porcs*, with the exception of known leaders, were given only suspended sentences.

Robert Pirault, continuing his discourse on the military, provides a trenchant description of the occupation:

> We got into the camp without any trouble. We went in at noon, when most French people think of only one thing: lunch! We could have blown up the camp. They never understood that we had a strategy. We were all assigned to different parts of the room. I had a window; another had a door. We knew exactly what to do while the soldiers did nothing at all to prevent our attack.

Pierre Burguière continues:

We all had our assignments. We tore up papers so fast that our hands hurt. When we were taken back to the camp during the trial to reenact the "crime," we saw a pile of shredded papers almost two meters high! During the action, one of us surveyed the work, and when interesting papers were found, they were photographed. We stuffed the originals under our belts. When we were finally arrested, we hid the film in our underpants and the two women [the only women taking part in the action] put them in their brassieres. They discovered the papers right away, but not the film. Because we were found in *flagrant délit*, we were not searched immediately. Instead, they took us down to Millau for booking. Before appearing in the courtroom, we asked permission to go to the bathroom and they let us go without a police escort. We unloaded the film in the john and were able to pass them to supporters who came with us. Marizette [Tarlier] was supposed to be searched by the wife of a policeman because there were no female cops available. When the woman approached her, she opened her blouse and said: "Go ahead, search me." The woman backed off, and Marizette was able to unload her film later. That way, we had a record of the papers we wanted to keep. When we were sentenced, the people of Millau and the surrounding area reacted with tremendous outrage. Everyone felt that the sentences were too harsh. The police and the court received threats [not from the Larzac peasants, however] and after three days, the peasants among us were freed. This was the first time in anyone's memory that such a thing had happened in Millau.

The seventeen peasants involved in the invasion of the camp appealed their sentences on November 24, 1976. On December 15, the Court of Appeals in Montpellier — apparently recognizing the political nature of the occupation — changed the terms of all seventeen to suspended sentences of five months.

Throughout the seventies, trials of objectors and those who had sent their military papers back to the government continued all over France. Whenever possible, Larzac militants attended the trials and offered themselves to the court as witnesses. On October 21, 1977, three objectors and Francis Moreau, who had sent back his military papers, were tried in Millau. Moreau describes the event:

We decided that the trial would be a kind of party. We knew that the judge sitting on the case was not a person willing to listen to us and we considered each trial a chance to get across our message. There was a group of witnesses present, including General Bollardière, we felt might be listened to. We appeared before the court in the morning with a group accused of common crimes. There was a woman, for example, who had taken something in a supermarket. Her husband worked but was an alcoholic and drank up his pay so that she had no money for food. She was fined 500 francs. Next up was a group from St. Sauveur that had blocked a military convoy. There was an error of procedure and their case was dropped. Next came an objector. He tried in vain to explain why he refused to serve. Then came the turn of the moral witnesses, but the judge did not want to hear them. He asked only if they had been present when the accused had received his call-up papers. He would not allow anything else, even from the general, who got very angry and demanded the right to speak. The judge commanded him to be silent. When we realized what was happening, we got ready to let a flock of sheep, which we had brought down to Millau for just such an occasion, into the courtroom. There were some local police in the room, but we kept them from shutting the doors and about sixty sheep came in. It was spectacular! There was sheep shit everywhere. The national police were finally called and it was they who were forced to clean up. The trials were restarted at three in the afternoon with the courtroom full of police. My turn came. I had prepared a defense, but the judge refused to hear it. I began my text and he told me to stop, but I gave my speech anyway. I was sentenced to a 500 franc fine, but the prosecutor thought that was too low and appealed to the court in Montpellier. I wrote a letter to the court saying that I refused to recognize their justice. My fine was increased to 1,000 francs. I finally paid it after the struggle was over and I had moved away from the Larzac.

As the protest continued, the army slowly gained on the legal front. Between October 1978 and January 1979, it successfully obtained expropriation orders in nine communes. The situation began to look desperate for the peasants. Although they had continued local actions throughout 1976–78 (fasts in Rodez; working and harvesting crops on land bought by the army; various construction projects sponsored by APAL, aided by volunteer labor from France and other parts of Europe), the peasants and their allies, the Larzac committees, felt that another spectacular national action was necessary. It was finally decided that they should once again take their protest to Paris. They had already gone on their tractors in 1973. This time, in 1978, they would go on foot.

Pierre Burguière was involved in the planning — in particular, coordinating the march with the welcoming committees the local residents had formed at each stop. Thus, he had to monitor the path of the marchers between the *causse* and the capitol — sometimes by automobile, sometimes by train and sometimes by air. In total, about a dozen peasants walked the entire distance from the Larzac to Paris, 710 kilometers with 23 stops. This core group was joined at different stages of the march by other peasants and their supporters. The FDSEA, charged with housing and feeding the marchers, generally arranged to accommodate the peasants but often refused aid to the nonpeasant supporters who accompanied them. Burguière had to find facilities for the latter as best he could.

According to our informants, the march was welcomed enthusiastically by the public along the way. In many cases, those who could not be present when the march passed their area left food and drinks, as well as notes of support for the participants. A passing train tooted its approval. Even the right-wing *Figaro* expressed sympathy for the action. In its December 1978 issue, it published a three-page, illustrated article with the headline, "Larzac: volem viure al pais" ("we want to live in our country"). In it, several marchers were interviewed, their words interspersed with positive comments from the journalist. The article ends, "Leaving la Resse, I turned around. A sign written in Occitan was nailed to the entrance of the farm. *Volem viure a la Resse. La terra e nostra. Sabes plan.* [We want to live at la Resse. The land is ours. You certainly know this.] One could not be more clear." Supporters of the camp extension also made their point when a group of them traveled halfway to Paris in order to paint anti-peasant graffiti along the path of the march.

Pierre Burguière describes the welcome received by the marchers along the route and the arrival in Paris:

> The newspapers paid no attention to us until the fifth day. Then they came and said, "You'll never go all the way to Paris." We assured them of our determination and they began to follow the progress of the march, but in my opinion the journalists treated us like some kind of quaint, regional event. Often, when there were trucks on the road, their drivers would toot their horns in support and frequently they escorted us, one truck in front of the march and one behind. People driving cars also encouraged us. Not one person insulted us along the entire march except the group from La Cavalerie that painted the anti-march graffiti.
>
> The arrival in Paris was frightening. There were police everywhere. We had negotiated our line of march with the police, but they did not respect the agreement. Orders had probably come down from the government to prevent our demonstration. Provocateurs infiltrated the march. Usually when troublemakers join a demonstration, they appear at the end of the line of march but that time they were in front. Later, some of us saw them talking with the police, and certain journalists told us that they were plainclothesmen. The objective was to break the Larzac. They wanted the demonstration to degenerate, but the *Ligue Communiste*

[a Trotskyite group, not known for nonviolence] protected us. They took many blows and gave some themselves. There were other nonpeasants who helped by putting themselves between us and the police. On the way from the Porte d'Italie to the Porte d'Orléans, we passed under the headquarters of a company of national police. We could see them on the roof of their building, firing tear gas at us. But the real tone of the demonstration was set by the marchers, who maintained total silence throughout the whole affair. All you could hear was the tapping of our walking sticks on the pavement and, now and then, our one bullhorn giving instructions to the marchers. That silence was tremendously impressive. I'll never forget it.

By November 5, 1980, the procedures necessary to evaluate the farms already condemned by the government had been completed. Expulsions were the next step. But on the twenty-sixth of the same month, the good news arrived that François Roux had won an important court decision. In effect, he had proved that the government had committed a procedural fault concerning a large number of farms in its request for a declaration of public utility (the first step in expropriation procedures). Legally the government was forced back to square one. It was determined to pursue the extension at all costs, however, and in short order it began the entire procedure again. At the same time, the presidential election of 1981 was fast approaching. A group of officials from the Aveyron, fearing that Giscard d'Estaing would be reelected, continued negotiating with the government, hoping that they could work out an agreement for a mini-extension in which both sides could save face. It is widely believed in the Aveyron and even among some on the Larzac that several peasants were in favor of this move.

Rumors of negotiation, particularly those concerning a mini-extension, were quite divisive on the plateau. The most militant of the Larzac supporters feared that the poorer eastern sector — including La Blaquière, Montredon with its squatters and Pierrefiche — would be the areas sacrificed in order to save the larger farms in the west. Public statements made by the peasants as a group, however, held to the line that no agreement would be signed that would force peasants to leave without their consent.

It was against this background of crisis that the last great national action was organized for December 1980. Susana Moreau of Les Truels suggested that a group of Larzac families go to Paris and camp opposite the military academy on the Champs de Mars. This action was planned in total secrecy to avoid discovery by the Paris authorities, who would certainly have prevented it. Larzac families left from various parts of the Aveyron in small groups, some in cars, others in buses, and still others on the train. Françoise Alla, who went with her two children, recounts the experience:

> We arranged to leave in secret. Although it was very cold, we did not take any warm clothing with us because we were sure we would be expelled within a few hours. Instead, they let us stay for several days! We set up the Larzac school, right there under the Eiffel Tower, and Radio Free Larzac began to transmit its programs.

The group was expelled, but they were allowed to take up residence for another few days on a river barge lent to them by a town government in the Paris region, which was controlled by Michel Rocard, founder of the PSU (*Parti Socialiste Unifié* — a left-wing party) and future prime minister.

Written with exquisite irony, a mock news dispatch appeared on the first page of the December *GLL* concerning the occupation of the Champs de Mars:

> In virtue of the superior interest of French agriculture and of the entire nation, we have decided to cultivate the seventeen hectares of the Champs de Mars that have been left unproductive by the army. It is a question of making the government aware that extending cultivation to the Champs de Mars responds to a need created by modern agriculture. We must extend cultivation over a wider and wider area to keep up with the constant progress that has taken place in the development of agricultural machinery.
>
> Now that this decision has been taken, it should be clear that the time for negotiation has begun. We have already appointed the Larzac committee from Paris to set up a schedule of working sessions with the elected officials of the Paris region, concerned military officers and those responsible for public parks. This is being undertaken with the hope of finding a quick solution to the problem of using the area for agriculture, while leaving the military the greatest opportunity possible to continue its own activities in harmony with the public at large. Thus we will continue to work towards an agreement that both meets the technical needs imposed by agriculture and satisfies the preoccupations of the military.
>
> The realization of this objective will lead to the establishment of a military zone around the Champs as an example of good neighborliness. Once the land has been taken over, a contract will be signed with the army allowing it to maneuver when the farmers are willing to let them do so. In the area of employment, the city of Paris will benefit from a bonus of 25 percent, and the farmers agree to participate in improving the sporting equipment of the city by fencing in the municipal swimming pool.

The Champs de Mars will be open to the public on Saturday and Sunday and visits to the Eiffel Tower will be permitted two days a week when this does not interfere with heavy farmwork.

The necessary dialogue must be frank and in good faith, free of all partisan attitudes. It shall be further understood that no communications concerning the negotiations or related documents shall be released to the public for any reasons whatsoever. The project shall be maintained in all its aspects without modification and, besides, the expropriation is now in progress — if the opponents to it are not content, they can go and find other jobs for themselves somewhere else.

Although the peasants were cheered by the success of their demonstration, the situation looked grim on the eve of the election. The right-wing parties were divided between the followers of Jacques Chirac and Valéry Giscard d'Estaing, but few people gave François Mitterrand much chance of winning. Certain that if either right-wing party won the camp would be extended in short order, a group of local officials from the Aveyron went to Paris to negotiate a deal with the government, as I have already noted. These individuals felt they were on a salvage mission and were ready to compromise most of the plateau in order to save a few farms and, perhaps, shore up their own image in the area.

The March–April 1981 edition of *GLL* carried the following headline: "Our elected officials have acted alone." On February 24, an agreement had been signed between the government, representatives of the department of the Aveyron, and all the mayors of the concerned communes — with the exception of the mayor of La Roque Ste. Marguérite, who had promised the inhabitants of his village that he would not sign. The agreement redrew the boundaries of the extension, with the understanding that the adjustment would save seventy-one of the eighty-three affected farms. It provided for resettlement of expropriated farmers on or near the Larzac, outside the boundaries of the extended camp. In addition, it guaranteed special protection to the village of La Blaquière, including the right of farmers there to continue agricultural activities unless and until they agreed to be settled elsewhere.

The peasants responded, in a television interview, with a resounding "No!" According to their statement in the March–April *GLL*,

a close reading of the February 24 agreement . . . shows that it will lead ineluctably to the extension of the camp to the projected 17,000 hectares with no reduction of the perimeter at all and no retrocession of land to the concerned communes. It also shows that La Blaquière with its inhabitants is destined to disappear, and that there is no serious guarantee that the seventy-one farms concerned will continue to remain viable once the extension is in place. . . .

The only thing left was to wait for the election results. Mitterrand had promised that if elected, he would annul the extension plan. Would he be elected and if so, would he keep his word? French presidential elections take place in two stages. The first round eliminates all those who have won less than 10 percent of the vote and also gives minority parties the right to withdraw (often encouraging supporters to rally to another party with a similar ideology). A second ballot is taken a week later.

The first round in May 1981 led to a runoff between Giscard d'Estaing and François Mitterrand. The second round was to take place on May 10. The campaign on the right had been a bitter one and many of those who had voted for Jacques Chirac in the first round would vote for Mitterrand.

At eight o'clock, the evening of May 10, Mitterrand was declared the winner. The Socialists had come to power in France for the first time since the founding of the Fifth Republic under Charles de Gaulle. One of Mitterrand's first official acts, taken against the advice of his minister of defense, was to cancel the extension plan. He had kept his word. The June 1981 edition of *GLL* carried the headline in Occitan: *AVEM GARDAT LO LARZAC!*

CHAPTER FIVE
Planning for the Future

Ouf! Suddenly the long struggle was over. Léon Maillé, writing in the sixty-fourth issue of *GLL* (June 1981), described May 10 as follows:

As for many others, this May 10 was memorable. First of all it rained — it even rained a great deal — and after a very dry period. The peasants already had something to celebrate. But would it come out? [*va-t-il sortir?*] In spite of the rain, no one was thinking about mushrooms, but rather about François, the candidate. We waited for eight o'clock in the evening. Those who had to milk their animals took transistors with them to the milking sheds while the rest of the family was glued to the T.V. A quarter to eight in the evening. "Elkabach [a conservative television reporter] looks sad." It's not possible; that means we still have a chance. How long those few minutes before eight were . . . and then . . . the boom, the explosion, the cries, the joy, even the tears. Spontaneously, instinctively everyone cried, "We won." ["*On a gagné.*"] Those who were milking stopped. "My mouth fell open, I was so surprised," "Papa" Fabreguette confided to me. In no time at all many peasants found themselves at the farm of L'Hôpital. Everyone embraced, overwhelmed by the news. We celebrated with explosions (of champagne, of course). The telephone rang nonstop. Friends from everywhere (even from Abidjan!) were letting us know how happy they were. We even received a call around nine o'clock from a group so drunk they never managed to tell us who they were. . . . A little later a cortege of cars formed and set out for Creissels, where our valley friends were already celebrating and dancing the carmagnole [a dance popular during the French Revolution]. As we passed, the doors of the subprefecture changed color, completely redecorated. The dancing continued all night. . . . When we met the next day, we looked at one another with astonished expressions. We did not dare believe it; we had come out of the tunnel into the light—out of prison into freedom. Ten years of brotherly struggle were worth all this joy!

But there were still some doubts that needed to be cleared up. In spite of the presidential promise, the extension had not yet been officially annulled. Worse, on May 27, Mitterrand's newly appointed minister of defense, Charles Hernu, announced that he was still in favor of the extension. A worried delegation of peasants and

67

their lawyers met with Mitterrand on the next day. Finally on June 3, the president, meeting with his Council of Ministers, proclaimed the cancellation of the extension plan. A few days later, the army evacuated the five farms that it had occupied (four since October 1976 and one since October 1977). Mitterrand's decision was confirmed by the prefect of the Aveyron on July 8 in spite of a strong protest by the local military authorities. The official victory celebration, attended by 12,000 people from all over France and western Europe, took place at the Rajal del Gorp on August 23. The Japanese peasant movement opposing the construction of Narita Airport outside of Tokyo sent a delegation, and representatives of the Polish union, Solidarity — prevented by their government from participating — sent a telegram of support. Robert Gastal, who had given the first major speech for the Larzac in Rodez in 1972, was asked to welcome the crowd. In his address, he called for the active continuation of the movement to pursue goals that had developed during the struggle.

If the Larzac movement was to continue, it would have to do so essentially on its own. The effective support from outsiders during the struggle had come primarily from the activities of the Larzac committees, which were successful because of the heroic commitment of their members to a common cause. These committees consisted of groups ranging from a by-no-means unified collection of ultraleftists, on the one hand, to religiously inspired, highly committed pacifists, on the other. The fact that such people could cooperate so well over a ten-year period — particularly in France, where political and philosophical purism has reached the status of a fine art — is something of a miracle. With victory, the only thing that had held the radically heterogeneous committees together disappeared.

On November 21 and 22, 150 committee members from all over France met in Millau to discuss what steps they might take next. It was decided that outside support for the Larzac was no longer needed, and the assembly voted to dissolve the committees. Henceforth, the energy of individual members would be dispersed among the various causes they had supported in the past. Later, a relatively small number of former committee members were to join the *Fondation Larzac*, organized on the plateau in 1981 and dedicated to supporting peasant activities in other countries, primarily in the Third World. One can see the fall off in outside support in the precipitous drop in subscriptions to *GLL*, which had reached a high of 4,100 in 1981 and which presently total only about 1,200.

Late in 1981, a general assembly of APAL members voted to change their organization's name from *Association pour la Promotion de l'Agriculture sur le Larzac* to *Association pour l'Aménagement du Larzac*. This change in name signaled a new and wider orientation for the group. It was now to concentrate on culture, tourism and local development, as well as agriculture. If the Larzac was to continue as a social movement, it was natural that APAL, the financial core of the struggle, should take the lead in the post-struggle period.

In October of 1982, APAL distributed a bulletin, under the title, *Informations Larzac*, which described an ambitious plan for the future of the plateau. This report is now regarded as "utopian" by many plateau inhabitants, as well as those militants still involved in the economic, political and social activities of the Larzac. At the time, however, it inspired a great deal of hope that the Larzac could become exemplary. The bulletin emphasized that the movement had passed into a state of legality, which brought with it new opportunities and responsibilities. These would be carried out in cooperation with the local population, its elected officials and professional organizations. The responsibilities would grow out of the means by which the peasants would respond to the new situation.

In the preamble to the bulletin the authors, writing in the name of APAL, noted that there were two strengths left over from the struggle that could be put to good use: the existence of several thousand hectares, now owned by the state, available for innovative forms of agriculture; and a new spirit that had been created by ten years of struggle. It was now possible to develop an alternate agriculture based on ecological principles rather than high production, with the help of young farmers, who were to become rental candidates for available farms. This innovative spirit would affect all aspects of rural development.

Many of the projects described in *Informations Larzac* were brought to fruition in one form or another. In almost every case, however, they were due to the actions of one or at most a few dynamic individuals working within what many critics called personal fiefs. Furthermore, it is true that with the end of the conflict, agriculture came to be the major on-plateau concern of certain key figures — perhaps somewhat to the detriment, at least for a period of time, of other social and political activities.

In discussing post-struggle participation, it also needs to be said that when we began fieldwork in 1984 very few *purs porcs* were to be seen at the meetings of the various associations. Also frequently absent were a fair number of the post-struggle settlers. Criticism of the level of activity and the forms it had begun to take after 1981 was often voiced to us and came from a wide range of individuals who had been ardent supporters of the struggle.

One of the harshest criticisms came in 1986, in an article on the new APAL, "A Failed Utopia, 1981–1983," that was published in a special issue of *Amiras*, a journal dedicated to Occitan issues. Written by a former off-plateau militant, it was met with a good deal of anger from many on the plateau who felt that it was unjust and harmful.

> . . . in the beginning of 1982, APAL was transformed. The Association for the Promotion of Agriculture on the Larzac became the Association for the Development of the Larzac — to cover all the ideas and propositions that had bubbled up and, most of all, to announce an ambitious global project of development. The new ideas contained in this project were not exclusively concerned with agriculture, and agricultural development was not to be, at that moment, the major orientation of this new association. It was on this occasion, at this moment, that the first rupture occurred on the post-struggle Larzac. One could see, for the first time, a counter-reaction against the direction that the planning had taken. It was the "historic leaders" of the struggle who exerted a breaking action in deciding who the new directors of APAL were to be.
>
> The composition of this ten-member board of directors was to be totally different from the former board of directors of the "agricultural" APAL in which the *purs porcs* had been the masters of the game. The latter had agreed to the composition of the new board after a perfectly clear and democratic discussion of the question.
>
> And then! The night of the board of directors' meeting, while counting those present (as well as those absent), they decided that things had not worked out. "This is no good at all! There is a problem in the board of directors. You have stopped electing peasants!" This was the reaction among the oldest leaders of the struggle. This feeling was amplified during the course of a long series of meetings and private discussions. Visibly this was an important issue if one is to judge from the disturbance it caused. The "historical leaders" of the struggle wanted to go back on their decision or, at least, define the composition of the new board of directors so that it would conform to their wishes.
>
> What were their wishes? These can be summarized in three points: 1. An equilibrium between the peasants and nonpeasants had been broken and the peasants were no longer in the majority.

The majority had to be returned to the peasants. 2. The equilibrium between the old peasants and new arrivals was also unsatisfactory. Too many new arrivals [squatters during the struggle] were members of the board. The old leaders wanted to maintain a dominant position on the board for those who were long-term residents. 3. Basically they were shocked that "agriculture" had been transformed into "aménagement." (Boyer et al. 1986:43–44)

Our data show that many who were among the ordinary shock troops of the struggle, particularly squatters, often felt used during the heroic period of the seventies. Although consensus after free discussion was — and continues to be — an ideal on the plateau, the reality is that decisions were frequently made by a few leaders who were seen by others as members of an inner circle. The *Amiras* article reflects this situation, which continued into the immediate post-struggle years. Today, these leaders, many of whom are still active in plateau affairs, admit that it was often deemed necessary to make quick and sometimes secret decisions in the heat of the Larzac conflict. This situation, acceptable to many only under crisis conditions, is unacceptable today. As we shall see, when past and current conflicts are discussed in detail, these feelings, rooted in the past, exert a powerful influence on present-day events.

Up to this point, I have discussed the victory as seen through the eyes of the anti-camp peasant community and its supporters. Let me now turn to the reaction of the camp's supporters and of the new French government.

Although they had always been in the minority in the Aveyron, the supporters of the camp in La Cavalerie never lost faith that the national government would, sooner or later, bring the extension project to fruition. In the presidential election of 1981, they were solid in their support for the right wing candidates (either Giscard d'Estaing or Jacques Chirac in the first round; Giscard d'Estaing in the second), and they were quite confident that the Socialist party would never win on the national level. It is no exaggeration to say that they were stunned by Mitterrand's victory. Shortly after the official announcement of the annulment, a set of questions assembled by the municipal council of La Cavalerie was sent to the newly elected president of the Republic. It asked:

1. Will there be a plan to replace that part of the extension that had been designated for maneuvers?
2. Will there be any continuation of the work (much of which is already in progress) planned to improve the Larzac camp for expanded military use?

3. Will the existing camp continue to be used and if so, for what purposes?
4. Will a military unit larger than the one already in place in the camp be permanently stationed there?
5. Will individuals who have made considerable investments, in the expectation of the camp extension, be indemnified in any way?
6. Will the existing civilian workers for the camp have their positions guaranteed in the future?
7. Will those lands that have been amiably sold to the government be retroceded to those former owners who might wish to buy them back?

In addition to these questions, a motion — in the form of a petition — concerning the potential negative effects of the annulment on the local economy was sent to the prefect of the Aveyron on June 25, 1981. It was signed by 187 individuals and in the name of two professional associations from La Cavalerie and the surrounding area. It reminded the prefect that the extension plan had been approved by an edict of public utility that had been in effect for nearly ten years. It went on to state that the work already completed on the camp extension had led to considerable employment in La Cavalerie, as well as the opening of new businesses (some of which had been expanded through loans) that would be threatened by the cancellation of the extension. It asked that, in the light of these facts, the prefect intercede with the president of the Republic in order to reinstate the project.

In June or July of 1981 a Larzac militant from La Cavalerie sent an eleven-page letter to Louis Joinet, one of the principal advisors of then Prime Minister Pierre Mauroy and a supporter of the Larzac peasants.[1] The letter presented the government with an analysis of the state of affairs in La Cavalerie in the light of Mitterrand's decision to annul the camp extension. Its aim was to help the government in its effort to plan constructively for the entire region in the post-annulment period.

This letter began with a short history of the struggle, noting that several of the peasants of La Cavalerie, including the writer himself, detached themselves as early as 1974 from the movement. (The writer's own inactivity was temporary, if long. It lasted from 1974 until 1978, when he began, once again, to take part in various protest actions.) This part of the letter emphasized the pressure to negotiate with the government that was placed on the peasants of

La Cavalerie by the camp commander, as well as by the leader of the branch of the national police. It is also pointed out that the struggle had only weak and ambivalent support from some local centrist officials and the leaders of the FDSEA, the majority agricultural union. The writer notes that, as the La Cavalerie peasants' opposition to the extension weakened, a movement in favor of it began to take shape, primarily among the business people of the village. The mayor and the municipal council supported the project as well. The members of this group are described as having

> demonstrated a few times in the area, exclusively against the peasants. Certain among them used obscene language when referring to us. Michel Rocard [who would become prime minister in Mitterrand's second term], as well as some of his comrades in the Socialist party can bear witness to this behavior for they were treated to it when they visited La Cavalerie on June 12.

The writer then expresses his opinion, backed up by some convincing evidence, that this group, which never had much influence outside of the village during the ten years of the struggle, had been supported and probably organized by the government in Paris.

The most important pro-camp activists in La Cavalerie itself were then listed. The names and professions of these individuals included, besides the by-then previous mayor of La Cavalerie and a civilian employee of the camp, many of the hotel and café owners in the village, as well as the local pharmacist and a few other business people. The writer added that not all of the business class supported the extension. Many, he wrote, observed a certain neutrality and some had a negative opinion of the existing camp. The night of Mitterrand's election, his victory was actually celebrated at the local *gendarmerie* and at the Café de la Poste. The festivity caused a small scandal among the supporters of the extension.

After the election, the village remained calm until the announcement of the annulment. At that point, the MPOL (the pro-camp organization) set about systematically to tear all the Socialist posters off the walls of the village. On June 6, the MPOL met in the café of a local member, Robert Muret, and voted to participate in a punitive expedition against the peasants in order to "burn down all the farms," but they were dissuaded by the new mayor. On the same night, the Larzac peasants held a general assembly. The writer notes that afterwards, when returning to their cars, many of the anti-camp activists found their tires slashed.

A meeting of local politicians — including Jacques Godfrain, the local deputy to the national assembly and staunch conservative — was then called. At that point, according to the writer, no one, not even Deputy Godfrain, contested Mitterrand's decision. Instead, the pro-camp partisans formed a new group, *Le Larzac Pour Tous* (The Larzac for Everyone). These people had apparently decided to cut their losses by cooperating with the government, providing, of course, that the government made concessions to them. It was also in their interest to have as wide a membership as possible in La Cavalerie and its surrounding area.

The writer, however, while not wishing to appear nasty in his comments, was unable to find anything positive to say about either the members of *Le Larzac Pour Tous* or its activities. Instead, he could only state:

> Perhaps [my judgment] comes from not having much contact with them. Are they a race of humans that have cultivated meanness and hatred? I don't believe that this is the case for all of them. But some of them have a very primitive attitude and most of them don't think very much. They are driven by greed, particularly profit that comes from the exploitation of others [the expropriated peasants].

Yet, the writer did agree that the government should make an effort to indemnify those private contractors in La Cavalerie hurt by the cancellation of building projects in the camp. To not do so would, he wrote, bring unnecessary hardship to the community.

On July 13, 1982 the Millau edition of *Midi Libre* carried an article (similarly covered in other local newspapers) reflecting sadly upon the "bittersweet" departure of a detachment of legionnaires (the sixty-first *Bataillon Mixte Génie*) from the Larzac camp. This unit had been engaged in construction work associated with the extension. An open letter from the people of La Cavalerie to the soldiers was published elsewhere in the same paper. What follows is an excerpt from this letter reflecting the usual bitterness among local business people that occurs when a military base is closed:

> Next to the risks of politics and in this world sick from ambition, vengeance and lies sometimes leading to the destruction of what has been built, you represent the opposite, something that is true and founded on the best of values. Yes, we regret seeing you leave, but are we all not a bit guilty of not being able to keep you here? Will not your departure . . . also be the prelude to an exodus of many of our compatriots who are native to this region and who will no longer, for economic reasons, be able to work here?

Actually only one of the three components of our community appears to have won, but what taste can we attribute to a victory if it can only be established on the death of a village or the decline of a region?

Tomorrow, in spite of our bitterness, we must guard the firm desire and hope that things will come out otherwise. We must demand that our representatives (elected and appointed) make sure that the solutions chosen do not have as their consequences a simple multiplication and change of victims as is currently the case. Thus, perhaps this good-by today will become only a simple "till we meet again" and the region we all love will no longer merit the title given to it by a journalist in the national press: "The Larzac, what a waste."

What the people of La Cavalerie who had supported the camp extension did not know was that even before the public declaration of the annulment, the government in Paris had begun to study the potential economic fallout from the decision. The new government was sympathetic to the peasants but also wanted to show its overall good intentions by aiding La Cavalerie and the entire south Aveyron. By July 3, 1981, Michel Rocard, the then minister of planning (and, as we have noted, Mitterrand's first prime minister in the president's second term), had already sketched out a plan for the development of the post-struggle Larzac region. In it, his first priority was the maintenance of agricultural activity, which after all had always been the mainstay of the region. It was his opinion that, to facilitate agriculture, the government should retain title to most of the land that had been expropriated, insuring the creation of viable units instead of the traditional farms consisting of scattered fields. Re-apportionment and friendly exchange of certain parcels were seen as an absolute necessity.

Rocard went on to suggest that a global plan was needed to develop the Larzac and its region to include — in addition to agriculture — artisans, employment in small- and medium-sized industries, and jobs in the public sector. In order to avoid bankruptcies and layoffs in Millau, the plan needed to consider businesses that had been involved in extension-related contracts with the army.

Tourism was seen as another priority. To meet this need, a developmental program would be designed to better exploit this "rich region," which, in addition to the Larzac, included the Gorges of the Tarn and other natural areas. The possible creation of a nature park was not excluded from the planning effort.

The minister emphasized that the reduction of military activity should not be allowed to lead to a deterioration of such public services as transport and education. In the case of the latter, he suggested that particular attention should be paid to keeping schools adjacent to the camp open, even if they were to suffer a demographic crisis with the outmigration of younger couples with children who were no longer employable.

The Rocard report made it clear that any plan developed for the region would require considerable governmental financing, as well as cooperation among all the groups concerned. This could best be accomplished by placing the program under the direction of a governmentally appointed coordinator attached to the local administrative structure that already existed.

The report, which was apparently never made public, ended with a passage that was undoubtedly intended to calm the fears of the people of La Cavalerie. This final paragraph, if it had become official policy, would have been responded to with shock and anger by the anti-militarist peasants.

> The quality of relations between the minister of defense and the different local groups will condition the success of this reconversion project. Agricultural activity is not incompatible with the military camp. A certain expansion of the camp (smaller, of course, than under the original plan) could, without doubt, be acceptable to the farmers if it were to be negotiated with them and were to take their needs into account when deciding upon the definitive configurations of the camp. It seems to us that the eventual extension, even if it is to be limited, cannot be defined *a priori*.

In August of 1981, in keeping with the Rocard report, the government assigned two officials — Henri Demange of the Aveyron Department of Agriculture and François Pingaud from the Ministry of Agriculture in Paris — the task of planning for the resolution of political, social and economic problems on the Larzac and its wider region. They were to act as midwives to the area's development and help to heal the still open wounds between partisans and enemies of the extension plan.

On June 1, 1982, Henri Demange submitted his report to the national government. It covered the points made previously by Michel Rocard but in greater detail, and outlined those steps that had been taken, as well as those that would need to be taken in the near future, to insure regional development. The plan set a target date of 1985 for its completion. Its first priority was the regulation of problems concerning land ownership in relation to the expropriations that had taken place during the struggle.

The Demange report also dealt with the specific needs of La Cavalerie. It stated that the activity of the existing camp should be maintained, that the maintenance of public services had to be assured, and that a dialogue with local business people and the peasants had already begun. Additionally, the report noted that special attention had been given to assure that local banks would help those few individuals in financial difficulty because of the annulment.

The last section of the report dealt with industrial development. It stressed the need to support Millau's traditional industries: tanning, leather manufacture and glove-making. Spinning and weaving of locally produced wool fiber was also mentioned, but these activities have never been a major part of Millau's economy. One could only be pessimistic about Millau's contemporary industrial potential.

While Henri Demange was charged with the development of a plan for the recovery of the Larzac and the entire south Aveyron, François Pingaud's mission was to work primarily with the Larzac peasants and local officials on the development of economic, social and cultural projects in the immediate region. His attempt led to the signing of an intercommunal charter by the mayors of the communes that contained the Larzac territory. Although the charter still exists on paper, it has had little effect on regional development or politics. This failure was due, in large measure, to the political and demographic facts already discussed in chapter one. Once the Larzac struggle was over, the interests of the nonpeasant majority in the valleys turned away from the plateau. In Pingaud's opinion, however, it was the peasants themselves who were at least partially to blame for the general failure of his mission because of what he felt was their overly exclusive attention to agricultural problems in planning for the post-struggle Larzac.

The only part of the government's plan that came to fruition was the formation of the SCTL, the Larzac's own land-management association. The 1980s and the early 1990s have been an economically difficult period for France in general. In addition, the European Community's overall agricultural policy is not kind to marginal agricultural areas like the Larzac. The Socialist governments that followed Mitterrand's election were financially unable and sometimes politically unmotivated to pay much attention to the needs of the southern Aveyron. The Larzac community did, nevertheless, remain mobilized and has attempted, largely on its own, to deal with a range of problems impeding development in the region.

NOTES

1. These documents, as well as those cited below, were found in government papers during my visit to Paris in the winter of 1989.

A former farm situated within the Larzac camp, after maneuvers. Credit: Le Cun

La Salvetat, 1987. Credit: S. Alland

Lanza del Vasto. Credit: *GLL*

A historical photograph of Jeanne and Elie Jonquet, Auguste Guiraud, Pierre Burguière, Lucien Alla and Léon Burguière taken at the beginning of the struggle. Credit: Jacques Houzel for *La Vie*

Lucien Alla, José Bové, Jean-Marie Burguière and Guy Tarlier discuss strategy during the struggle. Credit: *GLL*

Building the illegal *bergerie* at La Blaquière, 1973. Credit: *GLL*

Robert Gastal gives the first major speech at Rodez, 1972. Credit: Collection of Christiane and Pierre Burguière

Marizette Tarlier on her way to judgment after camp "invasion," 1976. Credit: Collection of Christiane and Pierre Burguière

Tractor march to Paris, 1973. Credit: Collection of Christiane and Pierre Burguière

The Larzac occupies the Champs de Mars, 1980. Credit: *GLL*

Nicole Bernard making sheep-cheese at Les Truels, 1990. Credit: A. Alland

A demonstration against quotas. Millau, 1988. Credit: A. Alland

Larzac militants in Japan support protest against Narita airport, 1981. Credit: Collection of Christiane and Pierre Burguière

Jean-Marie Tjibaou "takes possession" of the Larzac, 1988. Credit: A. Alland

Children of the Larzac. Credit: Michel Marguerite

The Gardarem Lo Larzac stand. Demonstration in Millau, June 30, 2000, to support those charged in McDonald dismantlement. Credit: *A. Alland*

José Bové and other activists arrive for trial, Millau, June 30, 2000. Credit: *A. Alland*

During the trial in Papeete, Larzac militants demonstrate at the Tahiti House in Paris, May 11, 2000. Alain Desjardin stands in front of banner. Credit: *Gilles Gesson*

Dismantling at the McDonald construction site. "MacDo Out. We stand by Roquefort." Millau August 12, 1999. Credit: *Gilles Gesson*

CHAPTER SIX
The Future Unfolds

Was it unexpected that, with victory, the immediate attention of the Larzac peasants would turn to agriculture? And can this turn be seen as a reactionary move as the writer of the *Amiras* article cited in the last chapter suggests? My answer to both questions would be no. After all, if the battle of the Larzac came to be seen as a struggle between national power and local control, local control meant the right to remain on the land — a right that, in the final analysis, even after the victory, would have to be proved through successful farming. Besides, the Socialists had already made a commitment to agriculture. In their campaign, they had promised to create an *office foncier* (land office) that would, in some undetermined form, provide land to newly installed farmers lacking the means for high capital investment.[1] Some in the government saw the Larzac as the perfect place for the experimental implementation of such a program. Although, by 1983, the idea of creating of a national land office had been definitively abandoned (Crisenoy and Boscheron 1986:106), the reforms that would have been provided *were* carried out on the Larzac.

We have already seen that the attention of both the peasants and the government was quickly focused on the 6,300 hectares that had been bought for the camp extension from retired farmers or non-farmers and now had to be disposed of in some way. (Land bought from still-active farmers was in most cases retroceded to the original owners. Communal land was returned as well.) Under existing French law, *all* former owners had a right to reclaim their land. However, the non-farmers who had profited from the inflated prices paid under the unusual conditions of the extension were generally not interested in buying back their properties.

By September of 1981, the peasants had created a charter for new installations on the Larzac. The preamble to the charter reminded the reader that during the ten years of the struggle the peasants had helped to set up seven farms in the total absence of state aid. It then went on to propose the installation of fifteen more families as renters on available land. In order to establish a positive climate for these new farmers it would, the charter stated, be necessary to

79

offer long-term leases that would free them to make economically wise investments without fear of losing their land in the short run. Under these conditions the new farmers could expect to attain a reasonable economic return and adequate living conditions without an inordinate delay.

The peasants also hoped that these new farms would avoid the trap of productivism, which was seen as dependent upon heavy investment and, therefore, high indebtedness. Many farmers in France were already perceived as being in the hands of the *Crédit Agricole*. With a renewed emphasis on small-scale, environmentally sound farming, the Larzac peasants hoped to make an ecological point as well. The current model for farming in France, and in the rest of the EC for that matter, involves capital intensive production on large farms and, as a corollary, the eventual disappearance of small farms, most of which are now in less favorable environmental zones. The Larzac provided an experimental laboratory to prove the value of small-scale farming in marginal areas.

In the light of this double orientation, the charter called for a new form of agriculture in which ecological principles would be followed and attention would be given to the quality of life of those farming the plateau.

> Therefore: 1. We will work against the accumulation of land by individual farmers. 2. We will not allow farms to be divided. There is enough land on the Larzac to restructure existing farms when necessary. 3. We demand that, in order to insure an effective social life, all farmers live on their farms. 4. When it is deemed necessary, we favor reapportionment of land. 5. When examining the candidates for these farms we hope to maintain a spirit of openness and tolerance that was the principle factor in the dynamic of the Larzac. No segregation will be accepted *a priori* on the part of either the veterans of the struggle, or the *purs porcs*.

To implement these local reforms, the peasants asked that 1. the state create adequate laws for the acquisition of land and its rental to appropriate candidates, as well as financial support for young farmers; 2. the *Crédit Agricole* adapt its norms concerning loans to young farmers and development plans to accommodate agricultural experiments. Noting that ten years of experience can be called upon to prove that local control over monies used in agricultural development would be more efficient, the charter also asked that 3. credit be decentralized and put under the supervision of such local organizations as APAL and the various CUMA.

The charter ended by suggesting how important the Larzac could become as a model for agriculture in France. Success on the Larzac could be applied to

> . . . other areas, now in the process of becoming depopulated and which require an important economic revival. This type of action could slow down the flow of people from rural areas that contributes to the plague of unemployment. Such action could bring about the reversal of what, for the past fifty years, has been an ineluctable tendency of the rural world to become a desert. Would this not be, for all French people, a beautiful illustration of change in our society?

On May 27, 1983 an agreement was signed between Michel Rocard, who had become minister of agriculture, and the SAFALT (*Société d'Aménagement Foncier Aveyron-Lot-Tarn*), giving the SAFALT the right to manage government land bought for the extension. According to Rocard, this agreement concretized the government's promise to return Larzac land to agriculture and to insure the installation of young farmers. (In actuality, the SAFALT legal structure only allowed, at best, short-term rentals.)

On September 29 of the same year, a meeting was held in Paris between a delegation from the Larzac and the minister of agriculture with the view of creating the *Société Civile des Terres du Larzac* (SCTL). Another meeting on the same subject was held in the prime minister's office on June 5, 1984. The agreement to form the SCTL — finally signed in the summer of 1984, just two days before the replacement of the prime minister, Pierre Mauroy, by Laurent Fabius — was worked out with the cooperation of a close associate of Mauroy and two Larzac militants, Chantal de Crisenoy, a researcher for INRA (the National Agricultural Research Institute), and Daniel Boscheron, a lawyer and judge of the Court of Appeals in Paris.

The basic principle of the agreement was that the SCTL would be granted an *emphytéotique* (long-term) lease — in this case, sixty years (with a possible thirty year renewal) — on the 6,300 hectares available. This lease would allow the SCTL to rent land parcels (with dwellings and farm buildings), for farming purposes only, to individuals for the entire length of their professional lives. It would also oblige renters to quit their farms on retirement, thus avoiding the future demographic problems of an aging farming population. The agreement also stipulated that the SCTL could lease buildings under its control that were not attached to farms at no rental cost to non-farmers for periods specified by both lessor and lessee. The latter, in all cases, would be obliged to improve the buildings on the allocated property within two years and to pay property and residence taxes. Once in operation, the SCTL developed a means for amortizing improvements (on the basis of "use value") to be made on farms. This was done to make it possible for those who left the area before retirement to recuperate a fair return and was keyed to both the amount invested in repairs and the length of time between such investment and leave-taking.

Everything was in place by the spring of 1985. (Previously on November 29, 1984, the SCTL had elected its first board of directors consisting of seven farmers, three artisans and three representatives of the communal commissions charged with agricultural land management.) Finally on April 29, the prefect of the Aveyron and three delegates from the SCTL signed the statutes of the new organization, which thereby formally assumed the long-term lease of state property. The SCTL was to pay 25,000 francs per year rent on its 6,300 hectares, as well as land taxes and certain types of insurance.

During the struggle, José Bové, along with his wife, Alice Monier, squatted a farm in Montredon. He was a militant in the minority worker-peasants union, the *Travailleurs-Paysans*. With François Mathey, Alain Desjardin and others, Bové played a major role in the organization and founding of the SCTL. According to him:

> In 1983 the *Travailleurs-Paysans* held a meeting to discuss how the expropriated land on the Larzac might be used and how a solution might be found to the problem of retrocession. Previous owners, of course, have the right to buy their land back as well as a priority right to rent their former property. These rights last for thirty years. We were against these rights, but we had to find a legal means of getting around them. Mitterrand had promised to create a land office but the FDSEA was against the idea. We had to find a way to avoid the sale of the land by the SAFALT. The solution was to rent the land to the SCTL with a nonagricultural lease, but one that gives the SCTL the right to rent land to farmers. This solution did not come from the government, which, for three years, did nothing. It was our idea. We did have a friend in Mauroy's cabinet and he helped us work out the agreement.

All holders of SCTL leases must buy one share of the association. They have the right to elect members of the board of directors that governs the association and to attend the annual shareholders' meeting. Each shareholder has only one vote in these meetings and, in addition, can hold a maximum of one proxy for an absent shareholder. Initially, there were seventy-one shareholders. Of the total land under SCTL control, 4,664 hectares make up whole farms. (Votes by the board to allocate farms must be unanimous or the question must be brought before a shareholders' meeting.) In a few cases, the SCTL controls just the major portions of farms. In the latter situation, some of the property of the farm may belong to the individual farmer, be leased from private owners or belong to one of the Larzac GFAs. In one case the SCTL has only thirty-nine hectares of a large farm (the rest is owned by a Larzac GFA), but the dwelling on this property is rented under an SCTL lease. There are twenty-nine complete, or practically complete, SCTL farms. Among the farmers occupying these farms eight are *purs porcs* (counting two brothers in a GAEC who also have substantial GFA land). Ten are former militants of the Larzac struggle and eleven are new arrivals. Of the latter, several have agricultural backgrounds.

The most active members of the SCTL board of directors have always been farmers. In 1989 the statutes were modified to exclude from the board individuals who were not lessees of SCTL land or houses. This step was undertaken not to inhibit the participation of outsiders but rather because such outsiders consistently failed to attend board meetings. Until recent years, the board was made up of both old and new farmers, including a fair representation of *purs porcs,* former Larzac militants and new arrivals. (At present, younger farmers predominate.) In addition, with the exception of the first board, there has always been at least a minority representation of women. In 1989 there were three women, each representing one of the three categories of inhabitants currently living on the plateau. Under the SCTL statutes one-third of the board is renewed through election by shareholders every three years.

One of the first tasks undertaken by the SCTL was to determine a fair rent-scale for farms of different size and agricultural quality. Under its statutes, the SCTL was required to base rents upon the prices paid to farmers in a given year for sheep's milk, wheat and mutton. (Rents for GFA farms are based exclusively on the price of sheep's milk. As we shall see later, this difference was partially responsible for a major conflict on the plateau, which began in 1986 and was resolved only in the spring of 1990.) Crop land is more valuable than pasture and wood land, but all three categories also vary in quality. The SCTL developed a system of points for each category so that an overall evaluation could be derived. These are useful not only for determining rents, but also serve in the difficult process of reapportioning plots. As such, the system stands as a model for other regions of France where farms need to be concentrated through the recombination of scattered parcels.

As we have already seen, a fair amount of Larzac land was also owned by the three GFAs created to buy land from those who did not wish to sell to the army. By the end of the struggle there were over 1,000 hectares in GFA hands, including two large farms, one in the south and the other in the northwest of the extension area. In 1982 the peasants decided to create a fourth GFA, which in 1984 bought Les Aussedats (114 hectares) in the northwest. Since Les Aussedats consisted of rather poor quality land and was small by modern Larzac standards, it needed to be expanded. The members of two neighboring GAECs (Tarlier and his partners, and the Alla brothers, who were *purs porcs*) agreed to contribute land by signing over rental plots from their own farms. It was plain that the commitment to the GFAs had not died with victory. The continuation of the precedent GFAs and the creation of GFA 4 would, it was hoped, help to impede land speculation on the plateau. We shall see later that structural and historical differences between the SCTL and the GFAs would lead to conflicts between some of the more traditional farmers on the plateau and some of the radical newcomers, even though each group counted among its members supporters of these two rather different types of institutions.

Though the future of agriculture on the plateau was a main concern, at no time after 1981 did the Larzac movement turn its back on off-plateau social and political problems. In March of 1982, five Larzac peasants (a *pur porc* couple and three militants), two ex-Larzac committee members, and the Larzac's lawyer, François Roux, visited Japan as an official delegation to support Japanese peasants who had been fighting against the construction of Narita Airport on their land. A major portion of the May 1982 issue of *GLL* was devoted to this action.

Peace activities were to continue as well. On August 6 and 7, 1981 (the traditional time for demonstrations on the plateau), a rally was held at the Rajal in favor of a nuclear freeze. Clearly the Larzac peasants' awareness of problems elsewhere in the world, as well as their readiness to engage themselves in militant actions, was to continue along with their aid to projects in the Third World, funded by the Larzac Foundation (*Fondation Larzac*). Today the Foundation is run by a small group of individuals living on the plateau and the surrounding area, but it receives contributions from a wide range of outsiders, for the most part former supporters of the Larzac community.

In 1984, the Foundation published a book that recounts the history of the Larzac struggle (see chapter seven), entitled *Alors la Paix Viendra* (*Then Peace Will Come*), with text by Pierre Bonnefous and photographs by Raymond Martin. The latter, who died in 1989, was a long-term supporter of the struggle and a friend of Bonnefous. Profits from sales of this book are used by the Foundation to fund its projects. Aware that their financial resources would always be relatively small, the members of the Foundation agreed that they would limit their support to worthy projects proposed by a member or friend of the Foundation who would, in turn, serve as the link between the association and those receiving aid.

Peace oriented activities and militant support for the Third World continue at Le Cun, the center on the plateau founded during the struggle that runs seminars on topics related to nonviolence in addition to maintaining a large library on peace and nonviolent issues. Along with the seminars, Le Cun has provided training in nonviolence to the Kanak community by hosting young Kanaks at its center and through training sessions conducted in New Caledonia itself. Members of the Basque movement for local rights have requested similar instruction as well. Recently Le Cun became associated with the Palestinian Center for the Study of Nonviolence — the first step in developing a shared program of seminars and workshops in support of the Center's nonviolent approach to the resolution of the Palestinian-Israeli conflict. Le Cun has also helped finance the participation of one of its members in the International Peace Brigade. Though its concerns with peace and nonviolence involve it in regions far from the plateau, Le Cun also makes its own facilities available for Larzac social gatherings and militant actions. It hosted, for example, a seminar, Women in the Rural World, in the fall of 1990 (organized by the CIR — *Centre d'Initiatives Rurales*, the successor to *Larzac Universités*) and, every year, invites the entire community to a New Year's celebration.

The community of Les Truels in cooperation with *L'Arche* also continues as a center for the propagation of nonviolence on the plateau and elsewhere. In addition, the farm of La Salvetat, under the direction of Alain Desjardin and a recent associate, pursues its role as a center for meetings and discussion of a wide range of militant issues. In 1987 it welcomed a delegation of farm-labor militants who met to create the new left-wing farm union, the *Confédération Paysanne*. In 1988 La Salvetat was chosen by the CIR as the place for its second seminar on Women in the Rural World. In the summer of 1989, La Salvetat hosted a youth group of over 200 young men and women from western Europe and Hungary, which met to discuss common interests.

Between 1982 and 1989, the major off-plateau political concern of Larzac militants became the struggle for independence waged in New Caledonia (a large island off the coast of Australia) by the majority of the indigenous Kanak people led by Jean-Marie Tjibaou. Before this issue can be discussed, however, it will be necessary to digress somewhat and examine both the number and the type of individuals who were to continue on the militant path after the camp extension was annulled.

After the struggle, sympathy for this or that specific cause remained rather wide spread, if not unanimous. Though the continuation of actions, particularly their planning, generally depended on a small minority of indefatigable people (rarely more than thirty and sometimes as few as eight), if one were to total up those different individuals who participated more sporadically in the planning of one or another type of action, the number reached about sixty. This larger number was due, I believe, to a unique feature of the overall social structure of the Larzac: the variety of associations that exist on the plateau.

Some of these associations are leftovers from the struggle, while others were created in the post-struggle period. Although the total membership in each association is relatively low (not counting shareholders of the SCTL and the GFAs), individuals have a wide choice of associations in which to participate. Thus, they are able to match their convictions and energy to a comparatively narrow range of interests.

Each Larzac association is run by its most active members, who constitute its board of directors. There is some overlap in the personnel of these. Nevertheless, as one looks over the total range of associations, different faces appear in each of the specific groups.

Although a minority of *purs porcs* and pre-struggle "pioneers" remain active, the majority of the contemporary Larzac activists are those who settled on the plateau after participating in the struggle. In addition to them, the inhabitants of Le Cun also participate in many Larzac activities, although they are — with the exception of its founder, Hervé Ott — more or less transient residents. Mention should also be made of the members of Les Truels. The original squatters have left, but the community is still active in Larzac associations.

The sizable group of true newcomers are those farmers who have settled on the Larzac since 1981, primarily on SCTL land. They are present on the SCTL board, in the CUMAs and the *Confédération Paysanne* (the recently formed left-wing agricultural union), and have participated in the Roquefort Committee (the precursor of the SPLB) — activities that help secure their economic survival. Yet, though they have developed strong social ties among themselves, they are conspicuously absent from such Larzac associations as APAL, the Foundation and *GLL*, which they tend to identify with the "war veterans" of the struggle. Along with the absent *purs porcs*, they have divorced themselves from much of the political life on the plateau. It seems to me, however, that there is nothing unusual in the fact that participation in political and community-wide social activities has fallen off since the victory. What is impressive is the fact that so many individuals still participate in community life, including those militants who never settled on the *causse* but who return from time to time and who contribute their services with commendable faithfulness.

Now let us return to the struggle for independence in New Caledonia. Beginning in 1984, this issue became the major rallying point for those on the plateau interested in politics beyond the boundaries of the Aveyron. (With François Roux's involvement — he was the first to raise the issue of Kanaky on the Larzac — and the successive visits of Jean-Marie Tjibaou, a current of sympathy swept the plateau and engulfed many of those not normally attracted to politics.) Here is an extract of our interview with Roux in which we see him serving as an intermediary between the Larzac and the Kanaks.

> Since 1979 when, along with de Felice, I defended separatists from Polynesia, I had raised problems concerning the Pacific territories with the people of the Larzac. I brought a Kanak to the plateau in 1982 but it was not until the events of '84 [two brothers of Jean-Marie Tjibaou, among other Kanaks, were killed in an ambush by whites] that people became really interested and said that they might be able to help. It was through the good offices of *L'Arche* that I became really involved. Pierre Parody [the leader of *L'Arche* after the death of Lanza del Vasto] and I visited the island and while

there I talked to Tjibaou, whose brother had just been killed, about nonviolence. I told him about the struggle on the Larzac and about *L'Arche*. I suggested that the Kanaks attempt to achieve independence nonviolently. He told me to write a letter to him on my return to France and I did so. On my return I got together with Hervé Ott and Pierre Parody in the Cévennes. In our letter we proposed an exchange between the Kanaks and the plateau. The Kanaks wrote to us accepting our proposition and then Hervé went there and did an excellent job teaching nonviolence. After that, a Kanak delegation came to the Larzac where they were very well received.

Visits between the plateau and the island have continued. In addition to François Roux and Hervé Ott, Guy and Marizette Tarlier visited in 1987 and again in the fall of 1989, as did Elizabeth Baillon in 1987. Jean-Marie Tjibaou and his wife, Marie-Claude — along with the vice president of the FLNKS (the Kanak independence alliance) as well as other less well-known Kanaks, including students studying at the University of Montpellier — have visited the plateau on several occasions. In the summer of 1988 the people of the Larzac, as a symbolic act, presented a small parcel of land belonging to Le Cun to the Kanak people as "their territory." Jean-Marie Tjibaou officiated at the ceremony. About to cut the ribbon at the entrance to Kanaky-Larzac, he said — with that ironic sense of humor much appreciated by those who knew him — "I take possession of France." Very warm relations between the people of the Larzac and the people of Kanaky continue to the present.

The first Socialist government (in power from 1981 to 1986) encouraged a dialogue between the Kanaks and whites (Caldoches) living in New Caledonia. When the conservatives won the parliamentary elections in 1986, President Mitterrand was forced to appoint a right-wing government. The new head of this government, Prime Minister Jacques Chirac, named Bernard Pons as minister of overseas territories. Pons was clearly against independence for New Caledonia, and he immediately moved to keep it in French hands. In the fall of 1987 he arranged a referendum on independence for the mineral-rich island. The outcome of this vote was obvious from the beginning. Since the end of the Second World War, the French have encouraged immigration to New Caledonia by mainlanders as well as Polynesians from the Wallis and Futuna Islands. By the 1980s the Kanak constituted a minority (albeit a substantial one with about 45 percent of the population) in their own homeland. The Wallisians, a favored minority on the island, whose own territory consists of an extremely overpopulated, small, insular group, could be counted on to vote for the continuance of New Caledonia as an overseas French territory. The Kanaks called for a boycott of the referendum which, to no one's surprise, was won by those who wanted to remain under the French flag. A "yes" vote in the referendum had been endorsed officially by the RPCR, the colonial party supported by most, but not all, whites on the island.

Meanwhile the Caldoches who had been indicted for the killing of Tjibaou's brothers were found not guilty by reason of self-defense, in spite of overwhelming evidence that they had committed premeditated murder. François Roux spoke eloquently several times on the Larzac of this miscarriage of justice on the island and, in addition, described the conditions faced in New Caledonian jails by Kanak prisoners. It was evident that a double standard of justice existed in New Caledonia. The reaction on the Larzac, as well as among members of L'Arche and former militants elsewhere in France, was immediate. Taking their cue from Émile Zola's famous "J'accuse" (published during the Dreyfus affair), a considerable number of them signed a petition denouncing the judicial decision and waited for the government to take action against them. In France it is a crime to denounce judicial decisions and those who do so put themselves in immediate jeopardy of arrest and significant prison terms. The government, prudently enough, did not respond to the challenge; however, the action did draw the attention of many in France to the real conditions existing on the island.

At the end of April 1988, a group of Kanak militants killed three gendarmes in Kanaky and took a group hostage, holding them in a cave on the island of Ouvea. During the week between the two rounds of the ongoing presidential election in which he was a candidate, Prime Minister Jacques Chirac ordered an attack on the cave. The gendarmes were liberated, but several Kanaks were killed — some under suspicious circumstances. The next week, Mitterrand was reelected president and appointed Michel Rocard as his prime minister. A delegation of individuals representing various church groups was sent by the government to the island in an attempt to create an atmosphere of dialogue between the Kanak and Caldoche communities. A few months later, Jacques Lafleur, the head of the RPCR, came to Paris, where he met with Jean-Marie Tjibaou and representatives of the French government.

It was at this time that the Larzac presented the Kanaks with their symbolic bit of land on the plateau. Speaking at the ceremony accompanying the gift, Tjibaou said that while the talks were going well, the FLNKS would never agree to a suggested partition of the island. Later in the summer, an agreement was signed between Lafleur and Tjibaou. This agreement did include a temporary division of New Caledonia into three regions with the stipulation that considerable aid would be available for areas beyond the capitol, Numea (populated largely by whites and Wallisians). In addition, professional and administrative training would be made available to Kanaks. A new referendum on independence was scheduled for ten years after the signing of the agreement that froze the electoral roles as of the signing, so that the French could no longer pack the island with people hostile to independence. Finally, the agreement gave what amounted to amnesty to both Kanaks and Caldoches who had committed violent crimes. It will be news to the French public to discover that this agreement was written (with, to be sure the close consultation of Jacques Lafleur and Jean-Marie Tjibaou) by François Roux![2] It is no exaggeration to say that the Larzac played a major role in bringing peace to New Caledonia.

In May of 1989, Jean-Marie Tjibaou and his second in command, Yéiwéné Yéiwéné, were assassinated by a young Kanak extremist. The Larzac went into a state of shock. Calls of sympathy and support went out immediately from the plateau to Marie-Claude Tjibaou, to Yéiwéné's family, and other Kanak friends. Later that summer Mrs. Tjibaou visited the Larzac and joined a large gathering of peasants at the Kanak grounds adjacent to Le Cun to commemorate the death of her husband and, of much importance as well, the deep friendship that had developed between her people and the people of the plateau.

If Kanaky represents the major effort in foreign affairs of the post-struggle period on the Larzac and the foundation of the SCTL represents the major economic innovation on the plateau since the victory, community-based education, begun with the foundation of Larzac University (*Larzac Universités*), continues as a feature of post-struggle activities and remains an important dimension in the continuing dynamism of the plateau. Larzac University as a cooperative institution run by intellectuals—many of whom were centered in Paris — was almost entirely superseded at the end of the struggle by the *Centre d'Initiatives Rurales du Larzac*. In the beginning, the CIR consisted of three branches: 1. Larzac University, which has been reduced to running the *gite rural* (rural lodge) in Montredon, used by tourists — particularly hikers and school groups — and also as a meeting place by militants; 2. a cooperative veterinary group, established on the plateau during the struggle by Elizabeth Lepetitcolin, which has become independent in the last few years and 3. the CIR proper, which has continued the educational role of *Larzac U.*

The CIR owes its dynamism to its paid administrator, Alice Monier, a former squatter and Larzac militant, who lives with her husband, José Bové, in Montredon, a small village in the eastern sector of the plateau. At the outbreak of the struggle Montredon was an abandoned village, most of which was quickly bought by the army. Alice and José, along with the others who squatted army land, are a hardy couple. They were the first squatters in the village and from 1976 until the end of the struggle lived with their two little girls without running water, electricity or a decent road connection to the rest of the plateau. Since its inception, Alice has worked diligently and with ingenuity to keep the CIR alive and funded.

While the CIR has a healthy following on the plateau, its attempt to establish itself in the wider area of the southern Aveyron has been difficult. As already noted, the area is well known for its political and social conservatism. By 1987 it was the opinion of a considerable number of Larzac militants and outside supporters of the CIR that the association between it and the Larzac struggle was counterproductive. They felt that many who could profit from the activities of the CIR refused participation because of this connection.

The divorce came at the general assembly in the spring of 1988. Henceforth the *Centre d'Initiatives Rurales du Larzac* was to be known simply as *Centre d'Initiatives Rurales.* The official relationship with the plateau was abandoned to history. Easing this separation was the fact that as far back as 1984 the CIR, in order to increase its effectiveness, had joined a national organization, the FRCIVAM (*Fédération Régionale des Centres d'Information et de Vulgarisation pour l'Agriculture et le Milieu Rural*). In 1988, with the help of the local CIVAM and the CFPPA (*Centre de Formation Professionnelle et de Promotion Agricole*) of St. Affrique, the CIR received an important grant to conduct a 200-hour workshop on the transformation of sheep's milk into products other than Roquefort cheese. This project, originally conceived by APAL, which for lack of finances and other complications was unable to pursue it, gave the CIR a leg up on an important economic issue, particularly pertinent in the light of the approaching date for the full entry of French agriculture into the tariff-free and highly planned European Community. It was also to undercut, if inadvertently, the scope of APAL's activities on the plateau, at least as these concerned economic development and diversification.

From 1987 onward, APAL had replaced the *bureau* (the representative body created during the struggle) as the forum for the planning of most political actions and information sharing. APAL has continued to organize meetings around issues of general interest. However, by the end of our research period (1992), its focus had changed. Although its post-victory charter had given it wide-ranging powers to work for the economic and cultural development of the Larzac, its principal activity (and most visible success), besides the ongoing support of the newly installed farmers, has come to be the 1982 creation of the *écomusée du Larzac* (the Larzac ecological museum), headquartered in APAL's center, La Jasse, located on National Highway Nine. This is no small accomplishment, for the museum is not only one of the sources of revenue that enables APAL to make loans to the Larzac community; it is also a showcase for the post-struggle Larzac.

La Jasse (*sheepfold*, in Occitan), a huge, stone structure, formerly used as a collection station for milk on its way to Roquefort, is a magnificent example of Larzac architecture with its long gothic vault and typical heavy, gray limestone (*lauze*) roof. At present, the building is divided into three sections. At the entrance, facing the national highway, an area is reserved for the display and sale of farm products produced by a small post-struggle association, the *Produits Fermiers*. Items sold include locally made cheeses, pâté, jams and honey. The work of local artisans — jewelry, weaving, pottery, etc — is also displayed here. Books, postcards and posters relevant to the Larzac and its environs are on sale as well. The next long section of the building is reserved for museum exhibits, which have concentrated on various Larzac themes such as, the history of the struggle, economic life on the renewed plateau, Larzac architecture, photos of the plateau by well-known artists, the Larzac during the French Revolution, an exhibition of photos and texts dealing with the lives of women of the Larzac and the surrounding Aveyron and, at the twentieth anniversary celebration of the conflict, a collection of vivid posters from the struggle. A large room at the back is set aside for meetings of the many Larzac associations and as a snack bar for passing tourists and friends during the two summer months of the tourist season.

The Larzac museum was conceived as a place to exhibit important aspects of life on the plateau organized around a theme expressing the point of view of those active in the post-struggle community. It has had a political cast that has not pleased everyone. Opening ceremonies of new exhibitions have been well attended by left-wing politicians including, in many instances, delegates from Paris, but local right-wing officials generally have refused to participate. Thus, the museum has a clear political purpose. In order to showcase that part of the plateau that was active during the struggle, a permanent exhibition was planned extending beyond the walls of La Jasse to farms and other areas of the plateau that had been important between 1971 and 1981. To accomplish this goal, an itinerary was established for tourists leading them over a major portion of the northern Larzac. A brochure was prepared to guide tourists to these sites, each of which is marked by an illustrated panel explaining its relevance to the history of the struggle. Every summer since victory, a good number of tourists who first stop at La Jasse ask about these sites and visit many of them. Thus the écomusée serves to inform the public of the plateau's history, underscoring the symbolic significance of the Larzac movement.

The inspiration and major energy behind the ecological museum is Elizabeth Baillon, an artist and writer who lives with her husband, Claude, himself an artist, on the ancient, fortified farm of Brouzes in the extreme northwest of the plateau. Since the inception of the museum, Baillon has suggested exhibition themes to APAL and has personally worked on the installation of every show, except the one on the Larzac and the French Revolution.

Baillon has generally maintained a political focus in her choice of exhibits. In 1984 she proposed an exhibition of militant posters from the struggle period. Pierre Bonnefous, who was among those who wanted to see the Larzac move beyond its geographic and historical limits, convinced APAL that the theme was politically provocative and too focused on the past. After much debate, the exhibition theme was changed to feature current activities on the plateau. Baillon accepted the judgment of the APAL board and worked hard under rather extreme time constraints to bring the newly chosen theme to reality. As we have seen, however, the poster show did come to fruition in the summer of 1991, during the celebration of the twentieth anniversary of the beginning of the struggle.

Aside from the occasional conflict over choice of exhibit, the museum faces two other problems. Because it does not fit under either an artistic or ecological rubric, it has difficulty finding outside financial support for the preparation of its exhibits. At times, compromises have to be made to keep to tight budgets. In addition, the museum has never had much support from settlers who have taken up residence, largely on SCTL land, since 1981. These people feel alienated by their own lack of connection to the struggle. From their point of view, the museum, like some other associations mentioned earlier, is a place for "veterans" to reflect on their past glory.

When she looks back on the museum's early days, Baillon admits that the criticism (it was too parochial in scope and too focused on the struggle) had some validity. In 1984, however, she organized an exhibition on Larzac architecture that opened in La Cavalerie, where the mayor, who had been in favor of the extension, was willing to reestablish links with those who had opposed the military. (This successful exhibition was repeated at La Jasse in the summer of 1992.) In 1987, with the agreement of APAL, Baillon reached out to a broad segment of the plateau by arranging the publication of a leaflet highlighting tourist and commercial sites located in the various communes of the Larzac. This very successful project was paid for jointly by the communes concerned and APAL.

In 1989 Elizabeth Baillon was elected on the Socialist party ticket to the Millau municipal council. She now serves as adjunct mayor in charge of cultural activities. In this role, she has convinced the members of the municipal council to accept the Larzac Archives, collected by Robert Pirault, for the city library, and to recompense Pirault with a small honorarium for the work he has done over the years to preserve this material. She has also expressed interest in creating some kind of acceptable agreement between Millau and the Larzac *vis-à-vis* funding for the ecological museum.

The CIR, responsive to economic factors affecting the Larzac and its surrounding region, has organized workshops to help the farmers cope with the economic pressures specific to the area. The most militant peasants are also organizing themselves. Let us review the situation. During the 1970s, new feeding techniques and better genetics raised the productivity of sheep many fold; the average flock size was on the increase in the seventies as well. In the 1980s, the majority share in Roquefort Société, the major producer of Roquefort cheese, was bought by Perrier, a multinational company famous in the United States for its sparkling spring water. (Since then, it has changed hands twice — first being bought by Nestlé and later by the cheese producer Besniers.) What had always been a locally based industry, proud of its important place in the regional economy, would now, it was feared, ignore local interests. Rumors began to circulate in the Roquefort catchment basin that cheaper cows' milk from outside the area, perhaps even from foreign countries, would be substituted for more expensive sheep's milk. In 1985 the Roquefort industry, which up to then had an agreement with farmers to buy all milk produced locally, decided it needed to protect itself from over-production. Two solutions were envisaged. One was to decrease milk production and the other was to diversify the range of products made by Roquefort. Diversification was the first solution instituted. By 1987, 30 percent of all sheep's milk bought by Roquefort was being converted into feta cheese, yogurt and milk powder.

However, the farmers' fear of eventual quotas did not go away. In February of 1987, the CIR organized a two-day workshop on the future of sheep's milk production in the area. The possibility that quotas might soon be imposed was discussed. In the same year the association of milk producers, the SEB, and Roquefort agreed that steep price-differentials would be paid for milk used in different forms of production. Farmers would be paid a premium price for milk destined to be converted into Roquefort cheese, less for milk converted into feta and even less for milk destined to be made into powder. Although Roquefort would continued to buy all milk produced, a quota system was to be instituted on how much from each farmer would be used in making each of these three categories. The proposed system, to be based on past output, favored large, established producers at the expense of younger farmers who were beginning their careers. Many of them had recently received approval of local agricultural authorities to expand their enterprises and were burdened with the loans they had taken out at the *Crédit Agricole* to pay for the expansion.

In 1987 a Roquefort committee was formed under the stimulus of Guy Tarlier (himself a large producer little affected by the quotas) and José Bové — a member of the newly formed farm-labor union, the *Confédération Paysanne* (the successor to the *Travailleurs-Paysans*) — who is not personally affected as his farm does not supply milk to Roquefort. The committee's membership comes from a large number of small producers in the five departments supplying milk to Roquefort, but much of its energy is furnished by participating Larzac militants who are able to share their past organizational skills with those farmers little used to sustained actions. Under pressure from the committee, the Roquefort producers' association has modified the quota system on several occasions, but rarely to the satisfaction of small farmers. In 1988 the committee uncovered what it believed was a swindle on the part of the Roquefort producers' association. It accused the Roquefort industry of putting to illegal use monies that had been donated by farmers to a corporation founded to develop alternate forms of production for sheep's milk. As the result of a court case brought by the committee against the producers' association, the latter will have to provide financial data concerning these funds and reimburse those farmers who contributed to them. In the fall of 1990, the Roquefort committee was converted into a union, the SPLB, *Syndicat des Producteurs du Lait de Brebis* (Union of Sheep Milk Producers), giving the activists a legal status lacked by the committee.[3]

The Larzac has been the motor behind the smaller sheep farmers' demand for equality and an open policy in the use of their money. When asked by us if the Larzac movement will continue to serve as a moral force for social change, François Roux replied:

> I believe that on the level of ideas, the Larzac is very important. It remains a symbol for other people. It's not easy to live and be a symbol and it's often a heavy burden. If we look at daily life on the plateau now and see the conflicts that have developed among some people one could have doubts about the symbolic value of the Larzac. But the Larzac has gone beyond the level of these individuals. They have no choice. The symbol belongs to them and, at the same time, they have the responsibility to embody it. The interaction of the people of the Larzac with Kanaky has kept the symbol alive. After Kanaky, there will be other struggles. And the Larzac can count on me to solicit its help. We are all equally responsible, actually. The struggle, because of its exemplary nature, marked an entire generation of people beyond the plateau. It left its mark, even more, because, it succeeded! So much of the time — though, basically, our position is the right one — we activists feel we have lost the battle. But, here, we have won! It can't be denied. The effect will last a long time.

The future of Larzac militancy will certainly depend on the continuation of actions like those that have come to characterize the plateau in the last twenty years, but it will also depend on the children of the Larzac and how they assume their community's values. The nursery school in La Blaquererie and the Larzac elementary school, the first new school to open in rural France for more than thirty years, are in full swing. The elementary school at the farm of L'Hôpital enrolled over forty children in 1992. The entire plateau takes pride in these children who are essential to the future of the Larzac.

NOTES

1. In the 1980s, a lively debate occurred among agriculturists on the left, including FDSEA dissidents, with regard to reforming the financial control of land that had become too expensive for most young farmers. Many of the ideas generated during these debates were to be incorporated into the statutes created for the SCTL, the Larzac's solution to the problem.
2. Alain Ottan, Roux's law partner, also collaborated on the preparation of these accords.
3. The fight for economic survival continues in the face of overproduction in the European Community and falling prices for agricultural products. In April of 1992, a general meeting was called with the participation of a development committee — in name, affiliated with APAL but made up mainly of the younger generation, who did not belong to the association. It attracted an interesting mix of the different generations on the plateau and held promise of leadership and cooperation in new projects by the younger set.

Part Two
The Community Evolves

CHAPTER SEVEN
From History to Myth by Way of Symbols[1]

It is reported that when Jean-Marie Tjibaou met with President Mitterrand in 1988, after the signing of the Matignon Accords on New Caledonia, he said, "We won because we were the weakest." He had taken note of this aphorism during a visit to the *écomusée du Larzac*, where it was featured on panels celebrating the victory of 1981. By recalling it, he gave credit to the strategy of nonviolence and, at the same time, to his Larzac allies who had supported his cause since 1984. It was his way of expressing the *legitimacy* of the Kanak struggle against the *power* of the French state. As for Mitterrand, he is said to have replied, "Yes, you won because you were the weakest; but you also won because I am President." Thus Mitterrand reaffirmed state power as well as his own legitimacy in the exercise of that power.

As long as the social contract remains intact, those who govern exercise *legitimate* power. In totalitarian states where the contract has been broken, social protest movements often attack the legitimacy of the state. When these movements are even partially successful, the state tends to react with suppression, further weakening its claim to represent legitimate government. Even in non-totalitarian states, the best strategy available to minority-based social movements is to attack the state's legitimacy to deal with whatever issue the social movement claims as its own. If it does this successfully, the movement can turn the tide in its favor either through the elective process or by gaining the right to negotiate with the state.

When a movement lacks political power to achieve its ends, even where there is minimal freedom of expression, it can still attempt to operate in the domain of symbols. By manipulating the symbolic order, it is possible to develop a counterverity that challenges official doctrine. Since the battle is fought only on the level of symbols, victory can be achieved through sustained and clever campaigning, even when the two sides have highly unequal resources and access to the public.

The Larzac struggle, fought as it was in a democratic society and under the rule of law, took place on two fronts: the legal and the symbolic. The legal battle occurred over the details of the expropriation order as they were issued by the government. From 1971 to 1981, the Larzac peasants engaged in a holding action against the government. On the symbolic front, the first order of business for the Larzac was to counter the government's contention that the extension of the military camp was in the national and local interest and that, in any case, the extension only affected a small minority of backward farmers in a demographically sparse region of France.

The Larzac militants and their allies were conscious from the beginning that they were involved in making history — many of them have kept practically every scrap of paper generated during the ten years of the struggle. They began early in the struggle to pay selective attention to those parts of their past lives and present actions that would best serve the cause on the national level. The near beginning of this process is preserved in the first major national publication concerning the Larzac struggle, *Le Larzac Veut Vivre* (*The Larzac Wants to Live*), which appeared in 1973. This large format book, illustrated by well-known photographers, contains a record of how facts and symbols were used to capture the imagination of the French population. If one compares this book with two other key publications (the catalogue for the exhibition, *Larzac, Terre en Marche* and the book, *Alors la Paix Viendra*) to be discussed at the end of this chapter, written after the victory in 1982 and 1984, one sees a clear progression from what began as a conscious effort to write history from the inside, using selected but real events and people, to the creation of a timeless charter myth — just the kind of myth anthropologists find in the nonwestern, preliterate societies we are used to studying. The Larzac myth, of course, is the product of individual writers and was written at a particular time, with specific intentions. However, this product serves the same ends as myths generated in ancient oral traditions. In its mythic version, the Larzac struggle is taken out of the historical time frame and given to the "ancestors." It can then justify and guide present and future social and political action.

The Larzac mythmakers are clearly, as the Maori described by Marshall Sahlins,

> cunning mythologists, who are able to select from the supple body of traditions those most appropriate to the satisfaction of their current interests, as they conceive them. The distinctiveness of their mytho-praxis is not the existence (or the absence) of such interests, but exactly that they are so conceived. The Maori, as Johansen says, "find themselves in history." (1985:55)

What these three Larzac publications have in common, as they move from history to myth, is that they are structured so that what might seem to us as contradictory features of the Larzac are welded into a seamless argument against the camp extension. Thus, the first book, *Le Larzac Veut Vivre,* avoids commenting on the vast economic and social differences between the few large and highly mechanized modern farms, inhabited primarily by newcomers, and those small establishments, where most of the *purs porcs* live. It argues for both modern productivist agriculture and the timeless attachment to the land personified by the traditionalist *purs porcs.*

One sees this duality in the book's photographs. On one hand, the pictures of farms, for the most part, present the larger, more modern and more prosperous establishments in the northwestern part of the plateau, plus the successful GAEC of Du Clos at La Cavalerie. The photographs of individual peasants and their families, on the other hand, are limited almost exclusively to those *purs porcs* living on the smaller farms of the less developed northeastern sector. So the reader is introduced to farms without their farmers and farmers without their farms. Sandwiched between the illustrations of farms and farmers are photographs of the mythopoetic shepherd with his flock.

The front cover of the book has a large photograph of Robert Gastal in his sheepfold, holding a young lamb in his arms. The first page, before the title page, is blank, except for a small quote in the lower right-hand corner, taken from a speech given by President Georges Pompidou before the farmers of Perche on June 11, 1972. The quote reads, "We wish to protect family farms for obvious social, political and environmental reasons. It is important to preserve those natural areas that are lived in and cultivated. Any other kind of natural area is funereal." The title page is followed by a chronology presenting the history of the Larzac military camp, and maps of the region and the proposed extension.

The first section of the book is entitled *"La Vie sur le Plateau"* (Life on the Plateau). This title appears in large letters across the top of page 7. At the bottom of the same page is a short quote that then Minister of Defense Michel Debré made before the National Assembly on November 8, 1972: "The choice has imposed itself. The austerity of the countryside, the wind, the snow, leave little chance for the implantation of any activities."

The writers cleverly use the government's own arguments against itself. Pompidou emphasizes the importance of preserving the family farm. The book shows that, on the Larzac, there are family farms worth preserving. Debré claims that the Larzac is too harsh an environment to support normal activities. The book in itself serves as a glaring contradiction to this position. The plateau is also one of those impressive natural areas that Pompidou would like to see, in his words, "lived in and cultivated," precisely the environment that must be preserved.

Section one of the book documents the beauty of the Larzac environment, the region's artistic heritage preserved in its architecture and the importance of its agricultural activity. Among the architectural treasures, one finds a photograph of the fortified farm of Brouze, restored by Claude and Elizabeth Baillon in the late sixties and early seventies. Brouze won a national prize for the best restoration of the year among important architectural sites. Subheadings and photo captions such as, "An exceptional environment," "A pastoral life is the basis of the economy" and "A country that knows neither fences nor limits," highlight these themes.

It is not until the setting has been well established that the reader finds economic data on farms and milk production, presented in a small box on page 32. The data point out that the extension area of the Larzac is home to 16,500 sheep that produce 1,300,000 liters of milk per year, yielding 325 tons of Roquefort cheese. Meat production per year from the same area totals 13,000 lambs and 4,000 sheep.

These figures are followed by photographs of new farm buildings, shepherds at work with their flocks and lambing on the farm of L'Hôpital. More photos of agricultural activities follow with the caption, "Grain agriculture is necessary for the survival of the flocks." Other photographs in this section show modern milking rooms on various farms, including the prize winning rotating milking machine of the GAEC of which Guy Tarlier was a member.

On page 76, another box introduces further statistics on economic activity in the extension zone ("the menaced zone"). It notes that 30 percent of the agricultural land in the zone holds fertile soil. This second box is followed by photographs of the land being worked for production and, finally, pictures of individual farming families. All but two of these are of *purs porcs*. At the end of this section, after meeting the living, we are introduced to the dead in photographs of cemeteries and war memorials. The tombs and monuments are presented as reminders of both the horrors of war and the continuity between the living and the dead among those native to the plateau.

These photographs are the transition to the second part of the book, which contrasts sharply with the portrayal of agricultural life on the plateau we saw in the first section. Here we find photographs of the camp itself — the ruined desolation that once was the farms of Les Agastous and Cazalets, used by the army for artillery practice until reduced to piles of rubble. Other pictures show scarred trees and the damage inflicted on the land by tank treads — the results of routine maneuvers outside the camp's perimeters.

The conclusion of the book is a moving speech given by Janine Massebiau at the occasion of the planting of 103 trees along National Highway Nine just across from the military camp. In it, she celebrates the signing of the pledge not to sell to the army and the determination to resist the unjust decision of the national government. This text is followed by an appendix that documents militant actions. The back cover photograph is of the door to a traditional sheepfold painted with the slogan "Nous Garderons le Larzac."

Before continuing the discussion of the three books, let me digress to explain how the Larzac militants used symbols and symbolic actions to keep the cause before the French public at large.

Both local and national demonstrations were designed to sway opinion to the Larzac cause. Such actions, however, were not the only means used to this end. France is still a country in which wall posters provide a major and economical way to proffer political messages. Soon after the struggle began, a veritable industry developed around the Larzac issue. Over 150 different posters were used at one time or another to protest the camp extension, as well as to advertise coming events and demonstrations. Many became classics, expressing either of two primary themes — solidarity with the Larzac (the opposition between the life force of the plateau and the death image projected by the military) and, as the ten-year period unfolded, the strength, persistence and continuity of the movement.

From the very beginning, two major symbols — one animal and one plant — emerged on the protest posters as trademarks of the struggle. These were the sheep and the *cardabelle* (*cardabela* in Occitan). (When people occur in posters, which is rare, they appear either as types — peasants or soldiers — or as anonymous members of a crowd.) The *cardabela* is a large thistle, up to a foot across, that grows on the poorest land of the plateau. The flower, rooted directly in the ground with no visible stem, appears to cling to the rocky soil. The flat, round center, up to five or six inches in diameter, is surrounded by spiky leaves that radiate outward. The *cardabela* is a protected species, limited to areas of calcareous land, harsh and dry like the Larzac. When storms approach and the humidity mounts, the *cardabela*'s leaves curl inward. In dry, sunny weather, the leaves relax and flatten out once again. In former days, peasants used to dry it and nail it to the doors of their barns or sheepfolds, where it served as a barometer.

In the struggle, the *cardabela* served as a metonym for the land on which it grows — a symbol of the tenacity that is required to endure on that arid soil. Moreover, this spiky plant is well equipped to fend off its enemies. It thus speaks metaphorically of the right to self-defense, a right granted by nature itself.

The *cardabela* was also employed to stand for the sun. The most widely distributed poster of the entire Larzac struggle shows a single line of marchers with flags, spread out against the horizon, silhouetted in black. From the upper three-fourths of the poster a large, bright, Chinese-red *cardabela* shines down on the marchers. In other posters, the Larzac is depicted as a *cardabela* centered on a sketch of the region; and, in at least one case, it is in the center of a map of France, signaling that the movement is the number-one issue of the nation as a whole.

If the *cardabela* stands for tenacity, the sheep is the force that, for centuries, has supported human life on the plateau. Ewe's milk, converted into Roquefort cheese, is the major source of financial security on the Larzac — the economic base, in fact, for an entire region. Lambs are a source of meat and fine quality leather. The fertility of the land is maintained by the manure that is carried from the sheepfolds to the fields each spring. Like humans, sheep are social animals. Their flocks are tight-knit, creating a sense of security. Lambs, like children, are playful and carefree but also defenseless and foolish. They must be protected by the flock as a whole and by the shepherd. Apart from the Larzac struggle, the lamb, of course, has great significance in Catholic France, symbolizing Christ and his sacrifice.

It is no wonder that from the very beginning the sheep became the most visible symbol of the Larzac struggle. The first bumper sticker produced in support of the movement was of a sheep munching on a branch of ivy with the text *"Sauvons le Larzac"* (Save the Larzac). But it was on the protest posters that the sheep was pre-eminent. Flocks of sheep, or a single ram, chase tanks off the plateau. A single animal dressed in a trench coat likens the Larzac movement to the French resistance against the Nazis during the Second World War. A sheep stands in for the habitual dog listening to "his master's voice" on a poster advertising a concert to raise money for the cause. A flock with its shepherd leaves its Eiffel Tower sheepfold. A flock and its shepherd walk over the top of a hill into the gaping mouth of an enormous soldier. In various other posters, one finds sheep contentedly eating hay or, in contrast, biting down on barbed wire.

A version of the typical road sign signaling "men at work" with a sheep dressed in work clothes, digging a trench, became a poster advertising illegal work projects on the plateau. When the peasant commando was arrested after the invasion of the military camp, a poster showing a proud sheep behind prison bars appeared on walls all over France. A piggy bank became a sheep bank inviting people to withhold 3 percent of their income taxes for the good of the Larzac cause.

The Larzac militants also used the sheep as a negative symbol. In this guise, the animal stands for dependence, stupidity and lack of individuality. One poster suggests to the public that it "not pay its taxes like sheep." While one finds ewes and rams metamorphosed into Larzac militants, one also occasionally finds them as members of the French army. One poster depicts a sheep in officer's uniform. Another suggests that soldiers should refuse to serve in the armed forces: Men "are not sheep." Another shows an army tank inside a "Trojan sheep." Soldiers are seen holding sheep on their shoulders with the caption, "The new style Larzac peasant."

Aside from the *cardabela* and sheep, other objects and experiences intrinsic to life on the plateau are frequently encountered on the posters. Common tools of the farmer's trade such as, scythes, tractors and pitchforks appear, for example. A pitchfork held skyward, impaling a tangle of barbed wire — or even a tank — spells out the fierce determination to live off the land and the resolve to protect that way of life. Solidarity between the Larzac and the working class, as well as with ecological and class-oriented protest movements is, as I have pointed out, another favorite theme. One of the most impressive posters links the Larzac to the militant workers of the Lip watch factory, who had taken over their plant in order to protest its closing.

Numerous posters depict the forces of life and renewal pitted against the death and destruction associated with the materials of war. One poster in this vein announces a harvest for the Third

World in the summer of 1974. A slightly cracked army helmet turned upward serves as a planter for a flourishing patch of wheat. Another, celebrating the end of the struggle in 1981, shows an empty shell-case full of flowers. In still another poster, support for the Larzac and a request for members of the military reserves to return their service papers to the government is symbolized by a smiling infant in white breaking out of a black-silhouetted soldier standing at ease with his rifle. The caption reads, "Leave the Reserves."

The persistence and determination of the struggle is dramatically illustrated in a 1977 poster announcing a summer demonstration. Under the caption "Live and Work in the Country LARZAC," a wooden shoe sends roots deep into black earth. Another, announcing the 1978 foot march to Paris, is illustrated by a road spelling "Larzac" as it winds over the hills into the distance.

As already noted, the victory in 1981 was taken by many not as an end but rather as a new beginning for the plateau and its many associations. With the opening of the *écomusée* in 1982, the Larzac established a permanent window through which the public at large could look into the past and share the present with those in the Larzac community who were determined that the social movement created during the struggle would continue. The first post-struggle exhibition, entitled *Larzac, Terre en Marche* (*The Larzac, A Land Moving Forward*), was a recapitulation of the ten-year period of resistance. It constituted a first step in the process of consciously mythologizing the movement. The text accompanying the series of photographs (the second of the three texts under examination) reflects an ideological emphasis that was to become even stronger in a book to be published by the Larzac Foundation in 1984, *Alors la Paix Viendra*. The movement is represented, essentially, as the spontaneous uprising of a relatively amorphous group of peasantry without strong leadership, whose political authority was defined by the "morality" of their common cause. The exhibition emphasized the ideology of collective action — which had played a real, if ambiguous, role during the struggle — through a depersonalization of historical fact. A self-conscious charter myth, in literary form, was substituted for history.

The text of *Larzac, Terre en Marche* (written by Elizabeth Baillon) begins with a descriptive welcome to the visitor. "Unknown visitor, accidental voyager, inhabitants of lands near or far, supporters of the struggle, friends, the land towards which you have climbed, that on which you have posed your feet, this land is not like others, it is called the Larzac." In the next passage, the peasant uprising is presaged by the land itself: "A prophetic gesture had already taken place in a distant geological era when the Larzac rose up above the plains of the Midi." Human action is then introduced into the geologic metaphor: ". . . all one has to do is cut a few roads and this flat mountain becomes an impenetrable fortress. . . ." The struggle itself was a unique combination of ". . . the craziest actions and the most concrete ideas; ideas that originated in the land." These texts are accompanied first by a photograph of the empty, rocky plateau and then by a huge crowd at the Rajal del Gorp. The geologic metaphor continues with: "A human wave flows over the land of solitude. Human rivers from all sides flow towards this country without rivers." The Larzac movement then enters the domain of the sacred. Thus, ". . . the real dimension of our struggle is suddenly evident to us. The reason behind this struggle, this piece of land, the Larzac, our work-tool, our daily bread, has become a symbol for tens of thousands of our contemporaries. . . . This barren land of the Larzac becomes for them, for us, the living symbol of the 'promised land.'" Finally, the struggle assumes the form of the primordial mother: "Far from the cities and the society of consumption, it welcomes them, brings them together, mothers them in its peaceful immensity."

Just as *Le Larzac Veut Vivre* converted a contradiction (between modern farms and peasant tradition) into a unified argument against the extension, *Larzac, Terre en Marche* displaces historically real dissension on the plateau and converts it into a strength of the Larzac movement as a whole. Thus, the intermittent conflict between small farmers and their squatter allies in the northeast and owners of the larger establishments in the northwest over whether or not to accept a mini-extension through negotiations with the government is changed into a mythic alliance of two opposite facets of a unified resistance to the extension. The dogged opposition between the peasants and the state is called to our attention first with the heading, "In the face of the unchangeable discourse of the state — a peasant discourse." But of what is the peasant discourse made? It is, we are told, complex — the result of a dialogue internal to the plateau between two abstractions, the pragmatic plowman and the romantic shepherd. In the text, each becomes a stereo-type and each is said to have contributed a different voice to the struggle.

> Two forms of action affront one another, two energies come together and produce the discourse of the peasant of the Larzac, which, like a river enriched by its two branches, will finally speak out. In this land of subterranean rivers two discourses are born and mix together in an incessant dynamic. . . .

The shepherd is said to speak in a ". . . free, affective and poetic language, idealist and radical, an open form of speech without defense. It is expressed over time demanding an identity which has been denied." This voice speaks in Occitan and says, "GARDAREM LO LARZAC." The other voice, that of the plowman, is one that speaks of strategy. This is the voice that realistically perceives power relationships. "His language is pragmatic and structured. It assumes and personifies the power in the heart of the struggle. It is the plowman, therefore, who understands power and who, in the immediate present, is able to counter his adversary's use of it."

Once she has established the dichotomy, Baillon goes on to create a dialogue between the two protagonists.

> For ten years the pragmatic plowman said to the idealistic shepherd, "Be realistic. Save the bit of land that can be saved." The shepherd responded, "Yes, let's be realistic. A land that has become a symbol is like a living organism. If you excise a part of it, the rest of it will die." And the plowman replied, "We agree in principle, but what is to be done in the face of power?" For a little while, the Larzac was torn apart. And then unity was found again in a compromise limited to what was possible in the immediate. . . . It was agreed that the talks with the state had to continue. Thus, for ten years the power of the state understood the language of the plowman, listened to that of the shepherd, evaluated the weight of outside support, but never understood where the dynamic of the discourse originated: it was in the Larzac peasant. How could an urban and centralized power working from records and maps, how could it understand this day-to-day sensual relationship with a land which is cultivated, lived upon and loved? Thus we can now say: all of us, the thousands of defenders of the Larzac, we have won the land of the Larzac, not because we were the stronger but very simply because we love it!

Baillon's text continues.

> For ten years we have proved wrong the desperate words of Péguy, "Everything begins in mysticism and ends in politics."[2] Here the mystical was never separated from the political, the imaginary from the real, the symbolic from the daily routine. Each of these fed the other. This is the secret of our success. Ah, we never put the

same wooden shoe on both feet! We advanced as best we could: one foot in politics, one foot in poetry; one foot in the mud and manure and the other in a garden of flowers. Pragmatic and dreaming, at the same time, our Larzac struggle.

Towards the end of her text, Baillon states, unequivocally, that a myth has been created.

> With audacity we can say: Here we know how myths are born! We know what part comes from dreams and upon what modest reality they are built. . . .

> Here three desires confronted one another: that of the army, completely crazy, maladapted; ours, concrete and realistic — "*Gardarem Lo Larzac*"; and a third unexpected one, the one that came from the four corners of France reinforcing ours, giving it an opening to the world, a universal dimension. And the myth was born — it took! . . .

> The myth cleansed us, unified our diversities, reduced and censored our contradictions. Under its protective wind, under its totalitarian desire, many differences were lived in silence. . . .

The process of converting history into myth begun at the end of the struggle continued with the publication in 1984 of the last work under discussion. Looking for a way to raise money, the Larzac Foundation decided to publish a book on the struggle, using the profits to support its projects. The text that resulted, *Alors la Paix Viendra* (Then Peace Will Come), is purely and simply an origin myth into which the history of the struggle has been folded. Of the forty photographs in the book, most are of natural sites. Only five show human beings and in only three of these can one recognize a particular individual. All five humans are shown as shepherds tending their flocks. There are no photographs of tractors and only two show cultivated fields. The architecture depicted is all of the traditional type, stone-walled and roofed in the heavy, flat, rough slabs of raw limestone know as *lauzes*. Many of the photographs are shot in the early morning or late afternoon, and a significant portion was taken in winter light. These conditions all tend to heighten the mystery of an already spectacular landscape.

The text begins with a prologue:

> If you pass, one evening, by the Rajal del Gorp, clothe your heart with the sun and listen carefully to the wind: You will hear, perhaps, a strange story phantoms of stone tell to their children in the evening by the light of the moon.

Over the next four pages the phantoms' story is related. Beginning as a fairy tale, it creates the mythic community:

> Once upon a time in a country swept by the wind and inhabited by strange giants of rock, there was a group of peasants and shepherds composed in the beginning of 103 families plus a few relations. For centuries an absolute calm had reigned in this country, a country that one thought would be forever asleep.
>
> Everything seemed in its place in this marvelous country when, one day, the shepherds who are the eternal watchmen of the day and the night, noticed that the sky was not as it should be. *"Lo temps es malaute,"* ["the weather is sick," in Occitan] they said as they observed their animals.
>
> The inhabitants of this country had already noticed on several occasions in their past that, for them, danger came from the north. But up to that time no one dared to say so out loud for fear of "bringing bad luck."

Going to their sheepfolds, the shepherds find the doors blocked by huge boulders which they are unable to dislodge. People come from all over to offer advice. Some say the land is worth nothing anyway and so they might as well abandon it. Others say that they can move the rocks and secretly make an attempt to do it. During the night, a terrible explosion frightens everyone. Still the rocks would not move. And then:

> . . . a strange old man — coming, one might say, from a distant planet — arrived. He asked permission to stay. The inhabitants agreed to take care of him and lend him one of their houses. For fifteen days this strange person refused to eat anything. In the morning he remained alone thinking to himself with his head between his hands. In the evening he explained his ideas to the people.

Taking his advice, the people work together to make links for a long chain and harness, which, when placed around the rocks — though slowly, almost imperceptibly — does succeed in pulling them away.

News of this first success spreads and people come from everywhere to learn about the story of the chain and harness. They listen and take copious notes. They want to recount all the details to their friends who have stayed behind in their own country.

> Little by little, people everywhere began to make links for the chain. And each time they were ready, they harnessed themselves

to a rock and moved it. These events ended in a huge celebration, there at the Rajal del Gorp, under a starry sky where the phantoms of stone still keep watch.

The story begins again somewhat further along, but this time, realistically. It is told from the point of view of a single peasant, Emilien, a fictional composite character who is modeled primarily on Robert Gastal. The book ends with a chronology of the struggle, a bibliography and a filmography.

The three publications presented in this chapter were all written by nonpeasant militants and are meant to be read by a public not limited to the confines of the plateau. However, they reflect a conscious effort on the part of militants in the post-struggle period to maintain the particular sense of community and engagement that developed during the struggle. Taken chronologically, we see a movement in these publications from the presentation of reality, albeit a highly selective one, in *Le Larzac Veut Vivre* toward the creation of abstract idealized entities in the two post-struggle publications. By denying conflict and creating a single voice in the person of the fictitious Emilien, *Alors La Paix Viendra* seeks to universalize the Larzac experience and preserve it for the contemporary community.

NOTES

1. By *history*, I mean a description and/or explanation (accurate or not) of events based on real dates, persons and events, located in specified geographical areas. By *myth*, I mean a description and/or explanation that has been taken out of time, and often out of place, to become an abstract justification for a real or imaginary past and, as is so often the case, for present and further action.
2. Charles Péguy (1873–1914). French poet and one of France's foremost Catholic writers. Supporter of Dreyfus. One-time Socialist. Sought to infuse spirituality into all aspects of life.

CHAPTER EIGHT
Discords

Before the struggle there was little, if any, evidence of overt class antagonism on the Larzac. Some farmers may have exploited their shepherds as evidenced by low pay, long hours and no vacations. However, if the shepherds felt exploited, this feeling was rarely, if ever, articulated (at least publicly). It was assumed that shepherds would accept their putative and traditional status as subservient members of geographically scattered farming families. By 1981, the enclosure of pasture land and/or the incorporation of remaining shepherds into GAECs removed this potential cause of tension from the social and economic life of the plateau. As for the small-scale farmers of Pierrefiche, though they voted Socialist by tradition, this did not mean that they stood in overt opposition to the larger and more successful farmers of the northwest and south, who voted for right-wing parties. The natives of Pierrefiche lived more or less in their own world until the struggle both united the farmers of the extension zone in common combat and brought potential conflicts into focus.

Thus, on the Larzac, class was never an important issue although, as we have seen, a reflection of pre-struggle class antagonism did exist between the workers in Millau and the farmers of the plateau. It was the militant squatters of the struggle period who raised the class issue. Articulating a politics of the left, the squatters identified with agricultural workers and small farmers and attempted to mobilize these two groups into an agricultural union, which was rejected by the more successful farmers. Ironically, most of these militants were from middle-class urban backgrounds. Hence, what to a casual observer might look like class conflict on the plateau, during and after the struggle, can best be seen as one between affectives and politicals (to be defined in chapter nine). If the Larzac was not as a society divided into classes, it was — with the arrival of the squatters in 1972 — very definitely a political society in which social and economic differences provided the material for internal conflict.

In his analysis of the Larzac struggle, *Le Larzac: Utopies et Réalités*, Didier Martin takes note of the geographic and ideological conflicts that existed on the plateau between 1971 and 1981. The problems that were ultimately ideological, but which had a strong geographic component (a subject I touched upon in an earlier chapter), had two sources. One source was a shift in leadership to the north of the extension area that occurred early in the struggle, which caused a partial break between the north and the south. The other was a persistent undertow of mistrust between the smaller, poorer and more traditional farmers in the northeast, and the richer, larger farmers in the northwest. Besides cultural differences between the two groups, friction was caused by the former suspecting the latter of favoring a mini-extension that would sacrifice the small farmers in order to save the larger farms.

Although the mistrust that developed between the farmers of the northeast and northwest is easy to understand on the basis of differences in tradition and wealth, we have not been able to comprehend fully the power shift from south to north that occurred long before we began fieldwork. We spoke to Janine Massebiau whose husband, Loulou Massebiau, was one of the original leaders among the peasants of La Cavalerie and, at the beginning of the protest, a dominant force in the south. She refused to discuss their joint participation in the struggle, and we felt it would be impolitic to approach her husband separately, after that. In addition, Robert Gastal — Massebiau's GAEC associate, who withdrew from the struggle for several years and who has always been discreet when questioned about conflict — was also reluctant to talk about this power shift, which continues to be an emotionally disturbing issue. It is clear, however, that living on a daily and intimate basis with both the army and its supporters in the village must have been very trying for the peasants of La Cavalerie. Furthermore, before and during the struggle, these individuals were active in the FDSEA, which — although it opposed the extension — became at most an ambivalent supporter of the growing movement that it was unable to control.

More purely ideological conflicts, this time between the peasants and outside supporters, are immediately comprehensible when examined in the context of the struggle's expansion to the national level and the formation of the Larzac committees with their mixed membership of assorted radicals and pacifists. Throughout the struggle, the committees remained more radical than the peasants. The peasants were strongly influenced by the committees and dependent upon them for financial support and manpower. Nevertheless, they also felt a strong need to maintain ultimate control over the movement and the decision-making process. In this, they were successful, but the effort was costly. It created deep and constant strains between the peasants and their supporters. What the committees did succeed in doing, however — besides spreading the Larzac gospel throughout France and beyond — was to strengthen the peasants' resistance to the national government in times of real crisis and doubt, ultimately radicalizing a large segment of the indigenous population on the plateau.

The ex-committee members we interviewed, in spite of their fidelity to the Larzac, do not always have pleasant memories of their experience. They remember the many disputatious meetings that occurred during the struggle. There is also frequent and somewhat bitter mention of the less-than-gracious hospitality offered them by the majority of peasants. We were told that, with few exceptions, they found scant welcome in peasant houses when they were called to the plateau by an emergency situation, even when this meant dropping everything at home and driving through the night to the Larzac. They admit that the struggle, coupled with the exigencies of farming, made daily life extremely difficult for the peasants. Yet, they recall the Larzac during this period as preoccupied and rather selfish toward those outsiders who came to help and who proved their worth through steadfast participation in a wide range of protest activities. If this was the case among the working- and middle-class committee members, it was — as we have seen in the interview of a volunteer worker on the sheepfold at La Blaquière cited in chapter three — an even more general feeling among the students, "hippies" and assorted volunteers who gave freely to the Larzac in its time of need.

On the other side, the peasants express ambivalent feelings toward these outsiders in their midst, who were seen at first as the equivalent of creatures from outer space and whose comportment went far beyond the limits of the peasants' morality. Though we know that the peasants, with time, became more tolerant of other lifestyles and even acquired a certain respect for the work capacity of many volunteers, their hospitality remained uneven. In their interviews, the peasants continue to defend their relative inattention to the volunteers. They point out that they lived under the pressure of continual farmwork made even more burdensome by the trying conditions of the struggle, which demanded constant meetings and frequent militant actions.

There was another important conflict that I have alluded to in various chapters. This is the one that involved a major contradiction between the radicalized ideology that formed during the Larzac movement's development and the treatment of its own agricultural workers. But, as I have noted above, this conflict was due more to the militancy of squatters than to pre-struggle conditions. However, the situation of the agricultural workers highlights the contradiction between the ideal of participatory democracy, which was fostered as a major feature of the new Larzac, and the emergence of strong individuals as leaders. These leaders (some *purs porcs,* others not) were also the richer farmers, most of whom were concentrated in the northwest of the plateau. Everyone admits that, to win, the movement needed strong leaders, but many also believe that the emergence of such individuals and the continuation of their leadership after the victory have diminished the chance for real participatory democracy on the post-struggle plateau.

We have already seen how the Larzac peasants developed an early alliance with the working class in Millau, as well as with the Millau chapter of the CFDT. The close ties that were established during the struggle between the Lip workers and Larzac peasants have also been mentioned as an important element in the successful move that brought the predicament of the Larzac to national attention and expanded its base of support. The alliance with workers in Millau and the connection with the Lip protest were real attempts to forge a general alliance between peasants and the working class. Although such an alliance never really materialized, it was highly satisfying to Larzac militants (who were pacifists and members of the noncommunist left, let us remember) both on and off the plateau to see the first steps of mutual support that, it was hoped, would develop further. This is perhaps why, to this day, most of the peasant militants on the plateau, who in the past hired agricultural workers, attempt to explain away or deny their own conflicts with, and possible mistreatment of, these workers on the Larzac. The rest of this chapter is devoted to passages extracted from a number of interviews we had with individuals who experienced these and related conflicts either as workers or as their supporters. These interviews also show that, while the protestors followed his lead, the admiration for Lanza del Vasto was not unanimous on the plateau, at least among those who were not *purs porcs.*

Francis Moreau, although from a solid middle-class background, turned leftward politically after performing compulsory military service. He lived first at St. Martin where Robert Pirault, who had directed the construction of the illegal sheepfold at La Blaquière, had set himself up as a squatter and was engaged in a range of militant activities. Later, Moreau moved to La Blaquière. Toward the end of the struggle, he joined a group of artisans — masons and carpenters — that offered its services at reasonable rates to the peasants, who had, up to that time in the struggle, benefitted from a great deal of volunteer labor. In Moreau's opinion, a set of problems existed between the peasants, on one side, and artisans, agricultural workers and shepherds, on the other. He also spoke of other factors that he felt were responsible for social divisions on the Larzac.

Our association of nonagricultural workers was not accepted by the peasants. They did not want to be bothered by the problems of residents who were not farmers. We were considered an unstable element. This did not come out during meetings — after all, the common enemy was the army — but it did spread as gossip. The peasants welcomed workers but only when they worked for nothing. During the construction of the sheepfold, there were no problems with the work but there were cultural problems. All of a sudden the village was full of "hippies."

There was always a difference between the big and the small peasants. The big ones were defined by the size of their farms and their style of life. All the big ones were on the northwest of the plateau. Tarlier's farm is colonial in type. It is large with a great deal of modern machinery. He is the inventor of the *rotolactor*. The Burguières are a family of *notables*. The father is very important in the region. These are the big ones. Michel Courtin was assimilated to this group because of his culture. [Michel Courtin has a university degree in history. During the struggle he was a member of the GAEC of Les Baumes in the northeast.] His father was the *chatelain* ["lord of the manor"] of St. Tropez.

Here is an example of how the cleavage between the big and the little operated. Pierrefiche is a village of small farmers. They are simple people. Culturally they live like traditional farmers. Pierrefiche was always jealous of its independence. At times during the struggle, the people there felt that they were not consulted enough. When Hervé Ott decided to build the straw house at Le Cun, he did not consult with Pierrefiche even though Le Cun is in their territory. He was installed by Léon Maillé, the Burguières and Tarlier. One day the construction, which was illegal, was discussed at a meeting. The argument was over whether people should be willing to face sanctions by helping with the construction. No one spoke up in public but the people of Pierrefiche were angry because they had not been consulted about the construction, and now that there was a problem they were being asked to join with the others. They were against the action. They also disagreed with the non-violent stance of the movement. As for the construction, the people at La Blaquière were also against it for the same reasons as the people of Pierrefiche. Auguste Guiraud said that he was afraid that the army would react violently to the action. Elie Jonquet said, "Hervé goes too far. He does not ask anyone for advice. He collects money and does not consult anyone." I had told these people to speak up at the meeting on the issue and that provoked a reaction against me. Pierre Burguière was very angry. Normally if Léon Burguière, Pierre Burguière and Tarlier were for something it was done. Auguste Guiraud was also a star of the struggle, but only for the outside. I don't wish to condemn the "big chiefs" because they kept us all on the move. It was they who had all the new ideas, but we need to realize that during those times there was not enough dialogue. The leaders were not really concerned about what the little people were thinking.

The Larzac struggle did change the peasants politically. They have moved from the right to the left. But there are many contradictions, even here. Robert Pirault found that, in their religious faith, they tend not to question the power of the Church and do not fight for democracy within it. People like Bonnefous, working with the CMR, could not change this, even though he probably wanted to. He is very prudent and in no way a revolutionary. Before the struggle, the Christian message he attempted to spread was not enough. There had to be another shock. This was, of course, the extension plan.

A major negative point concerns the shepherds. There was a type of traditional relationship between the farmer and "his" shepherd. The shepherd is considered to be part of the family, but he has a very low status and little individuality. He works all the time and earns very little. Traditionally the only day off he had was on the festival day of *la loue* [when work contracts are renewed]. The shepherd was content with his lot in the old days. Now things have changed. During the Larzac struggle, new people came to work as shepherds. They were hired by the peasants. Often they had more education than their employers. They spoke out against their working conditions. Moreover, they wanted to participate in the struggle. They also decided to form a union. There was a meeting at the Jonquets' where the peasants made it clear that they would not accept a union. They were unanimous in this rejection. There was a great deal of tension. L. changed shepherds every three months. G. also had enormous problems with his shepherds. The B. family also had problems but finally took someone from *L'Arche*. Later their shepherd became an associate of the GAEC. Others have fenced in their fields and in most cases the need for shepherds has been eliminated.

The artisans also had problems related to economic survival that the peasants never accepted. There were even conflicts between the old farmers and the squatters because the new arrivals upset the strategy of the traditionalists. The squatters at Montredon were not well received. Their customs differed from those of the peasants. They were considered foreigners. Couples were not married. Frequent confrontations between them and the army occurred in and around Montredon because they lived very close to the camp. Whenever there was talk of a mini-extension the people at Montredon were afraid that they would be abandoned to the army. And there were often rumors about a mini-extension. Most of the conversations that took place between the peasants and the government involved the big farmers, the leaders, only. Small farmers never really knew what had been said between the parties. Gossip was common on the plateau at the time. For example it was said that Tarlier had been invited to dinner by the prefect at Rodez the previous week.

The mistrust that was apparently in the air found its appropriate expression in this bit of gossip. In France — at least traditionally — a dinner invitation is never casual and, in these circumstances, would have been fraught with significance.

Additional comments reflecting social divisions were made to us by a former squatter, who had worked as a volunteer on the sheepfold at La Blaquière and now occupies a successful farm in the northeast of the plateau. He told us that when he worked on a large farm in the northwest, he was paid very little. One day he asked if he could have some straw as food for his animals. His employer agreed but, although he did not use it as feed on his farm, deducted its cost from our informant's pay. This strict accounting of "extras" and the low wages must be understood (though not necessarily condoned) in the context of the bitter struggle that was costing the "successful" farmers, as well as the small ones, a high price. In addition, the long tradition of the underpaid shepherd was a custom that was slow to change in spite of growing political awareness.

Another militant and former labor leader with farming roots, Alain Desjardin, was one of the most active outside supporters during the struggle. He is now a farmer as well as a moral and political force on the plateau. When he spoke of the past, he alluded, with some irony, to inequalities that existed during the struggle. He said that the Larzac "always was a war of little chiefs" and went on to stress the difficulty of solving problems in a group. He noted that some of the present-day ill feelings on the Larzac are due to cultural differences between the *purs porcs* and recent settlers. When the former feel insulted, they never forget but find it difficult to discuss their grievances with others. Instead, he said, they tend to sulk. On the other hand, they reappear at meetings when they feel that their principles are at stake.

> There is a general incapacity among the people of the plateau to debate issues normally, even when there are differences among them. The conflicts are left to drag on and on and if a solution is finally reached, it is usually proposed by someone who has stepped in to solve it. Certain people have left the Larzac because of their negative feelings about the ways the various associations are run.

Another interviewee, a militant who is still active in several associations, expressed his own negative feelings about how decisions were made during the struggle. He also remains bitter about the way outsiders — even those who, like himself, settled on the plateau during the struggle and contributed to the movement — were treated.

> I can't say that the Larzac was democratic during the struggle. All the important information was passed through the farms of L'Hôpital [the Burguière family] or Devez Nouvel [Tarlier]. That's where the only phones were. In the beginning L'Hôpital was the only farm with a phone. Tarlier must have pulled strings to get his installed. The meetings consisted of agreeing to decisions that had already been made. There were confrontations at these meetings and some of them were very tumultuous. All the relations that we had with the prefect went through Tarlier. The latter was very clever. When he dealt with an important official, he always had another person with him, like me, who was a strong militant. But during these discussions it was only he who talked. We were there as witnesses. When there was a meeting afterwards to discuss what had happened and people disagreed with what he had said, he would always reply, "But so and so was present and he did not say anything." But what power did I have to speak? Everything took place that way. For example, the head of APAL arranged a loan for a peasant who was in trouble. A few weeks later the board of APAL heard about it. I was furious. The board agreed to legalize the action retroactively. Even Tarlier was against this but he had to accept it as a fait accompli. If the board has been asked before the loan was given, everyone would have voted in its favor.

> Now that it's over, I can't accept the same kind of politics. I don't feel that I'm obliged to follow the leaders. I'm a member of the

board of the GFAs, and I take a bit more responsibility there because the association is going through a crisis. I believe that the SCTL is a very interesting initiative. Like all associations there are certainly some faults with it due to its newness, but these are not serious. Besides the SCTL does not have the same problems as the GFAs. The SCTL is structured according to strictly legal principles. The other associations are very informal. During the struggle the GFAs functioned with a family spirit. Now it will have to be run with a more formal structure. The shareholders are not interested in the quarrels that take place among board members. I have not been to an APAL meeting since 1981. I see APAL as a seat of power for the leaders and that does not interest me. I lived the struggle very deeply. It was very rich. It made me into what I am today. I met a wide variety of people, very different people from different regions and with different professions. I still have contacts with people from the exterior.

This interviewee, in spite of his reservations, has made a place for himself in plateau life and is committed to collective work. He is an important member of the CIR as well as the *CUMA des Grands Causses* (a cooperative that was organized to sell various farm products produced on the Larzac and the nearby *Causse Noir*). In fact, he was one of the people who organized this CUMA but was against using the title "Larzac" in its name. In his associative activities, he resists the Larzac's tendency to become too self-involved and to underestimate the importance of collaborating with neighboring areas. "I'm tired of the language used on the Larzac — it's the best, the most beautiful, etc. Now that the struggle is over, we have to move on and establish connections with other parts of the region."

Still another former militant, a pre-struggle settler on the plateau who is no longer farming in the proposed extension zone, gave us his opinion from the perspective of the far left. Saying that he was one of the few who opposed the power of the large farmers, he went on:

For the generation of 1960 the Larzac was the promised land. It was a place where they could put their ideas into practice. There could have been no Larzac without 1968. I was on the far left. I cut myself free of the group when there was a move in 1975 for a mini-extension. That was the idea of the people on the west wide of the plateau along with Michel Courtin. [The latter has confirmed to us that he was indeed in favor of some kind of mini-extension, but one to be negotiated between the Larzac and the government, because he felt that the peasants could not win against the army.] The people in Pierrefiche were unanimous in their opposition to that.

Tarlier was ready to give a piece of the Larzac to save the rest. Only the large farms would have been saved.

For me the Larzac was Léon Burguière [the archetypical *pur porc* and patriarchal figure of the struggle], but the only really pure person was Jean-Marie Burguière [one of Léon Burguière's sons]. He was ready to die for the Larzac. But he could not be a chief. He was not pragmatic like Tarlier. It was necessary to have someone like Tarlier.

Afterwards they said it was only a pretext to keep the struggle going. [Tarlier told us that a mini-extension would have been acceptable only under the condition that no farmer who wished to stay would be expropriated.] The people of Pierrefiche did not express their feelings at meetings. I spoke up and Tarlier left the room. On the eve of the 1981 election, the Larzac had already ended. If Mitterrand had not won, the camp would have been extended.

The fast of Lanza del Vasto made the struggle into a holy war. It was the key to the struggle. I fasted with him. He was a man of tremendous pride, a terrible egotist. I did not like him at all. He was a teacher but did not interact with people on a human level. Mitterrand's visit to the Tarlier's house [to be discussed in the next chapter] was terrible. It was a typical "thing" for the *notables*. It's just like elsewhere. The old leaders have become *notables*.

Another interview was held with a man who was an agricultural worker during the struggle. He has remained on the plateau and is one of the few experienced workers available to replace temporarily sick or absent farmers. He told us about the aborted attempt to form a union on the plateau before 1981.

During the struggle, it was very difficult for me because I was an agricultural worker. Workers did not have the right to speak out at meetings. We were the "crowd." In 1977 we created a union. There were twenty-seven of us [most from the extension zone]. All have either left the Larzac or have been fired. The union asked for proper salaries and one day off each weekend. At the time we were given only one day off a month — in the milking season we had to finish milking before we could even have that day off. That is to say, I had only eight hours a month off, one Sunday per month. We also asked to be included in the discussions of actions to be taken against the extension. Positive reactions to the union came from Ti-Clo Galtier and Philippe Fauchot [pre-struggle, GAEC partners on the farm of Les Baumes]. The Burguières and Tarlier said that they understood our demands but that the struggle came first and we would have to wait until it was over. They told us that we could not be included in the leadership meetings because the group had to be kept small in order to guarantee that secrets would not leak out to the authorities. Towards the end of the struggle we *were* more involved. The only person really with us was Jeanine Boubal [an outside militant and anarchist].

This individual ended his interview with the observation,

I do think that the struggle changed people's outlook. I am very busy but do go to meetings when I can. I'm particularly interested in the problems of the Kanaks.

A farmer from a middle-class, urban background, who came to the Larzac before the struggle and who participated in actions against the extension, was very severe in his criticisms of the social life on the plateau. He is generally known as a cynic, yet even he made it clear that people did work together when necessary.

The Larzac is a basket of crabs like anywhere else. What was important, however, is that we could yell at each other and still get things done. There were many things about which Tarlier and I were not in agreement. He's a chief and I'm against that. Lanza was an elitist. I didn't like him, but he did have considerable influence. He was very "Hollywood." For me the struggle was more anti-central power than anti-military. Tarlier and I are different temperamentally too. There were times when I saw things more clearly than he did, but there were other times when he was right and I was wrong.

A young couple (he working class and she from a farming background), newly installed on an SCTL farm, who also lived on the plateau during the struggle and participated in it, expressed their feelings about leaders, traditional peasants and those among the last wave of settlers who rent SCTL land. They laid stress on the principles they adhere to in their own lives and work, shared by only a very few of their Larzac neighbors. The young man began:

The leaders of the struggle were Tarlier and Burguière. Now there is José Bové. There was strong opposition to this year's exhibit at the *écomusée* [the show of posters from the struggle years proposed by Elizabeth Baillon]. The new farmers here saw it as a show about veterans of the struggle. I didn't agree with them. There are lots of people here who criticize "Babbeth" [E. Baillon], but they don't do any work for the exhibitions. I am the secretary of the CUMA [for the collective use of farm machinery] and I have to make most decisions by myself. If people complain, I tell them that all the records are available to them and if they want to do something else they should go ahead and do it. In France there is a tendency to be very critical but to do nothing.

The traditional peasants on the Larzac are more likely to follow up their responsibilities than are the newcomers. There is theory and then there is practice.

At this point the young woman took over.

In many things we find that we are not like the others. They all go and get straw for their animals and treat it with ammonia gas [a means of converting straw into feed]. We think that this is a terrible practice and will not do it. The ammonia gets into the milk and the meat. [Many disagree.] We don't use weed killers either. The only people here who farm like us are those at Les Truels and Léon Maillé. That's why we feel separated from the others. We use antibiotics as little as possible too.

Her husband continued.

At least there is no contradiction because the rest don't pretend to do anything else. What is a contradiction is when they say one thing and do another. Some of them support unions but accept apprentices who work for little or nothing. During the struggle this was okay because there was a special need, but now the context has changed. There are farmers in France who, when they need a replacement worker, pay helpers what they should be paid. Another example is when their wives work off the plateau in order to support the farm. When there are two salaries at 10,000 francs per month [about $2,000] that's not woman's liberation — rather it's a lack of solidarity with the working class. We can live on less and support workers by not taking their work from them. Given the employment situation in France at present, only one family member should work.

François Giacobbi from Montpellier's urban middle class (who was expelled from an agricultural high school for his "big mouth") came to the Larzac as a shepherd in 1973. Before that he had worked as a researcher in agronomics. His original reason for settling there was professional, but he soon found himself on the front lines of the protest. In 1976, he and another militant, Christian Roqueirol, occupied the farm of Cavaliès, which had already been bought by the army. Strongly committed to his own brand of left politics, which includes *autogestion* (self-management) and consensus, he left the plateau in 1985 when he felt the ideals of the movement had been betrayed by the leadership. From his discussion, we can understand why he was considered a "gadfly" by many of the struggle leaders.

The farm of Cavaliès was bought by the army from a speculator. I occupied the farm with the agreement of the Larzac leadership, but against their better judgment. It was a fait accompli that they had to accept and they were never very happy about it. We were expelled by the army two days later. It was in 1976. With the help of volunteers we constructed a house and sheepfold next door, just over the property line. We were the only ones who were in constant contact with the army on a daily basis. I opposed the leaders of the Larzac toward the end of the struggle because I was not in agreement with their plans for the future. They fought over every inch of land that was to be distributed. All the differences between us were hidden during the struggle. How can people with 1,000 sheep discuss things honestly with people who have only 40 sheep? It's not possible. I wanted to discuss the project [what later became the SCTL]. I wanted to go further in the collective direction. For example, I was in favor of collective pasture land. After all, such use of pasture [as communal land] is a historical fact, and had actually been in effect during the struggle. Such collective use ended with the Larzac victory. Instead the leadership installed the newcomers on farms that were too small. It was ridiculous. It's not possible to have these small farms and others with 600 or more hectares. I was called a *communard*. I was called a bastard when I separated from Christian, but when P. separated from his brother that was okay.

We [Giacobbi and his wife, Joëlle Chancenotte, who also participated in the struggle] had, and still have, good relations with the people from Pierrefiche. They also needed land. When the Larzac got into the question of who needed land for agriculture, the whole thing fell apart. When the peasants of Pierrefiche wanted some of the land at La Clapade many people insulted them saying they had no culture, or that they were "rustics." [The major argument was over hunting rights on La Clapade's land. Hunting is a major form of recreation for traditional peasants and they guard their rights in this area jealously.] You can't work with people like that. Otherwise I would have stayed at Cavaliès. When I left, the leaders of the Larzac wanted me to return the sheep they had given me when I occupied the farm. They also wanted me to pay for the work that had been done in the construction of the sheepfold. [Difficult to verify as certain accounts contradict Giacobbi's version.] Cavaliès never had enough land to make a go of it. The new renters there have additional land at Pierrefiche so the farm is now large enough. The leaders always made it difficult for us to establish ourselves.

Nonviolence was an artificial glue for the struggle. When the Larzac was cut into zones [each sending representatives to meetings of the *bureau*] the people of Pierrefiche were opposed to any mini-extension and they were the ones who prevented it. They were quite violent about it. Once, when the army was on G.F.'s land, he called the prefect and asked that they be expelled. When nothing happened he called again and said that if the army did not leave he would get his gun. E.J. said that if his farm were expropriated he would fight the government physically. In the beginning of the struggle there were the Maoists, and then Lanza came. He told everyone that there was no more big and small. When you are nonviolent, you stop asking the true questions. Gastal is a person who asks true questions, and during the struggle there were times when one did not see him anymore.

One day there was a meeting to discuss the question of expropriation. The leaders were all there. The discussion was very important. I was sitting next to A.V. I asked him what he thought. He did not understand what was going on. That was when I realized that we had failed. There are no more *purs porcs* [involved in present-day meetings or associations — an exaggeration] because things were not properly explained. Another peasant who had profited from the struggle could not say what he thought because he *had* profited from it and had become a hostage of the leaders. It's a serious matter when people don't have control of discourse and are dominated by others.

M. could have done it well. He was honest and had a vision, but is no longer here. Let me give you an example of how people behave now. A former militant was working on water installation for a farmer and no one offered him a drink. People make a delivery and no one offers them a beer. A woman was stuck in the snow in a village and the farmer there offered her a shovel! He wouldn't help her. We support the Kanaks and that's wonderful. It makes me ashamed. A clinic [private hospital] is on strike in Millau and someone who lives on the Larzac asks a leader to sign a petition. The person refuses, asking why the women on strike had not helped the Larzac during the struggle. The Kanaks are far away, that's easy!

A young farmer, trained as an accountant, who settled on the Larzac in 1977 and who is now a member of the SCTL board, gave us a different perspective on the post-struggle Larzac.

I don't go to meetings of the *bureau* because I feel it's too theoretical. When they deal with something concrete I get involved. I like the SCTL because it has a real job to do. We have to deal with reality not with theory. We have to deal with neighbors and at the same time keep our principles. We don't feel that we are under pressure from interested parties. We listen to all points of view before making decisions.

Before 1981 we were held together by the struggle. Since the end of it life is different. We are free to do our work and whatever else interests us. I play soccer with villagers from L'Hospitalet. We do feel the ambiance of the struggle when there are demonstrations. Although there's not much that's happening right now I'm happy. What's left — the positive side — is that there are a lot of people we know and if something serious occurs we know that we can call on them. I can also ask people to lend me a hand on the farm.

I don't understand why people are not more positive about life and don't talk about such things as sports and village fairs. These things are an important part of life. Some individuals on the plateau spend too much time on politics. They are too theoretical.

Another interview was with a young anarchist couple, who did not move to the plateau until after the struggle when they were granted a lease on an SCTL farm and who, at present, participate in various economic and political activities. The young man's remarks reflect the couple's straightforward perception of both the pros and cons of life on the Larzac.

During the drought of 1984 we participated in *Action Paille* [a cooperative effort to get cheap straw from a neighboring department and distribute it on the plateau as feed to those in need of it]. We got to know lots of people. No matter what political label one has on the plateau one is accepted by the others. We have a viewpoint from the exterior. We had no problems getting a loan from the *Crédit Agricole* so we are less dependent than some on APAL [later they were also granted a loan at their request by APAL]. The SCTL is the major way young farmers can set themselves up on the Larzac. The SCTL was a bit euphoric in the beginning and wanted to maximize the number of people settling on the plateau. Some of the farms are too small. The farms should be large enough to support a family with children without outside work.

We have a past that is quite different from most of the people here. What is interesting is that things happen here even if some people are not in agreement with them. That's important. We are politically engaged and it's good that we are here, but not all of the newer farmers are politically active. Most of those who come to meetings now are either ex-squatters or some of the new people. Very few of the *purs porcs* are active any more.

This year [1986] Elizabeth Baillon presented a Larzac poster project to the *écomusée*. Many people were against it and there was a very passionate discussion. We feel that La Jasse and the museum are important but that they should deal with what is going on now. Elizabeth felt that she was being attacked personally, but in the end she accepted the decision. We also feel that the exhibition on sheep [presented instead of the poster project] is too idealistic. The Larzac should show what life here is really like. We must not give too idealistic an image of the Larzac to outsiders. People who have settled here must find the means to stay. That will be the best demonstration of success.

There have been failures. P-Y is selling out [he finally decided to stay] and the farm of Le Sot is a failure, but it's no worse here than elsewhere. We all have the minimum necessary to live. Unfortunately, the real problems facing the Larzac today are not discussed in meetings and it's always the same people who do the talking. For ten years there had to be a certain amount of unanimity but now things are different. In the name of unanimity one should not be a hypocrite. One should not use unanimity to destroy another person either.

In meetings it is often difficult to get to the bottom of a question. Tarlier has the power. He has a certain value but he tends to use his power of speech to put down others.

Finally, let me present the view of an outside militant who now owns a vacation house on the plateau and who is a member of the ecology movement in Germany.

The big people here *did* work hard for the little ones. Tarlier helped the small farmers on many occasions. But the volunteer workers, at least those 600 from Germany who came in 1978, were not welcomed very warmly. Of course, there were some who helped them. The people at La Blaquière did arrange some things for them but one cannot say it was a "welcome." It was more the outsiders, the Larzac committees, that arranged things. Joseph Pineau [from the Millau committee] was very strong organizing this. The volunteers did, after all, help people in restoration and farmwork. When we worked in Pierrefiche the peasants were with us all the time. The people of Pierrefiche have a different mentality. If they see someone working, they join in immediately. The Burguière brothers were also very welcoming.

The ten-year struggle and its aftermath of continuing political and economic militancy have left the Larzac with a uniquely heterogeneous population. It can be broken down roughly into *purs porcs*, "pioneers" who settled the plateau before the extension was announced, militants who came during the struggle (many as squatters) and, lastly, the post-1981 arrivals. Each group has its own social and cultural particularity. While most *purs porcs* among the original 103 signers of the pledge are no longer active in the movement (many have died, retired or moved away), a minority does continue to participate in one or more activities and a few others are ready to join in crisis periods. Several of the pioneers (two significant figures have left the plateau, two participate very little in community life and another has died) continue to play important roles. The majority of those militants who came to the

Larzac in the 1970s remain dynamic and politically active. The post-struggle settlers are, in many cases, deeply involved in trying to make a success of their farms, a problem exacerbated by quotas recently imposed by Roquefort, low prices for lamb and mutton, frequent and severe droughts and precarious financial situations. Most work SCTL farms and, although their rents are low, the buildings in which they live and work need a considerable amount of restoration, requiring an investment in time and money. Some of them were attracted to the Larzac because of its militant past, but others were eager to settle on the plateau because the SCTL offered a unique opportunity for the young without financial resources to begin farming on their own.

The interviews quoted in this chapter give voice to those of the above who began on the Larzac as outsiders. Some were involved during the struggle, while others came as settlers only after 1981. Most of them now live on, and are generally accepted as inhabitants of, the plateau. My purpose in presenting these interviews has not been to deconstruct the myth of the previous chapter but rather to express the complexity and potential fragility of the social tissue that exists on the Larzac today. Although cooperation on the individual and institutional levels continues, overt and hidden conflicts are also a real part of daily life.

Here, I have presented conflict from the viewpoint of individuals. The next chapter will examine the way feelings are played out among these individuals in the context of different institutional structures.

If the Larzac of today existed without strains and conflict, it would be more like a fictional utopia rather than a complex reality. In my opinion, the fact that social, political and economic militancy in the context of a great deal of cooperative action continues more than ten years after victory is a testimony to the strength and commitment of the new Larzac community. This community is young in terms of relative historical depth, but it was forged by a unique experience — ten years of praxis under exceptionally trying conditions. It is this praxis that has given it the strength and the means to continue.

CHAPTER NINE
The Structure of Conflict and Its Resolution

Geographical and economic differences aside, after 1981, a more general post-struggle cleavage became manifest on the plateau between those whom I shall call *affectives* and those whom I shall call *politicals*. (These terms were also used in conversation with us by some Larzac militants, who — though themselves in one category or the other — were aware of the overall picture.) To define the terms, affectives see problems in terms of human relationships, which generally take precedence over strictly political goals when decisions are made concerning on-plateau activities. The politicals see each local issue in the context of a larger framework consistent with the general desire on the plateau to press for social and political change — a desire shared by affectives as well, though not always given first priority. (On off-plateau issues, such as independence for New Caledonia, there is general agreement between these two groups.) For the politicals, it is of the utmost importance that the Larzac continue to serve as a pilot project for the rest of France. If this means discomforting certain individuals, even long-term militants, so be it. As one might imagine this cleavage is due, at least in part, to underlying cultural differences. The affectives are, in large measure, native to the Larzac, while the majority of the politicals are to be found among those militants who settled on the plateau during and, in a few cases, after the struggle.

In this chapter I will examine two major conflicts that erupted on the plateau between 1986 and 1990, one in the SCTL and the other in the GFAs. For the most part, in each case, affectives and politicals found themselves on different sides. To complicate matters, however, although the two disputes appeared on the surface to be political in nature, in each case personal friendships and animosities also played a significant role in the positions taken by many individuals in both camps. As long as there had been a common enemy, the Larzac could act with a high degree of internal unity. With victory, already existing differences rapidly came to the surface as some people attempted to settle old scores. Furthermore, differences in the history and structure of the SCTL and the GFAs played major roles in how and when the disputes were finally settled. The stories I am about to tell provide two contrasting case histories that show how structure and sentiment interact in an institutional framework, in the context of both personal and political divisions.

In the SCTL the dispute centered around who should be granted a lease to a farm in the hamlet of Montredon. The farm was made available in 1988 when the original lessee, who had been involved in lamb production, decided to leave. We were present when the various candidates interested in the farm were interviewed by the SCTL board. Of the five to be considered, three were outsiders to the plateau, one of whom seemed quite promising. The other two were already installed Larzac farmers. One on-plateau proposal was to expand the farm of La Clapade, where a strain of black face sheep had been introduced. These hardy sheep live out-of-doors year-round but need a great deal of pasture. The effects of a major drought had put the viability of La Clapade in doubt, and its farmers asked that the Montredon land, without the house, be attributed to them. The other on-plateau applicant, a veal producer living and farming with his father near Montredon, asked for the entire farm.

The politicals on the board tended to favor one of the off-plateau applicants, and no one on the board wanted to attribute all the land to the couple who needed extra pasture. It was agreed that to do so would reduce the number of farmers on the plateau and leave the newly restored house vacant. Some of the board members, particularly those living in Montredon, expressed adverse feelings concerning the other local candidate, the veal producer. His potential social integration into the hamlet (given his father's reputation as a loner) would, they felt, be problematic. This was an important factor. Montredon is a very small community inhabited full time by only four families (including the eventual inhabitants of the farm in question). These people have banded together in an Association for the Improvement of Montredon and, in cooperation with summer residents, have put a great deal of work into community projects. The affectives, however, felt that the veal producer, an inhabitant of the plateau and also the son of a former Larzac militant, should have priority over outsiders, particularly if, as he claimed, he would have to leave the area if the farm were not granted to him. At the same time, friendship between the young farmers on the board and the La Clapade couple played a vital role in the negotiations, exerting an influence on their choice of candidate.

As the discussions progressed, it became clear that the majority favored accommodation to the needs of the two local candidates. This, they felt, could be accomplished through a compromise that would divide the vacant farm, giving the house and about two-thirds of the land to the veal producer and the rest of the land to the sheep farmers. (One of the young farmers also added some of his own land to what was allotted the couple to induce them to accept the compromise.) Such a solution would save one farm in difficulty without destroying the viability of the other. The debate over this issue was quite heated, and unanimity was not reached for several weeks. In the words of one political who had opposed this decision, his vote was based on an unpleasant choice between "the plague and cholera." In voting yes, however, he accepted the inevitable and helped to maintain solidarity on the SCTL board.[1]

This decision did not go without criticism on the plateau. One SCTL farmer and member of the Green party wrote a stinging critique of the SCTL, accusing it of abandoning the raison d'être of the organization by allowing for the expansion of farms rather than the installation of new farmers. He attempted to get his attack published in *GLL*; however, the *GLL* editorial board refused the article, claiming that its tone was too polemical.

In the article, he likened the SCTL to a "typical adolescent who has rejected his parents." In the case of the Montredon farm he said,

> The latest [division] perfectly illustrates this deviation. It concerns a perfectly viable farm, which had just been restructured and restored, and for which there were several candidates from the outside who had coherent and justifiable projects. The inhabitants of the village were unanimous in their desire to see the farm remain whole and were favorable to one of the candidates. In spite of this the SCTL preferred to divide the property between two existing farms.

Believing that the GFAs were also abandoning the demographic policy outlined at the end of the struggle, this individual concluded that

> the GFAs, where the name SCTL brings on the hives, has followed the same political line. One farmer, wishing to help a neighboring farmer survive, had ceded some of his rented land over to him.

When the latter left the plateau, the donor asked the GFA board to reassign the lease to him, but the board refused preferring to favor an expansion of another farm. But don't be too disappointed. At least they did not sell the land off to the highest bidder.

The first major dispute in the GFAs is more complex and harder to describe. A preview of it erupted during 1987 among the members of the GFA board and came to a head at what, we are told, was a very tempestuous shareholders' meeting that spring. A group of younger farmers and militants on the board wanted the rent for GFA farms brought into line with those of SCTL. Many of those who took this position were also members of the SCTL board, or were involved in its creation.[2] They are all what I would call politicals. At the same time, some of these individuals became embroiled in a dispute with older, more conservative GFA board members (people I would class as affectives) over whether or not GFA funds should be used to reimburse a large number of shareholders who, the board was told, were asking that the GFAs buy back their shares.

These two issues — the second of which had emerged as soon as the struggle ended in 1981 — were tied together because SCTL rents are lower than those of the GFAs. If the GFA rents were brought into line with those of the SCTL, there would be even less money available for reimbursements. Under the normal rules governing GFAs, shares are treated as they are in any privately held corporation. Shareholders who wish to reclaim their money must find a willing buyer. There is no obligation, moral or otherwise, for GFA boards to buy such shares. But the Larzac GFAs were founded under the special circumstances of the struggle, and many board members felt that they had an obligation to honor requests for reimbursement.

We have read a considerable number of letters in the Larzac archives from perspective GFA shareholders. Many show that potential investors wanted to buy shares primarily to help the cause; indeed numerous individuals bought collective shares with like-minded people and had no intention of ever asking for reimbursement. A significant number, however, did inquire about the negotiability of shares, as well as profits that might accrue through time. The answers they received stated that, though they could not assure anyone of profits, in time the land held by the GFAs was likely to increase in value and likewise the value of individual shares. Those who posed the question of reimbursement were also promised that once the Larzac had won they could sell their shares back to the GFAs without difficulty.

GFA board members who saw reimbursement as the major issue contended that of the 5,950 shares outstanding in 1987, at least 1,000, perhaps even more, would have to be bought back in the near future. Over 400 of these shares were held by four individuals, all of whom were said to be either in need or inclined to use their money to support other causes. According to the secretary of the GFAs (one of three zealous advocates for reimbursement), all four of these individuals had specifically asked to be reimbursed as soon as possible. One of the secretary's allies (an important and long-standing moral leader of the Larzac struggle to whom correspondence concerning the GFAs was sent by shareholders) confirmed this, stating that he had received many letters from needy shareholders asking for immediate repayment. He refused, however, to make these letters available to the board.

Since the profits from rent paid to the GFAs could not cover more than about eighty reimbursements per year, the secretary's group explicitly favored the immediate sale of one or two complete farms. It was widely known that one of these farms was badly managed and, through neglect, decreasing in value. Other members of the board, who also considered reimbursement a primary moral issue, agreed that such sales might be necessary in the long run, but they were not as insistent as the secretary and his two allies that this was an immediate imperative. Those who put the integrity of the GFAs before reimbursement were against selling any farms. They argued that before any shares were bought back, all letters requesting this action should be examined by the entire board.

The fourteen individuals who saw reimbursement as the major issue confronting the GFAs (who, as we have seen, were themselves somewhat divided) held the majority among the twenty-one members of the GFA board. They came to be known as "tendency one." The minority side with six members, which came to be known as "tendency two," (one member of the board was inactive and was in neither group) agreed that reimbursement was an obligation, at least to those who were in real need and who specifically requested that shares be bought back. They felt, however, that before this was done the GFA board should declare its firm intention to continue the life of the GFAs, which (along with the SCTL) fulfilled the goal of providing land to farmers on the plateau at reasonable rents.

Tendency one was made up primarily of *purs porcs* and older, former Larzac militants living in nearby communities off the plateau. Tendency two was made up of younger, recent immigrants to the plateau, many of whom occupied SCTL farms. The one major exception to this was Guy Tarlier, whose GAEC occupied, as part of its total land, one important GFA farm. This property, Boissans, often came up in discussion as the other possible sale for the GFAs. During board meetings throughout the winter of 1987–88, Tarlier tried to get Boissans protected for his colleagues by having its lease shifted from his name (under which it was protected only until his retirement) to the name of the GAEC. If the lease were so transferred, it would remain in effect as long as the GAEC existed, and therefore, for all practical purposes, the farm could never be sold.

To complicate matters, the three major figures in tendency one disliked Tarlier immensely. The personal animosity between them and Tarlier amplified with increasing intensity during the tumultuous meetings of the GFA board that took place from 1987 to 1989. (The board finally voted in favor of the lease transfer in the fall of 1992, after the dispute in question here had ended and Tarlier had died.)

Throughout this period, the members of tendency two continued to demand that actual requests for reimbursement be made available as proof that the number of shares to be reimbursed was around 1,000. In this they were blocked by the secretary and his allies, who argued that accountability of officers had never been an issue on the GFAs before. Tendency two also objected to the secretary's power of deciding on his own who should be reimbursed and, even more, his buying shares back without consulting the board. They demanded that such requests be brought before the full board for a vote. The secretary argued that the imposition of accountability implied a lack of trust on the part of some board members toward people who over the years had freely given of their time and energy to the GFAs without any recompense. Members of tendency one went on to charge that the members of tendency two were speaking in bad faith; that, in fact, the latter were making their demands because they were against all reimbursement. Tarlier's main adversaries and some other members of tendency one also expressed the opinion (both to us and in public) that their opponents wanted to merge the GFAs into the

SCTL or, at least, convert them into an organization run like the SCTL. This, they felt, was inappropriate, because SCTL farms were owned by the government, while GFA farms were private property, owned collectively by shareholders. Meetings to discuss these issues often degenerated into shouting matches. Accusations began to spill out into the public arena and onto the pages of *GLL*. The 1988 annual shareholders' meeting of the GFAs, to be described in detail later, involved harsh recriminations between members of the two tendencies.

During the winter of 1987–88 two members of tendency two, both women, wrote summary articles in *GLL* that they felt were objective descriptions of the dispute in progress. Members of tendency one were also invited to submit articles but declined, accusing both the authors of the articles and *GLL*'s editorial board of presenting a prejudiced view of the GFA controversy. Later in the winter, two proposals stating the positions of the two tendencies to be debated at the spring 1988 shareholders' meeting were sent to all shareholders asking those who could not attend to send proxies to individuals pledged to vote their choice. Outsiders must have been somewhat bewildered by the two propositions, for both covered much of the same ground. They differed only in that tendency one's motion gave greater emphasis to the moral obligation to reimburse shares, even if that meant selling farms, while tendency two's motion put the integrity of the GFAs first, at the same time respecting the right of shareholders to be reimbursed. Many on the Larzac from both tendencies agreed that the two propositions were not very different. Nevertheless, it was the leader of tendency one who received a heavy majority of the proxies, probably because he was a well known and highly respected figure during the struggle.

There was, in our opinion, another complicating, if perhaps minor, factor involved in the division of the GFA board into warring camps. Although a surprising tolerance of diversity in personal lifestyles and political viewpoints developed on the Larzac during the struggle and continued thereafter, there were still echoes of traditional feelings, particularly towards women.

There are presently a number of unmarried couples on the plateau. They have contributed to the increase in population and decrease in average age, and are accepted by most traditional farmers. One of these farmers told us that for a farm to succeed on the Larzac, it had to be run by a tight-knit couple in which a woman backed her man in productive activities. Women's traditional farm tasks include taking care of the barnyard animals and kitchen garden, as well as accounting and helping out with such seasonal tasks as lambing. While this individual suggested that legal marriages provided greater long-term security, he accepted the fact that unmarried couples could also perform effectively. On the other hand, he expressed ambivalent feelings about women who were in legal partnership with their male companions (husbands or not), and noted that some farms where women played a major role in agriculture and/or animal husbandry (a role on which the viability of the farm depended) were fragile at best. He expressed the opinion that such farms were at risk because sooner or later the woman in the partnership would balk at hard labor. In addition, unsurprisingly, women who are often defined as "aggressive" by traditionalists are tolerated less well than men defined in the same way. Relative age also plays an important role among traditionalists when they define acceptable behavior in others, whatever their sex.

As I have noted above, tendency one on the GFA board consisted largely of traditionalists. These individuals were least likely to accept women as equal partners in the decision-making process. To make matters worse, two of the more radical board members in tendency two were rather young women, both of whom came to the Larzac as militants in the middle of the 1970s. They are highly articulate and competent politicals, not shy about questioning the wisdom of older male members of the board whom we would describe as affectives. These men were prone to follow emotion rather than reason in coming to decisions. As a consequence, during board debates, the arguments offered by the two women were frequently misunderstood or misinterpreted. In general, there was much less tolerance shown to them than to males, particularly when they became involved, as so often happened, in harsh disputes with certain older men. This was the case even when they were provoked by one of the more strident and undiplomatic male members of the board.

At the shareholders' meeting held in the spring of 1988, the leader of the majority faction tried to have these women and his major rival, Guy Tarlier, expelled from board membership. Opinions were clearly expressed at that time that the two women were not sufficiently "diplomatic" to serve the GFAs. (In the summer of 1989, when the situation was cooling down a bit, an important member of tendency one, who had agreed to a compromise with the members of tendency two, told us that he was pleased by the conciliatory behavior of one of these women at a meeting held to discuss the constitution of the second committee to resolve the conflict. Yet, several months later, his underlying feelings had changed his memory of the event and he referred to her behavior as having been "aggressive.")

In our opinion, the ongoing tensions between tendencies one and two were aggravated in advance of the 1988 meeting when one of the "aggressive" women, a former agricultural laborer on the plateau, Danièle Domeyne, wrote an article that appeared in the February 1987 issue of *GLL*. In a straightforward manner that did not exclude sarcasm, she presented a case for bringing the rents of the GFAs and the SCTL into alignment and addressed the subject of reimbursement. Coming from her, the article was like waving a red flag in front of a bull. In it, she said,

> And the supreme argument [against bringing the rent into alignment], the one that is brought up each time to make us shed tears, is the one in favor of those shareholders "who gave their blood in order to buy shares." They shake this image before our eyes like a scarecrow to make us feel bad about wanting, it would seem, to run the GFAs uniquely for the profit of the renters. I believe that I can speak about these shareholders, and I would be the last to show contempt for them, for, in fact, I am one of them. When I was a poor student I bought a tenth of a share to help the peasants of the Larzac whom I had never met, but who were fighting for ideas I agreed with. I am, I regret to say, neither a widow, nor indigent, capable of making you cry. But is it the fault of the GFA farmers that shareholders have never received a centime of profit and that their shares have never gone up in value? Be serious; there are no profitable GFAs in existence anywhere. I agree that it is necessary to operate the GFAs correctly, but stop using the shareholders to keep the GFAs in a state of total immobility and refuse the renters the progress to which they are entitled.

By 1987 the GFA board was a varied group made up of Larzac farmers and ex-militants with the majority of the latter living off the plateau. From 1979 or 1980, until the summer of 1989, the volunteer secretary of the GFAs was considered a member of the board. According to the rules governing the operation of GFAs (these corporations exist throughout France and must conform to government regulations), major decisions are to be made at annual shareholders' meetings. As in all public corporations, each shareholder has a number of votes equal to the number of his or her shares. In addition, an unlimited number of proxies can be transferred to another party so long as that party is also a shareholder. Power within the GFAs can, therefore, be concentrated in the hands of a small group or even a single individual.

As noted in an earlier chapter, the SCTL is governed by a board of directors elected at the annual meeting of shareholders. The term of office in the SCTL is limited to six years with a third of the board elected every three years. (GFA board members may serve for as long as they are elected to office.) The SCTL board is now made up of three nonfarming individuals living in SCTL houses without land and nine farmers holding SCTL leases. The association has no president and the secretary, a part-time, paid professional, is not a member of the board. As mentioned before, each shareholder in the SCTL (all either farmer or nonfarming Larzac residents) has — unlike the GFAs — only one vote at the annual shareholders' meeting and individuals present are allowed to hold only one proxy for an absent shareholder. Thus, in the SCTL's experiment in self-management there is a measure of built-in insurance that power will not be concentrated in one or two individuals.

The SCTL, as a structure created for the sole purpose of land management, is in a much less ambiguous position *vis-à-vis* its mandate than that of the GFAs. There are no private shares in the SCTL and the SCTL owns no land. Its charter, created at the end of the struggle against the camp extension, was the result of an agreement between Larzac militants and the then Socialist government to establish an experiment in land management through rental of public land to young farmers. The SCTL board is responsible to the government for prompt rental payment, proper insurance of rented property, the efficient management of the rentals, and the reconstruction or repair by lease-holders of buildings on rented farms.

There is no profit motive and no feeling of obligation, as in the GFAs, to repay needy shareholders who, in the past, extended moral and financial support. All members of the SCTL board live on the plateau and the same is true for individuals who have the right of shareholders to attend annual meetings of the association. Each, as I have noted above, has only a single vote based on his or her single share. The board is run predominantly by young farmers with shared concerns. By statute, nonfarmers constitute only a small minority of the board. Thus, even though there were serious disagreements over the attribution of the farm at Montredon, the historical and structural basis of the SCTL made it possible to reach agreement in a relatively short time. This was decidedly not the case in the GFAs, to which — after what may seem like a digression — I shall return. If the reader bears with me, he or she will shortly come to see its relevance to the issues under discussion.

In the spring of 1987, Guy Tarlier received a phone call from the Elysée Palace announcing that President François Mitterrand would be coming to the Aveyron on an official visit in April and that he would like to lunch at Tarlier's house on the Larzac. For security reasons and because his visit to the plateau was to be unofficial, the dinner was to take place in relative secrecy and under tight security arrangements. Thus, according to Tarlier, although Larzac militants were to be informed of the visit, the exact time of Mitterrand's arrival by helicopter had to remain a secret until the last moment. President Mitterrand, however, agreed to meet with anyone from the plateau who cared to come to a reception to be held after lunch in Tarlier's garden. Tarlier told us that his house was chosen because security for the presidential party could be arranged there with relative ease. (His house is located on a hill in an open area and is isolated from other farms.) He also said that he was instructed to invite only one couple of his choice to the meal. He realized that if he singled out a particular individual among the farmers, others might be jealous. To avoid this problem, he invited his close neighbors, nonpeasant residents and Larzac militants, Elizabeth and Claude Baillon. Later, he told us, he received another call advising him that one of the president's party would be unable to attend and that he could invite one other couple. Having just come back from a visit to New Caledonia, Tarlier was eager to inform Mitterrand of the Larzac's position on the issue of independence for the island. Therefore, he asked François Roux, who had long been involved in the independence movement, to join them. The choice was a good one, since Elizabeth Baillon had herself just returned from New Caledonia where she had met with several Kanak leaders and interviewed Jean-Marie Tjibaou.

The presence of both the Baillon couple and Roux provided an opportunity to strengthen the case for the Kanak position on New Caledonia with the president. There was, however, a great deal of resentment on the plateau, particularly among *purs porcs*, and even some other militants, about the site chosen for the visit. Many felt that Auguste Guiraud's house would have been the ideal place, since it was there that Mitterrand had been treated after the attack on him in 1974. To make matters worse, a Larzac militant and good friend of Tarlier actually called the Tarlier house after the lunch had begun, to inquire about the time of the president's arrival. Tarlier, who said that he had a secret service agent at his side at the time and did not know how to respond, did not tell the caller that Mitterrand was already there.

Later, when this became known, the anger of those who felt snubbed and those who had scores to settle with Tarlier found an outlet in rumor, and a series of accusations against him began to circulate widely on the plateau. Few on the plateau would accept Tarlier's version of the events concerning the president's visit (which, I must add, was confirmed to me by a government official with whom I discussed the problem in the winter of 1989 when I was in Paris checking documents). Although Tarlier had been attacked before — particularly during the struggle when many came to believe he was in favor of a mini-extension (which is not totally false) — this was the first occasion in the post-struggle period that he was the major target of gossip — accusations that many people accepted too easily as fact. The virulence of these attacks was not unrelated to the conflict that was going on at the same time in the GFAs.

Tarlier had been a key figure during the struggle. Almost everyone on the plateau, even his enemies, agrees that without him, the peasants could never have won. He was widely recognized as the person who was best able to negotiate with government officials, utilizing his personal contacts with many of them to promote the peasants' point of view. He was also regarded as an innovative and fearless individual. Before the extension plan was announced, he was the only person ever to claim reparations for damage done to his land by army maneuvers beyond the confines of the camp. But Tarlier had always been the subject of controversy among a wide range of Larzac militants. Many of those we interviewed complained about his tendency to impose decisions on others. Furthermore, he had a reputation for treating people with contempt, particularly if they disagreed with him, a fault he admitted having. (Unfortunately his derisive remarks often occurred during meetings. The public humiliation of his victims did nothing to endear him.) Many, particularly traditionalists, also objected to his lifestyle.

Relatively neutral informants we queried (i.e., those who saw Tarlier's faults but felt that accusations against him were exaggerated) agree with our own view that resentment against him was based, at least partially, on the fact that he was a successful outsider. When he came to the Larzac in 1965, his farm had a small flock of sheep and a few hectares of cultivated land. By the end of the 1980s, the herd size approached 1,000 head and the amount of land in cultivation had increased many fold. Furthermore, Tarlier had a reputation for paying his debts at the last possible minute and for being a shrewd operator in running the affairs of the GAEC of which was a member. This behavior, perhaps acceptable in the business world, is frowned upon in the rural community. Adherence to the traditional values of the rural society in which he lived would have made him more predictable and, thereby, perhaps less threatening to his *purs porcs* neighbors. As for the Tarlier's residence, it was taken as a symbol of the couple's lifestyle which, like the running of the farm, was rather urbane in nature, contrasting with that of their more traditional neighbors. Their ancient house, in poor condition when they bought it, has been lovingly restored. Although the restoration cost no more than the construction of a comparatively modest new house, it looks expensive. For some, the house confirmed the fact that Tarlier was an outsider. Furthermore, he was physically an enormous man who, even when he did not want to, imposed himself on others. He also enjoyed a good verbal fight or a game of strategy, and seemed to welcome being in the forefront of controversy for a cause he considered just. Consequently, his actions were exposed to scrutiny and easy criticism.

The principle rumor that circulated widely on the *causse* and even in Millau after Mitterrand's visit concerned a sum of money (50,000 francs) Tarlier was said to have obtained from the GFAs in 1978 through shady practices. This accusation came to be joined to a rather long series of minor ones concerning financial matters and the way he dealt with others. Some of his enemies, for example, told us that Tarlier's GAEC co-members were nothing more than underpaid slaves, completely dominated by him. Also, one or two people in his employ during the struggle claimed that he had been unfair. Other informants among outside militants expressed the same opinion, but noted that Tarlier was not the only person who exploited agricultural workers in the period before 1981. Thus, this complaint, true or not, applies with equal justice to many other Larzac farmers. (Since the end of the struggle, the problem has been dealt with, first of all, by fencing in most pasture land, thus curtailing the need for shepherds. Secondly, those few agricultural workers who were left in the immediate post-struggle period have been taken into existing GAECs as members, converting workers into partners.)

The charge that Tarlier exploited his associates can be dealt with immediately. We know all three of them. Each is a highly independent individual and none is likely to be controlled or exploited by others. We observed them at meetings in Tarlier's presence and under circumstances when he was absent. Their behavior on these occasions gave us no indication that they were anything but their own persons. Furthermore, we have discussed this issue with two out of the three. Both were amused by the very thought that they might have been under Tarlier's thumb. But the argument against Tarlier cannot be put aside so easily in conversation with his enemies, for it is also claimed that Tarlier took people into his GAEC merely to save money. This is because, in the long run, partners in GAECs are cheaper than workers since the social taxes paid by employers in France are so high. In addition, individuals can bring substantial sums of money into GAECs because of the financial support that the government extends to young farmers. There are many of these partnerships on the Larzac and elsewhere in France, for that matter. With a rational division of labor and the opportunity for a vacation that they offer to their members, GAECs are widely considered to be an efficient way of running modern farms. Tarlier, like others who formed GAECs, would have recognized these advantages. Yet, he alone was accused of exploiting fellow members. Given what we know of Tarlier's associates, the charge was absurd.

The allegation that Tarlier had engaged in shady financial practices with GFA funds was made public at the 1988 annual shareholders' meeting. One of Tarlier's three major enemies (the person who held the requests for reimbursement from shareholders) read a tract claiming that Tarlier had essentially stolen the money for his own use and that he should pay it back immediately. To understand this accusation, the reader will need to be reminded that when a GFA is founded its initial shares must be created out of land exchanged for them. While many peasants donated small plots to found the Larzac GFAs, Tarlier was a major contributor, giving a substantial number of hectares. In 1978, when he needed money (for reasons that will be discussed shortly), Tarlier sold a proportion of his shares equal to 50,000 frances back to the GFAs. The number of shares he had received from the GFAs in the first place was based on the army's estimated value of the land. Everyone agrees that this value was two to two and one-half times the normal value. In selling his share back to the GFA, therefore, Tarlier was making a substantial profit from the inflationary prices created by the army.

He responded to this attack by saying that his need for the money at that time was directly related to the struggle. According to him, he had bought a tractor, for which the *Crédit Agricole* had ostensibly guaranteed a loan. However, after he had taken possession of the tractor, he said that the bank refused to pay the loan. Caught in an emergency in which he could be sued by the tractor dealer and having no other sources of money, he asked the GFA secretary to reimburse fifty of his shares at the standard price of 1,000 francs per share. This transaction evidently took place — as did so many others involving money, especially in the tense days of the protest — in less than public circumstances. (Furthermore, it is typical of the *purs porcs* themselves not to air money matters in the public arena.) Tarlier's accusers said that if he was short of money, he should have asked APAL for a loan. In this way no shares need have been sold back to the GFAs, and the money could have been used to buy more land from farmers wishing to sell. Tarlier claimed that, at the time, he was president of APAL and a loan from it would have looked more suspicious than the selling of shares. In his own words,

> Contrary to what some others think, I believed that this solution was much clearer than if I had borrowed the money directly from the funds of the GFAs, or worse, from APAL of which I was president. I believed absolutely, during that period, that I should not add another ambiguity to the suspicions that circulated on the plateau at that time about me. Afterwards other peasants or renters of GFA land, who had good reasons, have asked to be reimbursed by the GFAs. Among those who reproach me about this issue are some who actually were reimbursed in this way.

Bitterness among some Larzac farmers over this resale came, at least partially, from the fact that individuals who bought land to expand their farms during the struggle were obliged to pay the same inflated prices that Tarlier got for his land via the shares he sold back to the GFAs. What people tended to forget was the fact that the GFAs were created for the very purpose of helping those farmers who needed to sell their land but did not wish to sell to the army. Tarlier's holdings in the GFAs were very large. If he had wanted to, he could have sold everything to the army or even blackmailed the GFAs into buying him out. In either case, he would have made an enormous profit. This, however, was something that, given his personality and values, he would never have done. In any case, if he did make a profit on the deal, it was a modest one since on the open market the land in question was worth at least 18,000 francs. Many people on the Larzac admit that Tarlier was not the only militant to draw a small profit from the struggle and that, in each case, this fact had to be balanced against the sacrifice in time, energy and lost income these individuals had willingly made during ten years of anti-camp activity.

But the situation was even more complicated. When Tarlier responded to the charges made against him during the 1988 GFA shareholders' meeting, his accuser, who had been on the board of the *Crédit Agricole* at the time the loan was requested, said that it had, in fact, been granted immediately and that Tarlier had not needed the 50,000 francs he got from the sale of his shares. Tarlier answered that the loan was indeed granted but only in 1983, well after the struggle. We have copies of three documents that confirm Tarlier's version of the story. One is a bill for the tractor from *Rouergue Motoculture* for 113,000 francs, dated 1978. Another is a schedule of loan repayments to the bank, showing that Tarlier *had* received 150,000 francs but in 1983. The third document is a letter written by Tarlier to the director of the *Crédit Agricole* in 1979 in which he complains of the prejudicial treatment he had received at the hands of the bank, particularly in relation to the nonpayment of the loan destined for the tractor.

These documents provide strong evidence that Tarlier was telling the truth concerning this issue. I do not mean to imply, however, that his adversary was lying about the circumstances and the date on which the loan was finally granted. This person is a man of tremendous integrity and honesty. But he is also an old man, bitter and obsessed by his hatred of Tarlier. It may well be that his anger led him to forget certain details of what had transpired in 1978 and 1983. I will go so far as to say that, on the basis of our observations, all three of Tarlier's enemies became less and less rational during the two years that we spent in the field between 1987 and 1989. They are *all* men of honor but, as the dispute in the GFAs progressed, what had been an argument over reimbursement was turned into a personal vendetta against Tarlier. This is a fact that was finally to become evident to the other members of tendency one who, by the spring of 1989, had reached a compromise with the members of tendency two. But we have not reached that stage in our narrative yet.

Realizing that the 1988 shareholders' meeting of the GFAs was likely to stall under the burden of controversy and wishing to avoid the rancor that had occurred at the 1987 meeting, members of both tendencies agreed that François Boé, a member of the board of directors and neutral on the reimbursement issue, would chair the meeting. His strategy was to allow the expected personal attack on Tarlier to emerge early and then try to bring the group as a whole to a compromise. Sonia and I, who are in sympathy with the goals of the GFAs, had agreed between us that we would, while remaining neutral in the dispute, also try to calm the waters. In order to guarantee our admission to the annual meeting — open in principle only to shareholders — we had bought one share in the winter of 1987. We were, therefore, not only present legally but entitled to speak. Just after the bitter exchange between Tarlier and his enemy, I rose to read a short statement. In it I suggested that, without assigning guilt, the past be left to history and that the GFAs move toward the future. To help the GFAs repay shareholders who had requested reimbursement, Sonia and I pledged to buy one share per year over the coming five years and encouraged other shareholders' to do the same. This statement was met by general applause and appeared to relax tensions to some extent. Later, however, it became apparent that the attack on Tarlier would go on unabated. Our intervention had done nothing to bring the two sides together.

In the afternoon, the vote on the motions of tendencies one and two was recorded. Because of the large concentration of proxies held by one individual, Tarlier's main enemy among the peasants, tendency one carried the vote by a large majority: 900 votes to 170. Boé immediately asked, "Can't we get out of this bind by fixing a set of orientations for next year? Those present can vote amendments for proxies they hold and perhaps we can work together to unite our views." This was clearly unacceptable to tendency one, and they refused. At this point Tarlier interjected that motions presented in advance to the shareholders had to be passed by votes representing at least 50 percent of the total shares and that, on motions presented during the meeting, votes had to represent two-thirds. The secretary, infuriated, responded by saying that because of Tarlier's legalism, the GFAs were paralyzed. He announced his resignation from the GFAs and left the room only to return, quit again and return again, several times.

Tarlier's bombshell was followed by a long and indecisive discussion during which members of the two tendencies restated their positions. Tendency one stressed the need to reimburse; tendency two called for total transparency so that the facts concerning all financial matters could be known to all members of the board.

At this point the debate turned into a loud shouting match between the leader of tendency one and a former secretary of the GFAs, who supported tendency two. When things calmed down a bit, José Bové suggested that a meeting of the entire plateau be called to define the objectives of the GFAs. This suggestion, though, got nowhere and the meeting finally moved to the election of next year's board of directors. Most people in tendency two assumed that the board in place would be continued for another year. The leader of tendency one had other plans, however. He rose to present a list he had prepared in advance that excluded Tarlier and his most vocal allies on the board. In addition, his nominees included a person objectionable to many in tendency two as well as their supporters.

Boé again attempted to reach a compromise but the leader of tendency one insisted that as a minimum he did not want Tarlier, one other male farmer and the two women in tendency two on the board. When it became apparent that his list would pass — thanks to tendency one's proxies — Tarlier once again resorted to parliamentary tactics and announced that a majority of all outstanding shares would be needed to elect a new board. Tendency one, even with its large number of proxies, did not hold a majority. The election of their list was, therefore, invalid. This declaration was met with anger by the leaders of tendency one, who pointed out that strict adherence to legal procedures had never been employed in the GFAs before.

Tarlier, however, stuck to his position. A member of tendency one, who favored compromise, moved that the existing board be empowered to serve for another year with the exclusion of the most vociferous advocates of both tendencies and that a volunteer, not a member of the board, be found to serve as the new secretary. The secretary in place reacted angrily, threatening yet again to resign but that, first, he wanted the board to reimburse him for his shares. A member of tendency two who had been excluded from tendency one's list agreed to resign from the board, but said that she would not sell her share. The leader of tendency one refused all compromise, repeating that he held the necessary proxy votes to impose his list on the meeting. Boé again tried to calm the discussion by noting that there were names acceptable to both sides from among the old board and on the new list presented by tendency one. He suggested that these people be empowered as a "committee of experts" to deal with the impasse and to present their findings to the existing board at the end of the summer. This suggestion came very late in the meeting, when many shareholders were absent from the room. Most of those present from both tendencies greeted Boé's idea positively. Someone then suggested that Sonia and I be added to the committee as observers, which we agreed to do. There was a great deal of confusion and cross talk during this discussion. The leader of tendency one did not seem to understand or to be aware of what was going on. While other members of his tendency did agree to the formation of the committee (his ally, the secretary, was nowhere to be seen), he never gave his approval. Later, when he rejected the committee's findings, he claimed, with justification, that he had never agreed to its formation.

The committee of experts, with Boé as chair, met frequently during the summer of 1988. With the exception of Boé, its four members were all moderate adherents of tendency one. As observer-members of the committee of experts, Sonia and I witnessed interviews with farmers who rented most or all of their land from the GFAs — with the exception of one, whom the committee itself was never able to question. As committee members, we also read its correspondence over the succeeding weeks. Among the most interesting letters was a long series of exchanges between the committee and Tarlier's three adversaries, who progressively escalated and multiplied their charges against him. They were overplaying their hand. It became more and more obvious to the committee members that, whatever else was at stake, a good part of the dispute within the GFAs had been caused, or at least had been amplified, by personal dislike for Tarlier.

As chair of the committee, Boé visited the house of tendency one's leader, where he was allowed to read the letters asking for reimbursement. There were about 200 of them, and the total number of shares involved was between 400 and 600. According to Boé, the letters could be divided into three distinguishable categories. There were a significant number of letters from people who claimed real need and who asked to have their shares bought back immediately. There were other shareholders who said that they would like to be reimbursed eventually, but that they were in no hurry to get their money back. Finally, there were individuals who stated that if, as it appeared to them, the GFAs were being dissolved, they would like to be reimbursed. The last category was taken as evidence by the committee that at least some of the letters asking for reimbursement had been solicited.

To clarify the situation, it was decided that a questionnaire be sent to all shareholders, asking them when they had bought their shares, whether or not they wanted to be reimbursed and, if so, according to what schedule. The questionnaire was presented to and debated by the GFA board, and the final wording was agreed upon before it was to be sent to shareholders. In spite of this, when the committee asked the GFA secretary to provide it with the association's mailing list, he refused. Boé, however, had previously obtained a list of shareholders with five or more shares. The questionnaire could be sent to these individuals. In addition, in an attempt to capture the majority of shareholders, the committee decided to publish the questionnaire in *GLL*. It appeared in the December 1988 issue. The results obtained did show a clear commitment in favor of the GFAs, although they were undoubtedly skewed in favor of the continuation of the GFAs because readers of *GLL* are likely to be the most militant supporters of the Larzac. Few individuals asked to be reimbursed, and a significant number even offered to buy additional shares.

The old board continued to meet during the summer and fall of 1988. It became increasingly clear that most members hoped for some kind of compromise. Impassioned but civil discussion among the members of the two tendencies predominated during even the most difficult confrontations. However, Tarlier's three enemies were often absent from meetings. They were, instead, busy behind the scenes.

Meanwhile Boé had been encouraging Tarlier (without suggesting any wrong doing) to make the conciliatory gesture of reimbursing the 50,000 francs obtained from his sale in 1978. Boé pointed out that this money could be used to reimburse additional shares. When Tarlier acquiesced, Boé presented a package to the board including Tarlier's agreement; the suggestion that a new, paid, non-board member secretary be found for the association; and that an orderly means of reimbursing shares be instituted. Although some members objected to the repayment schedule offered by

Tarlier, the board finally voted unanimously to accept Boé's recommendations. With the exception of Tarlier's three enemies, tendencies one and two had, for all intents and purposes, merged.

In the spring of 1989, Tarlier's enemies mounted a counterattack by sending a letter and questionnaire to all shareholders (they had the complete GFA mailing list at their disposal). They asked that responses be sent directly to the Chamber of Agriculture of the Aveyron, at Rodez, putting them in the hands of an individual hostile to the Larzac community. To say the least, this questionnaire was worded specifically to encourage not only requests for reimbursement but also the total dissolution of the GFAs. The letter clearly stated that the committee of experts had never been accepted by tendency one and that Boé had acted in bad faith in order to save tendency two. All shares had to be reimbursed, and any leftover funds were to be given to charity. This letter and questionnaire aroused the consternation of a large number of people on the plateau.

Many now saw the renewed attack on the GFAs as an aggression not only against Tarlier personally but also against the Roquefort committee in which Tarlier was one of the dominant figures. This committee was then locked in a dispute with the industry and in a power struggle with the majority agricultural union, the FDSEA. The union opposed the actions of the Roquefort committee, which was allied with the Confédération Paysanne. Sending this questionnaire to the Chamber of Agriculture, dominated by the FDSEA, could put damaging information in its hands at a delicate time. At this point, Pierre Bonnefous stepped in and tried to mediate between the majority of the board and the leader of tendency one. He suggested that the latter step down from the GFA board. The leader of tendency one was intransigent, however. He saw no reason why he should withdraw from the GFAs, in spite of the suggestion that such a move would ease tensions and facilitate an accommodation between the two factions. For him, the only solution to the problem was the eventual dissolution of an institution that, he felt, had no purpose in the post-struggle Larzac. He reiterated his demand that Tarlier resign immediately from the GFAs and pay back the 50,000 francs.

At that point, another figure stepped into the fray. This was Hervé Ott, the founder of the nonviolent center of Le Cun. Ott took it upon himself to begin a fast to exert moral pressure on the two factions. At the same time, he sent a letter explaining his gesture to the GFA members asking that some form of compromise be found to end the dispute. This action was met with mixed feelings on the plateau. Some were convinced that the leader of tendency one was by now so isolated that he could no longer do much damage and that, in addition, there was an element of grandstanding in Ott's concern. The son of Tarlier's main adversary, however, was deeply moved by Ott's action and, to his great credit, convinced his father (with help from his brother who had also come to realize that his father's position was untenable) not only to accept a new committee of experts made up of outsiders to the GFAs — former militants and local *notables* — but to resign from the GFA board. While he felt that reimbursement was the first order of business for the GFAs, he also recognized that his father had become so obsessed with Tarlier that he was acting self-destructively. There was still some disagreement over who should serve on the new committee. A compromise was found when both tendencies agreed to accept all the candidates proposed by both sides.

Unanimity had finally been reached, and the new committee began its work in the fall of 1989. One of its tasks was to put the affairs of the GFAs in order. To do this, it needed the records of the association. Unfortunately, these remained with the former secretary, who was now no longer a member of the board. Nor did he hold GFA shares (he had reimbursed himself). Nevertheless, he refused to yield the books to the committee until he was paid 50,000 francs, which he would then give to charity. (This demand was a means of settling an old score with members of the Larzac Foundation to whom the secretary had lost a dispute two years previously.) Rather than make an issue of this refusal, the committee quietly set about its work and painstakingly reconstituted the GFA's books.

In the spring of 1990, the committee issued its report and called a shareholders' meeting for April 22 to regularize the operations of the GFAs. The report noted that while the GFAs had not operated in the past according to bureaucratic regulations (improvisation had always been the rule for running associations during the struggle), no fraud had been committed by anyone and all the accounts had been correctly kept. The committee was clearly in favor of the continuation of the Larzac GFAs.

The meeting in Millau, attended by about a hundred people, shareholders from the Larzac and elsewhere, began at ten in the morning. In the beginning some individuals, representing shareholders from other regions of France, questioned the past functioning of the GFAs and asked for reassurances that their continuation was in keeping with the goals of the post-struggle community. The committee responded positively to these questions, noting that after pending reimbursements, the GFAs could indeed continue to fulfill their useful role. One member of the committee, known for his conservative views, nevertheless spoke passionately of the need to maintain agricultural activity on the Larzac, as well as elsewhere in the Midi, to prevent the region from becoming nothing more than Europe's playground. After some discussion, the assembled shareholders voted unanimously to continue the Larzac GFAs.

In the afternoon session, the committee offered its suggestions for a slate of officers to guide the GFAs during their first year under the reorganization plan. The new board would be comprised of three farmers, three nonfarmers from the Larzac area and three outsiders. Former adversaries in the two tendencies were not among those nominated by the board. After acceptance of the slate, the meeting ended with everyone in good spirits and with the feeling that something memorable had been accomplished. All this was made possible by the selfless work of former militants dedicated to the viability of the Larzac "experiment" who, together with other expert members of the committee, helped to bring order to a tangle of difficult problems. Their efforts were encouraged by the cooperation of the old GFA board and its supporters and the goodwill of others concerned about the future of the GFAs. The Larzac had overcome a major problem as affectives and politicals had joined hands in a common cause — the saving of the GFAs and the equitable reimbursement of former militants.[3]

NOTES

1. François Pingaud, charged by the government to aid in the organization of the post-struggle community, was of the opinion that the SCTL board should include local elected officials as a balance against potential favoritism that might be expressed by farmer-members toward friends and colleagues within the association. The same point was made later by Agnès Bonnaud (1991). Another opinion was expressed by an agricultural researcher familiar with the functioning of the SCTL. According to this informant, José Bové, François Mathey, Alain Desjardin and others realized that an association of farmers without government participation would be more effective in protecting the interests of the local peasants if a right-wing party returned to political power. In fact, according to this informant, an SCTL composed of local people, exclusive of government officials, helped the peasants attain an important degree of social maturity, since they were obliged to

take individual and collective responsibility for the management of the association. We have seen that personal friendships, as well as loyalty to a past militant, did figure in the choosing of the successful candidate, as well as the allocation of some Montredon land to another farm. On balance, however, it must be stressed that the final decision also reflected a degree of realism, for it preserved two already existing farms, one of which might have failed if it were not allowed access to new grazing land.

2. According to a knowledgeable informant who was involved at the time, strong conflicts similar to those found in the GFAs occurred among power interests on the plateau when the SCTL was created.

3. Agnès Bonnaud (1991) points to a weakness in the democratic functioning of the GFAs. Due to the lack of quorums at annual shareholders' meeting, the board of directors is sometimes forced to make decisions that should be the prerogative of shareholders. For example, in 1991 board members voted to sell some GFA land to the government for the construction of the new *autoroute* that is to cross the Larzac. On the other hand, Bonnaud notes that since their reorganization, the combined GFA boards have decided to operate without a president so that actions can be taken collectively without ambiguity.

CHAPTER TEN
The Larzac and
the Tradition of the New

Returning to New York in 1989 was difficult for us. Our twenty-six months of research on the plateau had given rise to many close friendships, and although we knew we would be back the following summer, we realized that the intensity created by our long association was bound to diminish as we took up our off-plateau lives once again. Also, the GFA conflict had not yet been resolved, and new projects, such as a proposed *autoroute* that was to cross the plateau, were causing dissension. We would inevitably miss some of the new developments as they unfolded, though we made a point of returning for one week in the spring of 1990 to attend the climactic annual shareholders' meeting of the GFAs.

Our departure was marked by a huge party at Les Truels. We invited the seventy-five or so people present to visit us in New York if they had the chance but, "not all at once, if you please!" At different times, in the winter and spring of 1990–91, we were happy to welcome Pierre Burguière and his family; the Tarliers; and Alain Desjardin, his companion Michèle Vincent, and their daughter, Camille. We were amused by the reverse fieldwork that led us to see New York's positive qualities, as well as its defects, through the eyes of our observant guests.

We returned for the following summers, and in the academic year 1991–92 we were once again free to spend an entire year in Soubès. We resumed fieldwork, but except for social visits to our friends, on a far less intense level. We regularly attended only APAL meetings. In the early fall of 1991, Guy Tarlier began to show ominous medical symptoms, first diagnosed as an infection picked up from sheep. His condition worsened during the fall and winter, and in late winter, his illness was diagnosed as cancer. Tarlier's decline was rapid. It was very hard for his many friends to see this mountain of a man fade away so quickly. We visited him on May 2. Struggling out of bed for the first time in a week, he forced himself to have tea and cake with us. This was to be the last time we were to see him alive. He died on May 7, 1992, surrounded

157

by his wife, Marizette, other family members and several friends. Pierre Bonnefous remained at his side through the last days and administered the final rites.

Immediately, the Larzac community came together to plan the funeral of "their Prefect." One felt the sense of urgency that must have reigned during the tense strategy planning sessions of the struggle years. However, this time the "action" was not to protest but rather to accept a loss deeply felt — to affirm symbolically Tarlier's importance to the life of the plateau. The funeral was, in a very pure sense, a concentrated expression of the tradition *invented* by the Larzac peasants during and beyond the years of the struggle. Everyone knew exactly what to do. Committees were appointed, and responsibilities were divided rapidly among those best able to handle them. The family ordered a coffin from an undertaker in Millau, but the community took charge of everything else, including the digging of the grave in the cemetery of St. Martin. Three priests — Bonnefous and two other ex-plateau militants — said the Mass. Local and national figures — among the latter, a representative of the prime minister — spoke eloquently of Tarlier's many contributions to the struggle and to plateau life in general. As Marie-Claude Tjibaou (the wife of Jean-Marie Tjibaou, the assassinated president of the FLNKS) put it in her telegram of regret, "*La mort de Guy, c'est comme un grand sapin qui tombe et qui fait du bruit jusque chez nous.*" (Guy's death is like the falling of a great pine tree. The sound of its fall has reached us from across the ocean.)

* * *

Tarlier's funeral was a symbolic expression of the fact that, in spite of cracks and strains, the Larzac movement remained a viable social, political and economic force on the local scene. The Larzac community, a child of adversity, has matured through the long years that followed the announcement of the extension plan. The present community is founded on a "tradition of the new." It is characterized by a particularly flexible form of social structure, invented by strong individuals — each of whom made his or her own special contribution during and after the struggle. This did not happen in a vacuum, however. It occurred on the background of past culture and history expressed creatively through a long series of local and national actions taken by the community. While this new tradition must be seen as a dynamic and complex whole, it can best be understood if we break it down into its constituents — culture, history and social structure — each of which contributed to its unique success.

Two somewhat contradictory cultural-historical factors were of the utmost importance to the Larzac in 1972. One was the long-standing conservatism and regionalism of the Aveyron, while the other was the aftershock of the radical student revolt of 1968. The former was ready to be expressed, as it had been manifested before in other times of crisis, as a populist defense of local interests in the face of central power. It became the basis of broad local support for the peasants. The latter provided the creative and physical energy for the shock troops of intellectuals and former students in what was to grow into a movement national in scope. The deeply religious peasants — a few already aware of social injustice through their participation in the CMR well before the struggle began — were receptive to the concepts of nonviolence offered to them by Lanza del Vasto as well as attentive to his radical social ideas.[1] (This, in turn, may have encouraged their eventual responsiveness to the ideas of the outside militants.) The peasants' early commitment to nonviolence — for some an act of faith, for others a strategic means of combatting the overwhelming force of the army — provided the strength and unity necessary to control the movement as it took on national and international proportions. Nonviolence, at least in the context of the Larzac, also implied tolerance. This spirit of tolerance was essential in allowing the peasants to accept what they felt was the morally offensive and outlandish behavior of the "marginal" people (Maoists, "hippies," students and foreigners) who rushed to their aid.

The Larzac was lucky to benefit from what I have called the "cultural mode" of the late 1960s, a short-term and historically precise moment in which significant numbers of young French people were concerned with, and willing to act on, such problems as environmental pollution, disarmament and self-determination. The post-1968 period was one of disenchantment with the industrialized, highly centralized French state and a time of hope that alternate means to a better life could be found through a new and innovative praxis. The Larzac provided the perfect laboratory for people who held these views and aspired to put them into action in a meaningful way. As the historian, Jean Chesneaux, put it in the March–April 1990 issue of *GLL*,

It is my hypothesis that our militant actions in favor of the Larzac were stimulated by a singular moment in history, an ephemeral opening in time. Our generation of intellectuals was bathed in the fight against Nazism and our opposition to colonial wars ... we had just freed ourselves from the suffocating yoke of the Communist party. The Larzac brought us a breath of fresh air and an opportunity for creative action.

The effect of structure on the Larzac must be looked at from two perspectives: 1. the way in which local level political organization has helped or constrained the Larzac in its relations with the larger political-economic and social spheres of the Aveyron and beyond, and 2. the ways in which associative life on the plateau itself has evolved into a varied means of dealing with issues of local and international interest.

The problem of the Larzac's relations with local governments has already been mentioned. All the farms and communities on the plateau — with the exception of La Cavalerie, La Couvertoirade and L'Hospitalet — are small and demographically weak parts of larger entities centered in the surrounding valleys. La Cavalerie is controlled by the right wing, although its mayor, a political realist, is willing to cooperate with Larzac associations when they have something to offer his village. Thus, for example, he has helped pay for a brochure advertising various commercial and tourist amenities on the plateau and allowed the *écomusée* to use the town hall for an exhibition on local architecture. L'Hospitalet's mayor is friendly to the SCTL farmers in his jurisdiction; he is happy that a few, new, young farmers have taken up residence in his commune. At least initially, however, he failed to push for the regrouping of the local elementary schools from La Blaquererie and La Couvertoirade with L'Hospitalet's local school — a move that was eventually made to the benefit of the parents and children of all three villages. People in the area who are part of our Larzac community feel that L'Hospitalet residents, including their mayor, lack the dynamism necessary to accept change, which made them resistant even to such a beneficial one as the reorganization of the schools. La Couvertoirade's mayor, after supporting the peasants against the army throughout the struggle, has since 1981 caved into local conservatives (nonmilitant peasants) who were eager to divide the land abandoned by the army among themselves and who do not wish to share political power with the new settlers on the *causse*. In past local elections on the plateau, only one Larzac militant (the wife of a *pur porc* from La Blaquererie) has been elected to any municipal council whose territory covers a part of the extension zone. The attempt to create an intercommunal charter, grouping the various communes and the Larzac, led to the signing of a document, but to date that has been its only success. The power shift from La Cavalerie in the south to the north rim of the plateau that occurred early in the struggle has left the southern part of the former extension area without strong participation in the contemporary community. It was the hope of militants that the installation of Alain Desjardin at La Salvetat would provide a strong anchor in that zone. While Desjardin, himself, remains militant and has been successful at La Salvetat, his political orientation has, up to now, limited his ability to serve as a rallying point for the south.

Thus the Larzac, for structural reasons, remains politically weak in its own geographic region. Moreover, this weakness is compounded by the fact the the local deputy to the National Assembly is a powerful and popular conservative, an enemy of the Larzac and all that it stands for.

Now let us consider the Larzac's relations with Millau. During the struggle, a strong alliance developed between the Larzac peasants and militants in the city. The local branch of the noncommunist labor union, the CFDT, became closely associated with the struggle and a strong bond also developed between the members of the Millau Larzac committee and the peasants. The committee was made up of a mixed group of pacifists, Catholics of the left and assorted radicals. It was dissolved along with all the others at the end of the struggle, but in the municipal elections of 1982, two Larzac militants (one from the plateau and the other, an inhabitant of Millau) won seats on the municipal council. A firm supporter of the Larzac also became the first Socialist mayor to be elected in many years. In the elections of 1989, the two council members declined to run again, but Elizabeth Baillon agreed to be on the Socialist party's list and was voted in. The incumbent Socialist mayor, once again victorious, appointed her deputy mayor in charge of cultural affairs. In France, deputy mayors are the only members of municipal councils to have any real power in municipal government.

On the other hand, relations between other ex-militants in the city and the plateau have been, at best, tepid since 1981. The Millau residents maintain that the Larzac has lost interest in the problems of the city, and the plateau militants claim that the working class of Millau has been so decimated by years of depression and unemployment that only a small fragment of militant unionism remains. Although people from Millau and the *causse* have joined forces to demonstrate in favor of New Caledonian independence, the best relations between the Larzac and the city take place when environmental issues are at stake. In this domain militants from both areas have joined forces on various projects, including plans for the development of a regional natural park. The environmental issue has been poisoned somewhat, however, by the outcome of the municipal election of 1989. In the first round of that election, the Greens received about 8 percent of the vote. In negotiations with the Socialists, who came in first, they demanded at least five seats (out of about thirty) on the council and were offered only two — a proposal that was seen by the Socialists as adequate considering the percentage of votes the Greens had received. Delegates from the Green party, a recently installed Larzac farmer among them, then decided to negotiate with the right. Although these negotiations led to nothing, they caused a great deal of resentment on the plateau, particularly among those who normally support the Socialist party but who are advocates of the Greens' pro-ecology position and potential backers.

As the Larzac community evolved (in both the struggle and post-struggle periods), a set of voluntary associations developed to deal with specific problems. While a few of these dissolved immediately or shortly after the victory in 1981 (the Larzac committees and, except in name, *Larzac Universités*), most of the organizations that evolved between 1971 and 1981 are still in place. These, along with others that were organized since 1981 (the CIR, the Larzac Foundation, the SCTL, the Association for the Improvement of Montredon and *Taxus Baccata*, a plateau rock band — to name a few) play a vital role in both the social and political life of the plateau. Each, in a different way, provides militants and potential militants with a wide choice of activities. Since the members active in directing these associations also vary, people who join one or another of them can choose to work with individuals with whom they feel socially compatible and on projects that interest them specifically.

Animal husbandry is still the major economic activity on the plateau. If the Larzac's innovative social institutions are to survive in the future, they will do so only on the basis of economic success. This condition is problematic when one considers the problems inherent in agriculture in the local area and in the wider context of contemporary Europe. It remains to be seen whether or not the plateau — with its drought-ridden, marginal soils — will be able to compete with the larger, richer farms of nearby valleys — not to mention central and northern France and, in the near future, the farm products of other EC countries.

Under the coming economic situation, the Larzac is in real peril of extinction, but it does have some advantages that are not found in other similar areas. The post-struggle Larzac remains dynamic. Recent innovations in production and land management on the plateau have already shown that Larzac farmers are capable of taking the initiative to direct their own affairs. This fact has relevance for current thinking among European environmentalists. Experts have begun to worry about the problems posed by the need to protect the dry, marginal land of the Mediterranean basin, and now believe that such protection will have to be provided by farmers whose activity has an overall positive effect on the area's fragile ecology. Intelligent farming with proper land use keeps natural areas open and discourages the destructive brush fires that ravage abandoned fields in these zones. Land that is allowed to go wild is of little use to tourists and is a menace to reforestation.

The post-struggle Larzac is therefore a logical place to begin rethinking land management in marginal zones. Along side of farms worked by their owners and farms rented from private individuals, the SCTL and the Larzac GFAs, together, provide a significant amount of land (about 7,500 hectares) that they make available to young farmers on a rental basis. Outside of some meat production, the milk sheep continue to reign on the plateau with most of the milk going to the caves of Roquefort. The post-struggle plateau has seen a significant amount of diversification, however, with the creation of farm-made products (honey, pâté and cooked sheep's cheese). Through their association (*L'Agneau des Grands Causses*) many of the meat producers have joined their sales efforts with the producers of the farm-made products and have formed a GIE (*Groupement d'Intérêts Economics*). Unfortunately, lamb and mutton prices are low in France, and it is difficult for Larzac farmers to make a go of meat production, even though the members of *L'Agneau des Grands Causses* have attempted to market their product (lambs raised in the open by their mothers) on the basis of its high quality. There is hope, however. The GIE is beginning to widen the circle of clients for all concerned. In spite of the fact that the market for these quality products is limited and increasingly competitive, in joining forces, the members of the GIE will be in a better position to defend themselves.

It is somewhat ironic in the light of the politics of their struggle that most Larzac farmers — whether they produce for Roquefort or sell homemade products — provide luxury foods too expensive for working-class people. Many feel that survival on the Larzac will depend not only on this luxury production but also on low density, quality tourism (e.g., hiking, backpacking, horseback riding, camping in unspoiled natural zones or taking rooms with farm families who open their houses to paying guests, etc). While these activities need not be expensive — indeed they are often less costly than more traditional tourist activities — they tend to appeal mostly to relatively wealthy or educated segments of the population.

* * *

More than one Larzac militant told us that the success of the struggle was an extraordinary event created by ordinary people. Certainly a large number of ordinary people made important contributions to the movement, but we believe its ultimate success, as well as its continuation, are due to a set of extraordinary people who might have continued their "ordinary" lives if the plan to extend the Larzac military camp had not been pursued. Historical circumstances of the struggle provided the opportunity for these people to make their individual contributions to that whole that became the "Larzac." Thus, when it comes to the role of the individual in the making of history, I stand with Raymond Aron (1989) against both the extreme individualistic position of Karl Popper (1957) and the Marxist position exemplified in France by Louis Althuser. Ultimately it is true, as Popper claims, that individuals make history but not in a vacuum. They do so, as Aron points out, on the background of preexisting culture, social structure and the historical process itself.

Our data from the Larzac, which covers twenty-one years from 1971 to 1992, allow us to document specific contributions made by a large number of individuals, who each in his or her own way advanced the cause of the Larzac. While many of these people discovered strengths and talents they did not know they had, nothing they did was entirely new to the history of social protest in France (Tilly 1986). In addition, their movement came at the right time in French history — just after the widespread social unrest of 1968 — and in the right place — a region under extreme economic pressure, with rising unemployment and labor unrest in the cities, and a renewal of agriculture in a countryside tied to and supported by the powerful industrialists of Roquefort.

A considerable number of women figure in the militant life of the plateau. The traditional woman's role on the Larzac was in the house and the farmyard — a support for her husband, a mother to her children. During the struggle, most peasant wives supported the movement by taking on added burdens, serving as secretarial help and replacing their husbands in work or management when the latter were away at demonstrations. When they could, they attended meetings, but few of them spoke up either during planning sessions or at demonstrations. As the struggle progressed, the people of the Larzac rubbed shoulders with outside supporters, many of whom were radicals and some of whom were feminists. A few peasant women began to assert themselves in both the private and public arenas. Janine Massebiau and Jeanne Jonquet became eloquent speakers. One bachelor woman, a member of a *pur porc* family who had been an unequal partner in her unmarried brothers' GAEC, left the Larzac after the struggle to start a new and independent life in Millau. Many strong and independent women came to the Larzac alone or with companions, as militants and squatters. Many of these, like Suzanne Morain, Dominique Robin, Danièle Domeyne and Alice Monier — to mention only four — are a significant presence on the plateau today.[2] Nobué Darras, a political refugee of Brazilian origin, works with her husband, Daniel, in honey production and pottery making. She and Daniel currently edit *GLL* and are both active in other plateau associations. Among other newcomers are women farmers who are full legal partners with their husbands or male companions. During the protest, Elizabeth Baillon and Marizette Tarlier made their own valuable contributions to the movement, and both play substantial roles in the post-struggle community. Christiane Burguière has found her voice as an editor and regular contributor to *GLL*. The CIR has run three successful workshops on women in the rural world, during which problems were addressed by participants from the Larzac and the rest of France.

The paradox of the Larzac movement today, given its ideology of participatory democracy, is the continued presence of strong leaders who, for some at least, have inhibited the flowering of that democracy. As we have seen, real participatory democracy on the plateau was and is more ideal than real, because the legacy of strong leadership that formed during the struggle has continued since victory. Almost everyone admits that, for strategic reasons, there was a need for a leadership that could take swift and effective action against the government. Our informants are unanimous in saying that Guy Tarlier was a key figure without whom victory would not have been possible. Léon Burguière and his two sons, Pierre and Jean-Marie, also played vital roles during the struggle, and Pierre remains a major force in current plateau activities. Hervé Ott, as well, continues to have an important place in community affairs, particularly in relation to the Third World. Today's leaders — many of whom were yesterday's leaders as well — will say, with justification, that they are the ones willing to put in the time necessary for the operation of the various Larzac associations. At meetings, we have seen the reticence expressed by members of these associations when they are asked to contribute to the planning of this or that action. Even if the Larzac community had been able to function as a participatory democracy from the beginning, would there not have been those who were more quick to act and assume responsibility? At the same time, could it have won its difficult struggle against the weight of the French government with any means other than the ones developed out of necessity during the conflict?[3]

Another thorny issue was raised in discussion with one of the farmers who came to the plateau after 1981. A troublesome legacy of the ten-year struggle, he feels, is that people find it painful to disagree. They miss the consensus that was necessary before 1981 and cannot face the reality of possible conflict with their close friends and neighbors. We think that his point is well taken, as divisions will inevitably appear with regard to vital questions that concern the future of the *causse*. Indeed, the proposed *autoroute* that is to cross the plateau by the beginning of the next century has already caused considerable dissension. Will the Larzac be able to acknowledge differing points of view and still act on issues that will effect it in the coming years? Will it be able to face the fact that its "united front" is no longer united but that, nevertheless, decisions must be reached if actions on a community level are to be taken?

While we believe it is important to raise the above questions, we do not wish to diminish in any way the importance of what the Larzac has already accomplished. This accomplishment is real, not theoretical. The individuals named in this book and the thousands of others who collectively made the Larzac struggle a success worked together to build a movement that was formed under the constraints of local and national culture as well as national and regional history. Many of these individuals were also innovators who used the available cultural repertoire creatively and with great perseverance. We believe that it is fair to say that if the people of the Larzac were shaped by history and culture, they also *made* history and culture. Significant numbers of individuals rose to the occasion, taking charge of their lives and, in the process, changing them, we think forever.

NOTES

1. For a general introduction to the role of the Catholic Church in French society, see Donegani and Lescanne (1986). For a review of the 1968 period and its aftermath, see Delannoi (1990).
2. In the spring of 1991, Danièle Domeyne, who was one of the most controversial members of the old board, was once again elected as a director of the GFA board.
3. A more pessimistic point of view was expressed by an agricultural specialist and former Larzac militant. According to this person, the plateau was incapable of forming a society of equals even though it claims to be one. While it is true that this claim has not been fully realized, short of a utopian community, one would be hard pressed to find a society of equals anywhere.

   As one final note, it is interesting that in the meeting of April 1992 (referred to in endnote 3, chapter 6) there seemed to be a consensus among all present — including the younger farmers who are particularly sensitive to economic inequality, as well as the pre-struggle militants and the *purs porcs* who were in attendance — that all the farmers were more or less in the "same boat" given the economic pressures of the times. With the constitution of the GAECs and the elimination of hired agricultural workers, a leveling process has occurred. Even on the larger farms, because of the number of partners involved, the relationship between the number of sheep and the number of people who depend on them for their livelihood is about the same as on the smaller farms.

CHAPTER ELEVEN

INTO THE NEXT CENTURY

Crossing into the next century Larzac militants continue to press for the same goals that developed during the *lutte*. Their commitment to small scale, ecologically sound agriculture has strengthened as has their commitment to aid politically disenfranchised farming populations in the third world, particularly, but not exclusively, the French colonies in the Pacific. They also continue to press for the development of eco-tourism in their region and seek ways to maintain economic viability through activities in what, in spite of Roquefort, continues to be a marginal area for agriculture. Their commitment to nonviolence both as a core value and a strategic method remains the force that binds the community together. Throughout the period since this book was first published the Larzac has remained a point of reference for others engaged in the struggle for nonviolent self-determination in the face of state power on both local and international levels.

The most spectacular event in recent Larzac history, an event that brought the Larzac movement back into sharp focus within France and internationally, occurred in the summer of 1999. This was what I shall refer to here as the 'great hamburger war.'

In the middle of 1999 the United States, in protest against a French ban on the importation of beef treated with growth hormone, won a decision from the World Trade Organization that allowed it to place a 100% tariff on certain French luxury products, including Roquefort cheese. Besides their fear of negative health consequences from eating such beef the French saw the WTO decision as direct support for American-led multinational agro-business corporations at the expense of their own agriculture and food production. This was a highly charged affair. What better protest target to choose under the circumstances than McDonald's? It was David against Goliath. At the end of August 1999 a group of union militants from the *Confédération Paysanne* (an agricultural union representing small farmers), supported by a large group of Larzac militants, demonstrated against the installation of a new McDonald's franchise in Millau. It was there, for a series of reasons to be explained below, that the spotlight of the national and international media was to focus.

José Bové, Larzac militant and prominent leader of the *Confédération Paysanne*, "was a major instigator" of the Millau protest. An advocate of what he calls "active nonviolence", the demonstration was to include a symbolic dismantling of the uncompleted building. A few prefabricated walls were carefully taken down, the main door of the structure was removed, and the sign in front of the building site was cut down with a chain saw. The next day *Midi Libre*, a local newspaper, referred to the action as a "saccage" (trashing). This term was picked up by the national media and repeated even in the American press. It was immediately seized upon by the manager of the Millau McDonald's franchise to support his claim that major damage had been done to his future enterprise.

In point of fact, since the McDonald's corporation which owns the building refused to press civil charges against the demonstrators and no expert was ever appointed by the courts to objectively assess the damage, no legally valid estimate was ever taken. Additionally, most observers, including the prestigious national newspaper, *Le Monde*, reported the actual damage as slight. (I will return to some eye-witness accounts at the end of this chapter.) Although the police in Millau did not intervene directly they did photograph the participants. In the aftermath of the protest, five and, later, four more protesters were arrested and charged with the destruction of private property. To the surprise of many in Millau those arrested were incarcerated under a demand for bail of 105,000 francs, about $20,000. (It might surprise American readers but it is very unusual in France for such harsh judicial action to be taken after a political demonstration even when significant damage has occurred.) In this case the legal decision was taken by a young, inexperienced, newly appointed judge. The reaction of a large segment of the French public was instantaneous and negative. Later many were to say that the demonstrators could not have prayed for a better ally than this particular judge.

Bové was part of the first group charged by the judge although, because he was on vacation when the warrant was issued, his arrest did not occur until several days later when he returned home to give himself up. Taken to bail in the city of Montpellier, about 100 miles south of Millau on the Mediterranean coast, Bové refused to allow his union to pay bail. His release came only two weeks later when funds were donated by individuals, many of them Americans sympathetic to his cause. (Among them were members of a small-scale family-farmers union.)

Bové's stubbornness struck a chord of sympathy in a wide segment of the French public and he was hailed widely as a national hero. His instant popularity beyond the immediate Larzac area was helped along by his uncanny resemblance to a popular comic book character, *Asterix le Gaulois*, depicted as a short, wiry individual with a drooping mustache, a winning smile, and quick wit. To fully understand the success of the attack on McDonald's, however, we need to look back on a series of events that shook public confidence in the French government as well as its scientific establishment during the 1980s and into the 1990s.

Trouble began in the early 1980s when the HIV virus was discovered and its likely transmission through blood transfusions became known. The problem was particularly severe in the case of hemophiliacs who require treatment with a clotting factor made from blood drawn from multiple donors. Although American scientists had warned about this danger and early in the 1980s developed a method to avoid it involving heat pasteurization, the French government refused to adopt the method and continued to use the tainted product. As a result, many—up to a third of hemophiliacs in France—became infected with HIV and, of these, a large number have died. The Prime Minister, the Minister of Health, as well as a group of highly placed medical personnel were all implicated in the scandal. While some of the latter were judged responsible and sentenced to prison terms, the two ministers were cleared of all charges. The Health Minister involved when the scandal broke, Georgina Dufoix, remains infamous to this day for her remark about the tainted product: "I feel responsible but not guilty."

At the beginning of the 1990s a new form of Krutchfeld-Jacob's disease, a fatal central-nervous system disorder, suddenly appeared in a small percentage of the English population. It was not long before medical authorities in Great Britain began to speculate that the human pathology (soon to be known as 'mad cow disease') might be linked to the eating of meat from animals infected with a new cattle disorder known as bovine spongiform, a degeneration of the brain. It was further suggested that the appearance of the condition in cows was caused by their ingesting a new high-protein feed made in part from the bones and carcasses of sick animals, particularly sheep, who had long been known to be susceptible to a similar brain disorder known as scrapie. Because the disease has a long incubation period, meat from asymptomatic infected animals could have found its way into the market. Shortly after the link was suggested British beef was banned for sale anywhere in the European Community and, by law, whenever a sign of mad cow disease appeared, entire herds were immediately destroyed and incinerated. The European public, and in particular the French, were scandalized and frightened by the affair and all beef sold in France was labeled to show its place of origin. To make matters worse it was discovered that illegal, potentially infected meat, was being smuggled into the European Community from the United Kingdom via Belgium.

Into the late 1990s, there were other food scares in Europe. In 1999, for example, it was revealed that animal feed made in France containing sewage, including human waste, was being sold to meat producers. The public no longer had to be paranoid to suspect that their food might be tainted. It was against this background that the World Trade Organization decision to require European acceptance of hormonally treated American beef was declared. Remember, it was the refusal to accept such meat that led to the imposition of 100% tariffs on certain French luxury foods in the United States. As far as the French were concerned insult was added to injury when another WTO decision refused to allow labeling on transgenic agricultural products imported into the European Community. Is it no wonder that in France, and later all over Europe, the action against McDonald's and Bové's refusal of bail became strong symbols for a growing protest movement against the imposition of rules concerning uncontrolled free trade in foodstuff; rules imposed by an organization, the WTO, that had wide supranational powers, little or no input from non-governmental organizations, and no transparency about how it arrived at its decisions?

The final step in José Bové's rise in popularity occurred in the aftermath of his leading role in the protests during the Seattle meeting of the WTO in the fall of 1999. Bové', who speaks English well, was perfectly suited to get his message to the media both at home *and* in the United States. On his return to France, he appeared frequently on news broadcasts, was solicited for talk shows, and was featured in a politically diverse set of popular magazines. Both Lionel Jospin, the Socialist Prime Minister, and Jack Chirac, the right wing President, spoke well of him as a defender of French interests in the face of rampant and uncontrolled free trade. Even the major producer of Roquefort cheese, the *Société Roquefort*, which considered him an enemy in negotiations with his union, hailed him as their savior in the face of American arrogance. Bové had arrived in the United States for the Seattle events with 50 kilos of Roquefort to be distributed free in front of local McDonald's outlets!

STABILITY AND CHANGE IN LARZAC ASSOCIATIONS

I shall return to the José Bové phenomenon later when I present parts of recent interviews with signifcant Larzac militants. First, I wish to summarize the current status of Larzac associations as well as offer a chronology of important events that have occurred since the first edition of this book.

Even though structural changes have taken place in some Larzac associations, all of those discussed in previous chapters continue to function. The conflicts that were so prominent during the late 80s and early 90s in the GFAs and between the GFAs and the SCTL have been resolved. For the past several years the two land holding associations have harmonized their systems for determining rents. GLL, with a strong editorial committee, continues to publish, although now on a bimonthly basis. The Larzac Foundation, which, for legal reasons, has changed its name to *Larzac Solidarité* has recently been reinvigorated. It plays a crucial role in providing funds for a range of militant activities, particularly in the third world. Les Truels has seen personnel changes, but most of its old and new residents continue to participate actively in a number of plateau associations. Le Cun, albeit with a small number of residents, continues its role as a center for nonviolent activity, and Hervé Ott is frequently solicited by NGOs in third world countries to lead seminars in nonviolence. Alain Desjardin has 'retired' as head of La Salvetat but continues to live and be a presence there. The vegetable garden is still under his care as well. He has extended his activities in the Green Party, is a member of the *Confédération Paysanne*, and continues to organize militants interested in protecting the local environment. La Salvetat, itself, is thriving. It maintains its popular role as a reasonably priced and convivial eco-vacation spot, while it continues as a center for cultural and political events including lectures on current topics of interest to guests and Larzac residents. La Salvetat also provides full and part-time employment for young people who, in some cases, are in social and/or economic difficulties.

The Association for the Development of Montredon continues its village restoration projects. In the summer of 1989 its residents inaugurated a farmer's market which takes place every Wednesday during the summer months. It has become popular with people from the surrounding areas, including Millau, providing entertainment, locally produced products, and a free barbecue for those who buy their meat from the GIE stand manned by one of its members. When he is free to do so José Bové is there to run the grill and provide the latest news concerning militant activities. Picnic tables are available in the center of the village for the 300 or more visitors who come not only to shop but also to meet friends, make new acquaintances, and enjoy the convivial ambiance.

APAL maintains its primary role as the umbrella and coordinator for social and political activities, serving as a clearing house for the many Larzac associations. It is concerned, as ever, with the development of eco-tourism in the region. Several committees function to improve La Jasse, not only as a show piece for Larzac crafts and farm products, but as a place to remind us of the Larzac's exemplary history. Since the death of its long-time president, Guy Tarlier, and being unable to find a replacement for him, the organization is run collectively by its Board. The APAL membership recognizes the current lack of a forceful spokesperson to represent it to the outside but to date they have been unable to find anyone willing to take on this onerous function. In spite of its cumbersome aspect, however, they are able to operate remarkably well under a collective leadership given their long experience in self-organizing.

In 1995 La Jasse changed its format and abolished the ecomusée. It had become increasingly difficult to organize new exhibitions. Moreover, some people in APAL expressed their discomfort with the fees charged for admission, although the funds generated were used to support new installations. Most of the space formerly occupied by the ecomusée is now devoted to an expanded sales area where a range of locally produced food, crafts, and books covering such topics as local geography, nature, architecture, and politics are offered. Although large exhibitions are no longer possible, some space has been set aside for illustrated panels from past expositions depicting the Larzac's opposition to the military as well as contemporary life on the plateau. Additionally, a video portraying the *lutte* can be viewed by visitors in a special section behind the commercial area. The rear third of the Jasse is still used as a restaurant featuring local products served in a congenial atmosphere. All of these facilities remain open during the summer months. Off season the restaurant area is used for meetings of the APAL Board and is available for rent to local groups looking for a place to hold meetings or social gatherings.

A major problem for the Jasse is the expected completion in approximately five years of the new four-lane limited-access highway, the A75. In expectation of this event, which under present conditions will probably lead to reduced tourist traffic on the old road, members of the APAL Board are currently participating in a seminar run by a non-Larzac professional specializing in local development. Various projects, including a possible expansion of the building to include better restaurant facilities, are being considered, as are other possible ways of increasing the facility's attraction to local people and vacationers in the region.

The CIR continues to own and run the *gite* (inn) at Montredon where a village resident has been hired to prepare meals for guests. Its other functions have been absorbed by a larger regional organization the FCIVAM (*Centre d'Information et de Vulgarisation pour l'Agriculture et le Milieu Rural*). The FCIVAM organizes workshops concerned with local development projects and job training for local people seeking new professional outlets. Alice Monier, formerly the CIR coordinator, now functions as the local FCIVAM administrator, continuing in her role as an advisor to Larzac associations and as a source for the preparation of grant proposals.

I should also note that the Larzac schools, in the north on the farm of L'Hôpital, and in the south, in La Blaquererie, both continue to function with approximately the same number of pupils, filled in part with offspring of the grown children of older farmers. This second generation, needless to say, was able to take over farms still intact because of the victory.

CURRENT PARTICIPATION IN LARZAC ASSOCIATIONS

Although the Larzac community remains strong today, nineteen years after the end of the struggle, most of the current active participants in Larzac associations are either former militants who came to the plateau between 1971 and 1981 or those who took up residence after the victory. Currently *purs porcs* rarely participate in planning sessions. This does not mean, however, that they have absented themselves from plateau affairs. At times of crisis the Larzac continues to count on most current and former militants, including *purs porcs*, to participate actively in its demonstrations. The McDonald's action is one case in point, out of many.

An important change on the Larzac and its neighboring areas is the growing influence of the *Confédération Paysanne*, particularly among younger farmers. Plateau veterans are not totally absent from this new and dynamic union, however. José Bové, Alain Desjardin, Christian Roqueirol, and Robert Calazel are among the many who are active participants. The *Confédération Paysanne* has also been joined by some older *purs porcs*, while others who have not yet joined have taken their first steps in this direction by quitting the FDSEA. Of these, many express their intention to shortly become members of the new union.

CHRONOLOGY OF EVENTS

In what follows I present a short chronology and summary of events that have taken place on the Larzac since the first edition of this book was published.

1990

Elizabeth Petitcolin who, with one other veterinarian, serves the Larzac community, traveled to the Near East where she established relations with a group of Palestinians in the occupied territories. This led to the formation of a support group on the Larzac and, more recently, the sale of crafts made by Palestinian women at La Jasse. As we shall see below, contacts between the Larzac and nonviolent Palestinian activists have continued ever since Elizabeth Petitcolin's first effort.

1992

On the 13th October, two representatives of the small milk producers' minority union, the SPLB (organized by Larzac militants, among them José Bové and Guy Tarlier), attempted to enter the building in which a meeting of the *Confédération Roquefort* was taking place. They were confronted by militants of the SEB (Union of Sheep Farmers) who blocked their entry by backing a car against the entrance. José Bové managed to get his leg in the door before it was blocked and, as a result, was injured in the confrontation. This led him to bring charges of assault against the SEB. Later in 1994, perhaps partially as a result of this incident, plus a later action in which members of the SPLB successfully occupied *Confédération* headquarters, the new union was finally recognized as a legitimate partner in the joint union-producers association, the *Confédération Roquefort*. Since that date they have exercised a minority representation at the negotiation table in which important decisions are taken jointly by milk producers and the industrialists of Roquefort.

On the 23rd October to the 4th November 1992, Pierre and Christiane Burguière and Marizette Tarlier flew to the Tuamotu archipelago in French Polynesia to demonstrate the Larzac's solidarity with the people of Matiava Island involved in a protest against the proposed development of a phosphate mine. Matiavans feared with good cause that the project would lead to significant environmental pollution of their island and its surrounding waters. This voyage, suggested by François Roux, the human rights advocate and long-term Larzac lawyer, was financed primarily by the Larzac Foundation (as it was still called). After their return from Polynesia Christiane Burguière described the situation in Matiava in an article she wrote for GLL. In this way she contributed to public awareness among militants in France of issues that are rarely, if ever, reported in the mainstream national media.

This first trip to Polynesia by Larzac militants began a continuing and increasingly intense relationship between the natives of this remote French colony and the Larzac which continues to this day. Typically, this first in a series of contacts between the Larzac and French Polynesia came to fruition as a result of actions instigated by one off-plateau Larzac militant, François Roux, was financed by one Larzac association, the Larzac Foundation, and was carried out by three inhabitants of the plateau. Finally the news of this event was brought to the attention of militants in other parts of France via GLL.

1993

Shortly after the struggle ended, farmers on the Larzac who sold to Roquefort were faced with milk quotas based on their previous milk production. Larzac militants who sold to Roquefort had agreed that 300 hectoliters of milk per season, per family, was the necessary minimum to support farmers and their families. Many of the new arrivals caught in a start up period when their production was low were assigned quotas well below the minimum. Other newly installed farmers arrived too late to even enter the quota system. Still other new arrivals had decided to go into meat production rather than milk their animals. This choice was disastrous since prices for lamb fell continuously from the 1980s onward.

It was André (Dédé) Parenti who decided to develop a project to help his less fortunate colleagues. Parenti came to the Larzac from a Paris working class suburb to occupy what would become an SCTL farm. A hard worker and devoted to his new profession, he was able to win an adequate quota from Roquefort in time to make a decent living in his new profession. To realize his project Parenti, with eventual financial aid from APAL, signed up in 1993 for a two-year management training course that would provide the expertise to set up a cooperative cheese production factory to be run jointly by himself and other farmers who, for the reasons mentioned above, had been excluded from Roquefort. His training completed and investments secure from loans offered by Larzac militants on and off the plateau, the Coop opened in 1995. In its first years severe financial problems emerged. Basically these were due to a lack of experience with the ins and outs of commercialization, making it hard to find retail outlets. But, by 1998, the situation improved as the Coop succeeded in finding a wholesale market for its cheeses. At present it is a going enterprise. Seven farms provide milk and eight employees work in production and sales. If the factory had not proved successful these individuals and their families would most likely have been obliged to abandon the Larzac. Of all the farmer-members of the Coop, Dédé is the only one to have risked his own secure quota for the unknowns of this new facility.

1994

In 1981, Francine Gellot and her companion, Jean-Claude Sanchez, took up residence at La Clapade, one of the farms the army had bought from a nonfarmer during the struggle. They proposed to raise blackface sheep for meat production. Under the expropriation rules former owners had the right to buy back properties from the government but, content with the profits they had drawn from the sales, most did not. La Clapade was an exception to the rule. When its former owner laid claim to it, threatening to expel Gellot and Sanchez by force, the Larzac responded with a massive protest. Organized under the aegis of APAL the participants, many of them former militants from the plateau and Millau, showed the continuing strength in the ranks of the movement. As a result the farm's original owner decided to quit the Larzac. In 1994 Gellot and Sanchez agreed to buy the farm buildings and, at the same time, just over 58 hectares of land were purchased by the GFAs for 215,245 francs, about $36,000. Today La Clapade occupies additional hectares rented from the SCTL and produces premium meat sold directly to consumers by way of the GIE.

A few years after the end of the struggle, Suzanna Moreau and her husband, Roger, both members of L'Arche and among the original settlers at Les Truels, moved to an indigenous community in Argentina near the borders with Bolivia and Chile. Their intention was to develop a range of self-help projects for the indigenous people. These included a bakery and the direct sale in France of locally-made woollen products. Suzanna, herself an Argentinean as well as a trained musician, set about organizing a performance group with the help of the Argentinean pianist, Miguel Angel Estrella and his association, *Musique Esperance* (Music Hope). In addition to children from Argentina the group has members form nearby border villages in

Bolivia and Chile. Their specialty is Andean folk-music. In the winter of 1994, the group gave several successful performances in France, including the Larzac, to raise money for the children's communities. The ties between the Moreaus and the Larzac remain strong as residents of the plateau continue to support their work.

On September 17th and 18th 1994, three Larzac associations, the CIR, Le Cun, and APAL welcomed two Palestinians, Judeh and Kwala Abdulla to the Larzac to study local agriculture. At the time Judeh was executive director of The Palestinian Agricultural Relief Committee and her husband worked for the International Family Planning Committee. This visit strengthened the ties between Palestinian militants and the Larzac that had been established earlier by Elizabeth Petitcolin.

1995

The French government announced its intention to conduct underground nuclear tests at its atomic laboratory in Moroa, French Polynesia. The Larzac, represented by APAL, sent five plateau militants to protest the tests. These were: José Bové, Jean-Luc Bernard, Alain Desjardin, Christine Thelen, and Christian Roqueirol. Jacques Barthélémy from Millau joined the group as did Thérèse Parodi from L'Arche and Pierre Bovy from *Stop Essais*. Funds for the trip were solicited by APAL via the Foundation Larzac.

In Papeete, the capital of Tahiti, the group met with Polynesian militants based in Faa'a, the second largest town on the main island. This contact was made through the good offices of François Roux, who had previously worked with a group of independentists led by the mayor of Faa'a, Oscar Temaru. Once on the island the Larzac group participated with the Polynesians in a series of anti-test demonstrations. A few days after the group's arrival Christian Roqueirol and Jose Bové set out for the test area, José on a Greenpeace ship that intended to enter the test area illegally, Christian on another vessel. When Greenpeace arrived at the edge of the forbidden zone, Bové joined a group of activists in a Zodiac (a rubber motorboat) which steered directly into the test area. After playing cat and mouse with the French Marines their boat was sunk and they were arrested. Bové was fished out of the water by his hair and, with the others, brought back to Papeete in handcuffs. He was later released without charges.

As the protest against the tests heated up it was rumored that the head of the local government, Gaston Flosse, was ready to leave the island in order to avoid any confrontation that might take place against him personally. The Polynesian activists led by a union leader,

Hiro Tefaarere, decided to block the take off of Flosse's plane by staging a sit-in on the runway at the Faa'a airport. When they arrived they were met by a force of hostile *Garde Mobile* (national police) and a riot ensued during which some damage was done to the terminal. Four members of the Larzac contingent were arrested along with a large group of Polynesians. Although the Larzac militants had not participated in the riot—they were there to bear witness to any action that might take place—they were all charged with rioting and the destruction of property.

1996

The church at St. Martin du Larzac, an historic site for militants, was restored by a committee of Larzac activists and reconsecrated by a priest from La Cavalerie. Claude Baillon, whose designs for new stained-glass windows in the church won a competition organized by the *Pèlerin* magazine, contributed his skills as an artist and craftsman to the restoration. After the work was completed the church took on new life as both a religious and cultural center for the plateau. Concerts of sacred and folk music, as well as art exhibitions, are held there each year during the Christmas season and in the summer months.

In the same year Alain Desjardin was instrumental in the formation of a new association, *Environnement et Elevage*. (Environment and Animal Husbandry) to protest the installation of an industrial pig farm in the commune of Cornus at the foot of the Larzac. Successful in its attempt to stop the project the association has continued to look out for and protest against any other such potentially polluting installations in the ecologically fragile region.

1998

Two hundred militants from the *Confédération Paysanne*, José Bové among them, attacked a Novartis company store house for genetically modified corn seeds. After searching several buildings in the Novartis complex they successfully found their target. Crying "Death to transgenic corn!" the demonstrators sprayed the seeds with fire extinguishers. At four in the afternoon José Bové speaking for the *Confédération* of the Aveyron told the crowd that the then Minister of Agriculture, Louis Pansec, and the Minister of the Environment, Dominique Voynet, were both responsible for allowing the importation of transgenic corn into France "without the most elementary precautions" concerning its danger to the environment and to human consumers. On their way back to the Aveyron, three of the demonstrators, Bové among them, were arrested and charged with denaturing the seeds. Their trial took place on the third of February in the presence, according to GLL, of a thousand people. None of the accused were punished by the court.

On the 6th September, four Larzac militants charged in the rioting at the airport of Faa'a returned to French Polynesia for trial along with the more than 60 Tahitiens who were also charged. All were found guilty but the members of the Larzac delegation were released without punishment. In contrast, a large number of the Tahitians were sentenced to long prison terms as well as the loss of civil privileges. After the trial the Larzac delegation announced that it would return to support the Tahitians when the appeals were heard by the court in the spring of the year 2000. [For a further discussion of these events see the extracts below drawn from the January 2000 interview with Alan Desjardin.]

A meeting of AC, an organization of unemployed people, took place at Le Cun on the 14th July, Bastille Day, the French national holiday. Since 1994 this group has been fighting for the rights of the unemployed and, according to GLL for September–October 1998, "have, in spite of the difficulty organizing people in a situation of exclusion, achieved a significant amount of attention in the press, and have won some victories in certain departments of France. These include, for example: free public transpiration and Christmas bonuses." However, the GLL article goes on to regret "the overly Parisian aspect of the association and the fact that AC groups in the Aveyron were not invited to the meeting." The paper also notes that "A debate with the *Confédération* and the inhabitants of the Larzac would have been interesting for the assembled group." Here we note the Larzac's desire, as during the struggle, to be active participants with groups that come in from the outside.

1999

The Larzac and Le Cun welcomed a delegation of farmers from India who made up part of the 'Intercontinental Caravan' representing farmers from the state of Kamatalna who were to spend a month traveling in Europe in order to denounce the WTO, the production and use of genetically modified crops, as well as other problems of interest to the third world. A group of these peasants, along with representatives of the *Confédération Paysanne*, traveled to the city of

Montpellier where they destroyed a plantation of transgenic rice produced by the CIRAD (*Centre de Coopération Internationale en Agriculture pour le Développement*). Three members of the *Confédération* were arrested, among them José Bové.

As far back as 1997 some on the Larzac began to discuss a project that was to divide the plateau as never before. This was the proposed implantation of a large group of windmills. The Larzac is well known for its strong dominant north and south winds. Some inhabitants of the plateau see it as an ideal place for wind power, particularly since the plateau was already known publicly as a model for ecologically sound alternatives to mass production and consumption as well as for the adoption by some farms of alternative forms of energy. Le Cun, for example, has for several years drawn its electricity from a small wind generator and La Salvetat has generated hot water from solar power ever since its opening. Most, if not all, of the Larzac members of the *Confédération Paysanne* favored the project from the moment it was announced, as did Alain Desjardin (the local spokesperson for the Green Party), but the regional Party was not unanimous on this issue. Gerald Galtier, for example, a Larzac farmer and National Treasurer of the Party, expressed immediate hostility to the windmills, arguing that they would disfigure the *causse*. He went on to suggest that it would be better to install them on the sea coast in zones already industrialized.

The project presented by a non–Larzac industrialist originally concerned the east Larzac around Montredon near the military camp. There, villagers greeted the project positively even though it would be in their own backyard. The installation in Montredon was vetoed, however, by the military commander of the camp who feared that the high towers necessary for the windmills would interfere with the operation of aircraft as well as the use of high caliber artillery and missiles fired within the base. The project also aroused controversy at the annual meeting of the GFA General Assembly when it came up for discussion. Most of the GFA farmers present opposed the installation, while a majority of shareholders expressed dismay at the possibility that the ecological Larzac could reject it.

After the army had declared its opposition to the project in the eastern part of the plateau the proposal was reformulated and made to farmers in the west. There the majority was opposed from the start claiming that the installation would, according to the plan, be too close to a number of dwellings. Some also expressed the feeling that the windmills would disfigure the unique natural beauty of the plateau. A public meeting was held at La Jasse to discuss the issue and the assembled group was asked to fill out a ballot asking each respondent to rate a set of questions on a scale of one through five, with five representing the most positive attitude. The ballots were counted by adding all the numbers together. Although the majority of *individuals* present were *for* the project, the totaled numbers favored the opposition since, at least according to those in favor, those opposed had systematically placed zeros at each question.

When we asked informants about the debate, individuals on both sides expressed considerable anguish over the bitterness it had generated. Fortunately, however, the Larzac is by no means foreign to debates. The plateau has seen many other disagreements and has always managed to overcome them. Although this one was particularly rancorous, the vast majority of those concerned maintained their usual civility in later meetings and even during social gatherings. The restoration of tranquillity even in this difficult case would have eventually occurred, but the rapidity with which things calmed down was due, no doubt, to the next big unifying event on the Larzac, the 'hamburger war'.

EXTRACTS FROM RECENT INTERVIEWS

Although we have long since embarked on another project we have never lost contact with the Larzac. We are members of APAL and The Montredon Association, continue to subscribe to GLL, support La Salvetat, and continue to socialize with our many Larzac friends. In January 2000 we interviewed eleven Larzac militants, one a new arrival, and another a returnee who was among the first nonresidents to settle on the plateau during the struggle. What follows are extracts from these interviews that deal specifically with the divisive windmill question, the demonstration at McDonald's, the Seattle meeting of the WTO, José Bové as a leading Larzac militant, and the Tahiti trials and their aftermath. To clarify who is speaking, our own questions and occasional comments are placed within square brackets in each of the interview extracts.

PIERRE AND CHRISTIANE BURGUIÈRE

Windmills

[P.] It was a very hot discussion. Those who were for the project were scandalized by the attitude of those who were against it. [P. and C. are for the project.] Some even said that if EDF [the national electric company] was *for* the windmills it could *not* be a good idea. One couple living on a remote farm far from the electric lines asked for and were given a generator by EDF so that they could have electricity and now they are against the windmills. [The electricity generated by the windmills would ultimately be sold to EDF.] When we voted on the project at the Jasse we tried to be objective about each separate question rather than automatically marking all of them with a five. In contrast there were fifteen people present opposed to the windmills and all of them put a zero on every question. That falsified the total vote against. [We ask: What about the argument that wind power should come from off-shore installations] P. It has not been proved that sea platforms are ecologically neutral. Apparently there is some danger to fish life.

McDonald's

We did not participate in the demonstration. The problem at the beginning was the planning. Many of us were not informed what the precise limits of the action were to be. Afterwards, people told us that it was wonderful. Some even said that everything had been broken, which is not true. [C.] Pierre was asked to organize a 'service d'ordre' and refused because we were not informed about the plans. [P.] I have participated in many actions organized by the *Confédération Paysanne*, but not this one because they were not precise about what they were going to do. Things can get out of hand. That's the difference between their demonstrations and the way we used to do things during the struggle. [C. notes that] the only 'violent' action that took place during the Larzac struggle was the destruction of army records in the camp. [P. says:] I have often told members of the *Confédération* that they should be more careful when they organize a demonstration. I need to know exactly what we will do and what the limits are. The Larzac never went beyond the strict limits of what had been planned in advance. The new people [primarily members of the *Confédération*] want to have their own experience and, therefore, avoid using the Larzac struggle as a model. While it's true that we also made mistakes, it would be useful if the new militants would use our own past experiences. On the other hand, the demonstration was a success!

The fact that the judge arrested several demonstrators united us. It's the custom on the Larzac that when friends are in trouble we try to help them out. This case is no different. A recent settler on the plateau who doesn't like one of those arrested nonetheless telephoned around to see if he could enlist others to help to raise that person's bail money. When the McDonald's demonstrators were arrested we supported them without asking questions about who each of them was. This is just one example of the continuing solidarity on the Larzac.

It s true that many of the new people want to construct 'their own' Larzac, and it will not be the same as ours, but they forget that they are here thanks to the struggle. The fact that there are new settlers here is a good thing and I have nothing against them. But they should not forget what came before them. When there is a demonstration here we all [original militants] join in and don't look at the affliation of those involved in the planning. When the *Confédération* demonstrates I join in. [P. has quit the FDSEA but has not yet become a member of the new union although he tells us he plans to.] [C. adds:] There is another problem. The militants in Millau tend to resent the Larzac and want to act on their own initiative [an old problem that goes back to friction between militants on the plateau and the Millau Committees during the struggle].

José Bové

I am a peasant who, as a result of the Larzac struggle, has become a militant. José is just the opposite. He is a militant who has become a peasant. We need one another. He has spent more of his life here than in Bordeaux. He needs the Larzac as a point of reference. He will never miss a lambing on the farm.

ALAIN DESJARDIN

[Alain tells us that La Salvetat is in high gear and that he is very happy about his full-time replacements, but that he will continue to live there as well as continue his farming activities. (He is in charge of the gardening, including 800 trees, and the flowers.) With more time for political activity, he fights against the installation of non-ecological projects in the region and works hard to get the largest number and variety of people to support efforts. He has founded a new local political group, *Démocratie Municipale*. He will be head of the list in La Couvertoirade and hopes to be its next mayor. As a Green he has been involved in negotiations with the Socialist Party candidate for the mayoral election in Millau and the latter has agreed that the Millau list (the elections are by proportional representation), following the parliamentary majority, will include 15 Socialists, five

Greens, five Communists, and two Left Radicals. Alain serves as a national delegate to the Green Party Committee on Agriculture, is a member of the Aveyron Regional Committee and a reporter for the National Council of the Green Party.]

Polynesia

Four of us were at the Faa'a airport when there was a strong confrontation between the Polynesian union members and the police. Sixty-three Polynesians were arrested and charged. The Polynesians were tried in the local court and sentenced in 1998. All this is completely illegal. In organizing the demonstration, the union, A-Tia-i-mua, had followed correct legal procedure. They had informed the government of their intention to strike at the airport which is what the law states. Hiro Tefaarere, the head of the union, was given a prison sentence and deprived of his civil rights, including his right to vote, for five years.

The purpose of the demonstration was to block the departure of Gaston Flosse on a regular flight out of the territory. When we arrived, there was a mass of *Garde Mobile* already on the tarmac. To gain access the demonstrators broke down the fence onto the runway with a truck [Police in France often tolerate this type of action as long as no one is injured.] When we returned to France after the trial we felt that we had to demonstrate our solidarity with the Polynesians as well as inform the French public of what had really happened.

In 1999 we held a meeting at the Assemblée Nationale [the Fench Congress] with the Green Party and other concerned groups, including churches. We wanted to keep pressure on the government to admit that the punishments given by the judge were too severe. Additionally, we wanted to inform people that the atomic tests in Polynesia were for the protection of white people and had occurred in a foreign place colonized by France.

During the original trial we felt the need to support those Polynesians present who wished to assert their personal and cultural dignity. We suggested that their witnesses testify in their own language. When the women present in the audience were asked by the court to remove their hats, which is contrary to Polynesian custom, we protested against this request. The translators assigned by the court were unacceptable. The Polynesians said: "He does not translate what we feel in our guts." Our lawyer, François Roux, demanded a substitute translator. The new one was also unacceptable to the Polynesians, who they said was known to be a thief. Finally, a third person, a Protestant minister, was deemed acceptable. We felt that we had successfully helped the people to express their own culture during the trial.

When we addressed the Court we urged the Tahitians to stand up in the face of colonialism. We were there to encourage these Polynesians to speak for themselves. To our great joy we saw these people say to the three white French judges: "You should not be here! We are ready to be judged, but by judges from our own people." They went on to explain their actions, the result of a series of unanswered grievances, including: a loss of lives due to radiation poisoning, high unemployment on the islands without any insurance, grinding poverty, etc. When it was our turn to testify we told the judge why we were there. I spoke about my experience with French colonialism during the Algerian war. When we left the island a group of women told us: "When you return to France do at least one thing. Bear witness to what you have experienced here, to our frustrations, and the denial of our liberties."

We have continued to maintain contact with our Polynesian friends both officially as a Larzac group and through friendships forged during our joint actions. We returned to France with symbolic gifts, a sign of these ties. Each was given a shirt made by the wife of a condemned man. Additionally, as we were leaving the island, a black pearl wrapped in a bit of cotton was pressed into our hands by a fisherman, one of the condemned individuals. This was in recognition of the difference between us and those other whites who had colonized the islands. In the year 2000 we intend to return to Papeete for the appeal's hearing. The trip will allow us to witness the attitude of the present government towards the people of the islands as well as to make sure that these events will not be forgotten here in France.

We intend to fight to reduce the wounds caused by French colonialism and by the trial. Later we hope to welcome one or more of the Polynesians here on the Larzac where he or she can work as an apprentice in order to learn our farming methods. We need to help them achieve the right to live decently at home from their own productive activities in the full dignity they deserve.

Windmills

[When we ask him about this he makes a face and laughs.] At La Salvetat we are for the windmills. One of the founders of *La Cardabella*, Alain Cabanes, is a member of an orgnization that plans alternative energy projects for buildings in urban and rural areas. It was he who directed the installation of solar energy panels at La Salvetat and suggested other means for us to conserve energy. As a Green I have tried to remain consistent in my approach to problems. I agree with the current policy of the Minister of the Environment. [A member of the Green Party]. There are four or five tendencies in the Green Party. I see myself directly involved in these matters on the local level. When the windmill project was first proposed I found it interesting. I am with those ecologists who try to think in long range terms and recognize that at present France has the highest percentage of nuclear power anywhere in the world. I am for economizing energy as well as for changing to renewable forms. During the debate concerning the windmills I found myself in the midst of Greens who were against the project and who were also my friends. Their reasons include the belief that the windmills will be bad for both the fauna and flora of the Larzac as well as spoil the natural beauty of the *causse*. They also oppose energy production in an area that has a surplus. Some say that they would accept it if it were for local consumption. I agree that the Aveyron produces a surplus of energy, but why not send this excess power to other parts of France that are less well supplied. Other opponents of the windmills are Communist Party members in Millau. On the plateau some ecologists, some farmers, artists and people with secondary residences who opposed the project essentially said of it: "It's O.K but not in my garden".

Those of us for the project feel that the money generated could be redistributed through negotiations to various communes to be used for good works related to ecology. Additionally, we were ready to negotiate a reduction of 50% of the number of windmills in the several communes concerned. Besides there are windmills in Holland and artists come to paint them. No one claims that they are ugly, although I will admit that the modern ones are bigger. I feel that the people here were not prepared properly for the debate. Also the ones most listened to were those who made the most noise. As usual they were the ones picked out by the media.

McDonald's

[Alain tells us that he supported the McDonald's demonstration, but planning for the action could have been better organized. He agrees that old Larzac militants developed an efficient methodology that included careful advance planning.] Now, *some* of the younger people have a tendency to let things get out of hand. But it is also true that these people are searching to fnd their place in the social field. The problem should not be seen as a struggle among individuals. On the Larzac we now have three generations: the old ones who were the precursors, those who arrived during the struggle, and those who came after the victory. If the latter are now trying to assert their independence I'm not against it. I'm for tolerance as well as for an analysis of the present situation.

The Autoroute

The autoroute and its [massive] bridge project represent various dangers. Some on the plateau now realize that it's a stupid project. But we live in a culture that admires autoroutes. Many say that they are safer than secondary roads. But what they forget is that we need other methods to reduce accidents. Alcohol kills, speed kills! Yes, we live in a rural area and we do need cars here to get around, but there is little reflection concerning how we can reduce this need. More importantly we need to reduce our dependence on trucks. We need to reflect on the entire culture of the automobile! The bridge is a material representation of the force of modern technology, but in the name of what? We continually say we are the strongest, we have the best technology, without reflecting on its effects on the environment. We find the money for these projects but it takes money from other projects. All of this reinforces individual egotism.

Seattle and Beyond

We need to reflect on what will happen after events like Seattle. We need to pose questions about what we wish to construct over the long term. What alternatives can we propose? We need to invite people to discuss the meaning of 'progress' in order to control it. We need to raise the question of local autonomy. The autoroute, for example, is for long distance commerce—Dutch tomatoes to Spain and oranges from Spain to Holland. What will people do with the time they gain after the institution of the 35-hour week? [The French Government has passed legislation cutting the normal work week to 35 hours with the goal of stimulating employment.] What purpose does the extra time gained by using the autoroute serve? Many people now have highly mechanized kitchens which allow them to cook a meal rapidly, but what about the pleasure gained from taking the time to prepare an excellent meal? What in the end will we do with all the time promised by these modern developments? We go faster but where are we going? We use our free time to sit in front of the T.V. The *system* eats what we gain elsewhere!

GILLES GESSON

[Gilles Gesson is a recent arrival on the Larzac. A Parisian, university trained as an archivist and involved in journalism, he worked for a time in Paris for a newspaper dedicated to the support of homeless people. He discovered the Larzac while on vacation and fell in love with the region. He would like to stay on indefinitely and feels that he has been welcomed into the Larzac "family." At the time of writing he is living on unemployment benefit and working for GLL as a reporter. It was in this capacity that he went to Seattle with the Millau-Larzac delegation. He also participates at meetings of the APAL Board and in *Larzac Solidarité.*]

Seattle

Most of the French there were from rural areas and concerned with farm problems. These were not my issues but there were many other things happening. I spent a great deal of time with young activists [He speaks English] What astonished me was the average age of these people: between 18–20 years of age, mostly women. They had spent up to six months in Seattle preparing for the demonstrations. I thought at flrst that they had been inspired by Martin Luther King but, without rejecting the idea completely, they said, "not really." Yet, nonviolence was the major glue that tied them together. They were very well disciplined and totally nonviolent in their actions. My perception of them was that their action was totally natural: it was their way of being. Since returning to France I have become convinced that the victory in Seattle was the victory of these young people. Their demonstration was different from what we see in France. It was not a question of manifesting their disagreement with the meeting, but rather of blocking the event – always in a nonviolent way. There was almost no violence at all during the meetings and absolutely none from these young people. They did not throw anything at the police and they were not the ones who broke the display windows of a few shops. I saw a small group of anarchists trying to take down a NIKE sign and these young demonstrators responded by protecting the area, as they shouted "shame on you"! These young people had attended many weeks, in some cases, months of nonviolent workshops. They were sure that they would be arrested. All of them wore stickers on their shirts proclaiming nonviolence and giving their lawyer's phone number. Those who were arrested asked to be paroled immediately or to pay a small fine for what they contended were minor infractions.

The demonstration headquarters resembled a huge squat. People were constantly entering and leaving but everything was precisely organized. There was a huge map of Seattle on the wall. Each neighborhood of the city was indicated and each was assigned to a designated group. People chose their group by affinity—for example, students, pacifists, ecologists. Each group had its particular responsibilities. When the police cleared an area the group involved moved to another zone according to a preconceived plan. It was a kind of pacifistic harassment. There was an astonishing sense of organization!

McDonald's

When I came to the Larzac I said that if there is militant work to do I was ready. I chose the Larzac Foundation because it works for solidarity between the plateau and the outside. But I wondered where the solidarity was, for example, with the unemployed. When people began to talk about McDonald's I felt that it was not the most important thing to do given the other problems in the area. I was present the day of the demonstration as a reporter for GLL. After the event there was a debate on the plateau about whether or not the demonstration was violent or nonviolent. In my opinion it was nonviolent. The word 'saccage' to describe it is totally inappropriate. There were tractors present that could have been used to tear down the building but this, of course, did not happen. Some parts of the building were dismantled but these were prefabricated sections that were taken down carefully so as not to break them. Of course, there was some slight damage, but most of this was accidental. I believe that the demonstration was not really against McDonald's *per se*. It was actually carried out in reference to the tax imposed by the WTO on Roquefort cheese as well as a protest against the power of the multinational corporations. It was most certainly not anti-American.

Windmills

I do not have an opinion for or against the project. I did not participate in the discussions because I do not know enough about the issues. I did feel that there were valid arguments on both sides. I was, however, struck by two contradictory things. There was complete transparence concerning the project and the vote was certainly a very positive thing. That's normal on the *causse*. On the other hand I was surprised by the verbal violence that occurred during the debates. But it's also true that an immediate attempt at mediation occurred and that's very positive. In the end I think the debate showed that the people of the Larzac are as human as anyone else. That, after all, is a positive thing.

MARIZETTE TARLIER

José Bové and the McDonald's demonstration

I'm very fond of José—I'm a 'groupie'. We never imagined the degree of importance that the affair would achieve. People like José churn up the plateau. I am very thankful for this. He keeps us from falling asleep. It's a reminder of what we lived through. Heidi [a German militant during the struggle and co-author of a book about it who had just died and had asked that her ashes be buried on the Larzac] said that we must always remember the struggle. The day the demonstration occurred I called Jose and asked him if it was going to be violent and, if so, I said I would not participate. He assured me that there would be no violence, explaining that the plan was to symbolically dismantle part of the building without inflicting significant damage. It is true that it got a bit out of hand and some of the youngest demonstrators did break a few things, but Jose himself stopped them. The term 'saccage' is a terrible exaggeration. It was really a symbolic action. The judge in Millau was much too severe with the people involved. She only listened to the manager of the McDonald's who inflated the amount of monetary damage. There was never any official evaluation of it. The press spent a lot of time on the fact that Léon [Maillé] had come with his chain saw, but that was only to cut down the sign in front of the construction site. We drove through Millau afterwards and the ambiance was excellent. It is important to realize that this demonstration followed on the importation of hormonally treated beef from the U.S. and the 'mad cow' problem. It was time to act. If we had been there to prevent people from entering a working McDonald's I would not have participated.

José does tend to annoy some people, but few of these live on the Larzac. Those I know are in no way bothered by his prominence. Some people were upset when he appeared on the cover of VSD [a popular, generally unpolitical weekly] because the article was about French culinary products rather than McDonald's or Seattle. José himself was upset by this and told me that he had not been informed as to how his image was to be used. Lately his popularity has grown to the point where even some of the Roquefort producers see him as a hero. On the other hand there is a monstrous jealously between the

SPLB and the SEB and, of course, the FDSEA is very unhappy with José success. They spread all kinds of rumors about him the way they did about Guy—for example, during the struggle, there was even the charge that Guy had been trained by the German Red Brigades!

There is a problem between the *Confédération Paysanne* and the old militants. The *Confédération* asked us to participate in the demonstration but we were never informed about how things were supposed to go and that certainly bothered us. Also most members of the *Confédération* do not participate in APAL. We can understand that. It's not that the younger people here don't want to have anything to do with the Larzac, but they do say that the struggle is history and they do have a tendency to treat us like 'anciens combattants'. I don't feel that I personally fit into this category.

Windmills

There were conflicts. There was a group that had worked on the project for some time and, when they thought they were prepared, they informed other people on the plateau about the project. The information was not well thought out. I wanted to raise the issue at APAL but was discouraged from doing it. These feelings were shared by some others. In general whenever there was some information about the project it was poorly presented. People on the west of the plateau said. "We are going to suffer from the autoroute and we are now unhappy about the windmill project." It would be fine in Montredon, but there would have been windmills within 500 meters of the Boissans farm house [part of her GAEC, in the west of the plateau] and that's too close. There were those who were against it because they felt it would ruin the scenery here. No one said clearly that the project [had a positive side because it] would bring more people to the Jasse. The questionnaire was not well thought out. People tended to camp on their positions. Those against the project rated every question with a zero and that made the other side very angry. Now, considering what I have just lived through I don't want any more fights. The windmill question created a very bad atmosphere.

BERNARD AND GINETTE PARSY

Windmills

[B.] If one is against nuclear power one must be for renewable energy no matter what project. But in this case there were to be 44 windmills, many of them close to peoples' dwellings. The project also varied through time. The people at Montredon were for it but the army objected. If the power was to be used locally, in Millau, for example, we would have been for it, but there is more than is needed here and it would have been transported elsewhere, with a significant loss of energy along the transmission lines. The industrialist who presented the project admitted that the future of wind power was in offshore installations and that the Larzac was chosen for symbolic reasons, as a show place. The problem can be looked at from various points of view—political, economic, ecological. (Shareholders in the GFAs were shocked by those farmers on GFA land who opposed the project.) Since the vote at the Jasse, what remains of the project concerns neither the land of the GFAs or the SCTL. The windmills will only be set up on private property. But the debate did cause rancor and many people are bitter about it. The Larzac was divided 50–50 on this project. It is good, however, that there was an open debate on the issue. Perhaps we will eventually be able to reach a compromise.

McDonald's

There was no real violence. It was, however, a bit disagreeable. If I had known that there was be to any dismantling I would not have gone. But looking back now with a bit of distance I can say that nothing serious happened. A great deal of noise was generated in proportion to the actual damage that occurred at the site. McDonald's opened on the date originally announced. As the debate continued the manager kept lowering his estimate of the damage and the McDonald's never brought civil charges. I have nothing against McDonald's but it has symbolic significance in relation to multinational corporations. Since the demonstration there has been a snowball effect. The judge committed grave errors and thus put water in the millwheel of the *Confédération*. Her decisions were out of all proportion to the facts. The judge is new to this area—young and inexperienced. Perhaps she thinks the Larzac people are anarchists and revolutionaries.

For the news media, José is the leader and the Larzac is seen as being at the center of the demonstration even though it was planned by the *Confédération*. They sponsored other actions that were not reported in the press. The fuss over José helps the *Confédération* to gain new members. We are heading towards a situation in which there will be two major agricultural unions. We don't think that there should only be one union and the FDSEA must come to accept the existence of the *Confédération*. We are closer to the *Confédération* than to the FNSEA and we tend to support the former's actions.

Transgenics

We should not forbid all genetically modified products *a priori*. The problem should be treated on a case by case basis. It would be helpful, for example, if we could find a gene in a tropical plant that worked against cancer, that could be inserted into some crop. Why not put it into wheat? But I'm against it if it deregulates the natural system.

Current relations on the plateau

The people of the Larzac are very welcoming. When we arrived at the end of the struggle we were accepted immediately and this is still the rule. People here can have differences of opinion, even passionate differences, and yet invite home those with whom one disagrees. People here are able to talk to one another without aggression. The Larzac is like an extended family.

LÉON AND OSLA MAILLÉ

McDonald's

[L.] The action in Millau against McDonald's was completely ordinary, but what happened afterwards was extraordinary! The installation of McDonald's in Millau and the tax on Roquefort in the United States was a coincidence, but it was lucky for us. If the demonstration had been in Rodez [a city about 50 miles away] we probably would not have participated.

The McDonald's site was not 'trashed'. People took down some prefabricated parts of the building and put them in a trailer. That made a lot of noise but there was very little damage. We did cut down the sign in front of the site and for this I was imprisoned as a *casseur* (breaker of property). Christian Roqueirol was on the roof of the building painting slogans on it, but with water paint that was easily washed off the next day.

We were arrested five days after the action. The police came to my house at six in the morning. I was asleep and didn't hear them at the door. Finally they phoned the house. I looked out the window and saw them. I showered, ate my breakfast, and then went out and was arrested. The adventure came after that. As I see it, all those charged were enemies of Millau's mayor. The president of the tribunal and the judge are both his friends. Last week the judge was interviewed by *Humanité* [the Communist Party daily]. She admitted that she had just completed her training and knew nothing about the Larzac. The demonstration was organized by the *Confédération*, but many Larzac people who are not in the union participated.

Most people here are astonished by José and very proud of him. The members of the SEB are, of course, very angry with him. He is seen by the public as *Astérix le Gaulois*. He never wears a tie or a suit. He looks different. He's not the person one is used to seeing on T.V. The media loved the story. Last week we had two journalists from Canada at the house. José told me that he received a postcard from the president of the WTO saying that he was sorry to not have had more time to talk with him during the Seattle meetings.

[Earlier] José went with a group of Indians [from India] to Montpellier where they destroyed a planting of transgenic rice. If he hadn't been there to lead it the action would have been impossible. José has the skill to turn things against the enemy. Next week he is going to Paris to have lunch with the Minister of Agriculture and the Secretary of the Socialist Party! He's happy to visit such people because it annoys the majority union, but here no one is jealous of him.

[We ask: In your opinion, how has the Larzac changed since the struggle?] The Larzac has ripened. The original militants are now older and perhaps wiser. In the Larzac [elementary] school you now find the children of the children of the struggle. During these seventeen or eighteen years we have become calmer, but the rest of the country thinks we are still excited. When we meet them they say, "Ah, you are from the Larzac!" If you *are* from the plateau you have the right to speak differently. People from elsewhere often do not have the courage to speak up or to act. The Larzac was a school for all of us. The interest generated by the demonstration against McDonald's was certainly due to the fact that the Larzac was involved. Of course, we also thank the judge in Millau. Without her mistakes things would not have escalated as they did. Also there was a void in the media at the time. One year before or one year afterwards it would probably not have generated the same interest. It occurred just after the latest news broke concerning the 'mad cow' scare and the decision of Europe to require France to import English beef. Then there was the contaminated Coke scandal in Belgium. The demonstrations elsewhere against McDonald's did not get the same publicity that ours did but, then *we* know how to deal with the media. We had telephone calls from old supporters who told us they were happy to see that things were heating up again!

Windmills

Yes, there was a lot of tension over this issue. It was like a glass of water—half full or half empty. When a group of us went to see the windmills at Carcassonne [a city about 100 miles from the Larzac] some decided for the project immediately, but others were immediately against it. There are those who find the windmills ugly. They are not so ugly! But on the Larzac one would be able to see them from very far away. The question is, then, would they be ugly on the Larzac? I think they would. [His wife, Osla, says she does not agree.

The industrialist who proposed the windmill project admitted that he chose the Larzac for its positive image. The rent to be paid to the communes and to the land owners is to be 5000 francs per year [about $800] with an additional 40, 000 francs going to the commune. At the GFA annual meeting Francine Gellot and Jean-Paul Delaitte spoke against the project. The shareholders were surprised by the attitude expressed by those against the project.

MICHÈLE VINCENT

McDonald's

I was at work during the demonstration. I couldn't take time off that month since in August there are too many people on vacation. I arrived at the site when it was over. Nonetheless, I found the atmosphere vey positive. There were many people there, both from Millau and the Larzac. When I arrived they had just begun to load a trailor with the things they had taken down at the site to cart them to the sub-prefecture. In order to understand the action you have to see the context. There were many local people watching from their windows. The demonstrators were shouting slogans and playing gongs. José was careful to stop the demonstrators from throwing things into the courtyard of the subprefecture. José never lost control of the crowd.

One of those arrested was assigned to his residence rather than jailed. Later, films showed him with his hands in his pockets. It was clear that he had not broken anything. The demonstration was organized by the *Confédération*. The union wanted to be sure that they got the credit for the action against McDonald's. On the other hand, the practical experience of the Larzac veterans who participated was very important. Larzac militants often say that demonstrations should go according to rules developed during the struggle. The proof that this is correct is that when Léon [Maillé] was arrested no one was capable of dealing with the press. Léon has had 25 years experience with the media. José is the only other person capable of acting as a spokesperson and he too was in jail. Marizette [Tarlier] played an important role in organizing the support committee for those arrested. She was also capable of calling on the experience gained during the Larzac struggle. She reminded us to keep a list of all those who had sent support money and to be sure to thank them immediately for their donations.

Of course things happened so fast. Organizing the reaction after the arrests was not easy. Since the *Confédération* wanted to maintain control they refused to structure the movement that emerged to protest the judge's decision. We were in a hurry, given the necessity to act immediately, and it was very difficult for us to prepare meetings on the spur of the moment. Those who had the most experience and who could shout the loudest ended up taking over the meetings. Also, I felt that the women concerned were not respected for the role they played in developing support for those arrested. Under the *Confédération's* direction women are generally excluded from planning. F. [a male member of the *Confédération*] said that we would discuss this problem later. The wives of *Confédération* members are not themselves union members. We were insistent on showing that women formed the basis of the support committee. We organized two meetings of women who had participated in the actions. There were about fifteen people at the first meeting and ten at the second. We raised the question of violence because we had noted that the adolescents and children who had broken things during the McDonald's demonstration were not reigned in by their parents. We also raised the general question of women's participation.

When Richard Maillé [Léon's son] and Gilbert Fenestras [Larzac farmer and militant] were to appear in court the police in Millau were apparently afraid that some kind of violence might occur. There was a large crowd stationed in front of the tribunal. To avoid the crowd the police ushered Richard and Gilbert to the judges chambers by way of an adjacent high school courtyard. José realized what was happening and also tried to enter the building via the school yard. The school principal, a young pregnant woman, immediately protested against what she felt was an invasion of her domain. The discussion between José and the riot police became very heated to the point where a fight seemed imminent and the principal became very upset. We women decided to send three female delegates to talk with her. We explained that the action was not a provocation and that the group had no desire to invade the school. The principal was very touched by our intervention. Later José told us that he had felt very bad for her. I feel strongly that it is important to explain actions to those who are present but not directly involved in them. Some of the men said that this was the opinion of *les bonnes femmes* [just women]. From time to time things have to be dealt with for and by women in the movement.

José Bové

When José was jailed in Montpellier a big protest was organized in front of the prison in which he was held. It was hot and stormy that day. François Pingaud, [a former Larzac militant] who we knew was quite ill with leukemia, was there with his accordion. He was the only one who thought of bringing along an instrument. His presence contributed to the overall spirit of the event. He died a few weeks later. It was a very special moment. There were people there from departments other than the Avreyron—the Gard and the Hérault. I had never been involved with anyone in jail, except during the struggle when Marizette was locked up, and I have rarely been so moved. The building was surrounded by a high wall and José was on the first floor and could not see us. His guards took him up to the top floor of the jail so that he could watch the demonstration.

From time to time some people do express jealously of José, but most realize that he represents the general opinion of the majority. The mobilization for the McDonald's protest and its aftermath were fast and constant. This may have overshadowed some of the 'soldiers,' but it seems to me that there is a permanent dialog on the plateau with very few problems. Some people were shocked by the cover of VSD. [Michèle did not know that José was unaware of the contents of the article in question.] The problems with José are very limited and I believe that it is not a Larzac issue at all. If there is any jealously present it is within the *Confédération* itself. Everyone admits José has an extraordinary skill in mobilizing public opinion. He has considerable talent for pedagogy and a strong ability to analyze any situation. He never speaks out of turn. At one meeting in Millau he addressed the crowd for fifteen minutes with truly astonishing clarity. José carries an image. He is *Astérix*—his mustache—he speaks so well—he remains calm no matter what the situation. Twenty years ago he could not have done things the way he does them now. He is, in a way, the child of Guy Tarlier. During the struggle he would not have had the same capacity to organize or reflect on events. At the time he was in revolt against Guy, the son against the father, but he has matured as others have matured. His ability to reflect on, plan, and carry out events is outstanding.

Windmills

[Michèle does not want to speak about the windmills adding that she was ill at the time. (She had just had an operation and was recuperating). She adds that she heard about the debates and is thankful not to have had to participate.]

JOSÉ BOVÉ

Seattle

[We ask: What impressions did you come away with from Seattle?]
Many, many things. To summarize: 1. The number of people and associations that were present during the events in Seattle. We were told that there would be many but the actual number was unimaginable. There were tons of Americans and between 800 and 1000 from the rest of the world. People were there from many countries. The subjects discussed in meetings included: employment, agriculture, environment, salaries, problems of the third world, the participation of the churches. 2. There was impressive organization by the Americans. The organization was greatly aided by the internet and specifically e-mail. Each day there was a list of different programs. For five or six days there were debates on different subjects. It was impossible to participate in all of them. I stuck to discussions of agriculture and had no time for anything else. 3. The mobilization of the young Americans. We did not expect to see this degree of participation at all. I was astonished to see how strongly the different topics of concern were supported by these young people. We were familiar with many of the organizations represented, but were surprised by how well the ones we did not know of were also organized. For example, we were impressed by the radical discourse of Public Citizen, Ralph Nader's group. We were also gratified by the fact that the unions present did not take a protectionist position. They were for improved working conditions for workers in other countries. The

steel workers and the environmentalists were in general agreement on issues and that surprised us as well. For example there was a strong sense of unity expressed by everyone concerning the protection of salmon in the bay of Seattle. The steel workers union members sank a steel bar into the ocean—later removed to avoid pollution—symbolic of their support for the conservationists' concern for the fsh. There were Indians represented as well. The non-violence of it all was astonishing. In total we were about 80,000 people and those few who broke windows in stores downtown were a tiny minority, perhaps no more than fifteen or so. Not even one projectile was thrown against the police. In France things would not have turned out this way. People were glued in place for up to twelve hours in confrontation with the police. In France this would have resulted in some kind of violence. It was truly impressive.

The young people present came from all over the country. Some universities gave money for the trips and some of the groups were in the city for months. A large number of volunteers were there to organize the events. There was large attendance at each of the debates, showing that participants were not only there to take part in the demonstrations. There were big halls with up to 1600 seats available. Each day the places were full. People had to sign up for these sessions and even pay for tickets! This would have been impossible in France. The churches in the city were organized and used as centers for meetings or press briefings. This surprised the media and all the people from the outside. It was amazing! There were meetings three or four days before the WTO session began.

On differences between the Larzac and the *Confédération*

The differences are clear. They are, *a priori*, two different entities, but these are strongly united by the former actions of the Larzac militants. In my opinion, there is no problem between the *Confédération* and the veterans of the struggle, but, on the national level, the Larzac raises eyebrows among union members who feel that, here, the plateau is put before everything else. It is similar to the strains between the Larzac and the Millau committee that emerged during the struggle and still exist. In the relation to the committees we see the same feelings now that existed twenty years ago. It's simpler to say that any action here *is* a Larzac action, but nationally Larzac farmers are a minority within the *Confédération*.

[We ask: What are the current projects of the *Confédération* in which you are involved?]

There are ties with other countries. For example, I was in Brazil in 1988, to participate in a session on agricultural reform. I represented the *Confédération* at that meeting but my trip was paid for by the Larzac Foundation. The *Confédération* has established relations with 18 unions around Europe as well as the international organization, *Via Campasina*, the seat of which was recently moved from Central America to Asia. We have associates in Africa, South and Central America, Asia, and Russia. We have been working on common positions between the North [the rich nations] and the South [the poor nations]. This is the first time that farmers from around the world have been organized to fight for the same program.

In the years to come my role will be primarily in international relations. We also hope to create a Polynesian farmer's union and a Kanak branch as well. I will be going to New Caledonia, after my trip to Tahiti for the appeal this coming spring. Formerly there were no peasants among the Kanaks, but recently some of them have become involved in agriculture. We also hope to discuss land management with them and see if the SCTL model developed here might be useful there, particularly between the clans and individual producers. The SCTL is involved in all of this as well as the *Confédération*. The *Confédération* is now the majority union in Guyanne and La Réunion [two overseas territories of France] and are equal in numbers with the FDSEA in Guadaloupe and Martinique.

I may make a trip to the U.S. for the Farm-Family Coalition later in the year as well. *Larzac Solidarité* has been given a new stimulus and a new set of statutes and is going to extend its reach. This will be helpful in supporting our work outside of France.

Windmills

For me, it was a good project. It started here [in Montredon] by accident when the entrepreneur involved came to the village. None of us knew him before. There were reunions at Le Cun to explain the project. In the fall the army informed us that they would not accept the project in Montredon because of its proximity to the base. That led to a modification of the plan which caused a polemic between us and the people living on the west of the plateau. The opposition grew because of the blunders of the person presenting the project. He proposed a large number of windmills but did not explain how they would be distributed around the plateau. The Minister of the Environment also played a negative role. Nothing was explained clearly and all kinds of false information circulated. There was also a dispute inside the Green Party. Local opponents had different ideas about why they were against the project. Some felt that they had lost the battle against the autoroute but that perhaps they could win on this issue. There were environmental objections. There was an attempt to reach a consensus, but the vote was falsified by the way the ballot was organized. Some saw the ballot as a means to discussion, but others took it as definitive. Even if the idea was a good one it *was* poorly presented. There was a very difficult GFA meeting on this issue. GFA shareholders and others from outside the Larzac did not understand how the people here could be against wind power. I feel the Jasse could have become a window to demonstrate the usefulness of alternative energy methods. What's left now is a small project to install a few windmills on private land.

McDonald's

The term '*saccage*' came from *Midi Libre*. Everyone, including the police, knew exactly what our plans were. On the fifth of August, well before the demonstration, I announced at the Ministry of Agriculture what our plans were. The press was also informed about the proposed action. Before the demonstration I met with the *Renseignements Généraux* [a State agency that keeps track of political as well as potentially unlawful activities] two or three times. They informed me that they would ask the director of McDonald's for something symbolic that we could 'break' in front of the media. We informed them that we were going to 'dismantle' the building then a under construction. The RG agreed to inform McDonald's and suggest that the latter remove all the tools from the site and, to avoid any confrontation, be sure no construction workers would be present. Two days before the demonstration I had a press conference to discuss our plans. On their side the government decided not to call the *gendarmes* and, in fact, there were only a few uniformed police there when the action finally took place. There were some people with cameras who filmed the demonstration. We did exactly what we said we would do. It was like the Boston Tea Party. The term '*saccage*' was used by *Midi Libre* and was taken up by Agence France Press. People in the U.S. told us that they thought that our tractors had leveled McDonald's because of what they had read in the media. There were some youngsters present who did some slight damage— they broke some floor tiles, for example. Afterwards I met with a worker who had come to repair the walls. He told me it had taken him seven hours to get to Millau from the west of France and only two hours to do all the necessary work. McDonald's did not press civil charges and there was never an expert evaluation of the damages [the implication being that an honest evaluation would have been too low]. McDonald's paid for the repairs since the building belongs to the company and not to the franchise holder.

[We ask: After having participated in the Larzac struggle do you have the impression that you learned something? Have your militant actions been affected by your past participation in the Larzac movement?]

It's evident that the struggle was the foundation of the way I now act. I was always a militant. Before the Larzac Alice and I belonged to nonviolent groups. The Larzac inscribed our actions in a specific geographic space and in the context of a mass movement. The struggle required actions that we would never have been able to carry out elsewhere since the Larzac gave us our legitimacy. Attacking the military camp and destroying official papers was an extreme action. You can't compare the demonstration at McDonald's to that. The Larzac struggle allowed us to construct an active nonviolence and to blend it into social action, something that did not exist in France at the time, although it did in the U.S.

[We ask: Were you marked by your interaction with other militants such as Guy Tarlier and the Burguière, including the father?]

No, what struck me and marked me when we arrived from the outside was the fact that the same ideas could be taken up by people from a world totally different from our own, and that we could live and act with such a diverse group. We came to realize that we could construct a new means of reflection that allowed us to leave behind our former marginal status as nonviolent militants. That is what we are now trying to do with the *Confédération*.

We come to the present out of the ten years of the Larzac struggle. During the *lutte* we were confronted by the 'realists' who were willing to sacrifice some of the land to win a partial victory, but fortunately it never came to that. I was never forced to break with those who had opinions other than my own: Guy Tarlier and the Larzac Committees, for example. Even though we disagreed frequently, in the end we all fought the struggle together and won. Our differences did not have a negative effect because the victory belonged to all of us. No one could say: "It is my victory and not yours." That is the very important and unique thing about the Larzac struggle. The people of the plateau were united behind the militant actions taken during those ten years. Of course, we were united because we all agreed that our actions were just.

CONCLUSION

The Larzac struggle began in 1971 and ended in 1981. In the many years since the victory, the Larzac community has proved its staying power as a small but highly imaginative and influential population of activists. Clearly, the ideology of nonviolence has shown its worth as the plateau's central dogma and binding force. It is both an effective means of protest against perceived injustice and a guide to resolving internal conflict. But the Larzac has succeeded also socially and politically where so many other social movements have failed in France because it never ignored the need for a sustainable economic base. Milk production for Roquefort is no longer the exclusive way of making a living on the plateau. Farmers have found a range of alternative means for supporting themselves, primarily through the development of high quality agriculture products, the increased value of which goes to them rather than through external commercial outlets. Many of those who raise sheep or goats make their own cheese which is sold directly to consumers in local and regional markets. Some are members of the new cheese producing cooperative. Still others sell meat from small, carefully raised herds or flocks of cattle, pigs, and sheep. Their high quality lamb, mutton, beef, and pork (as well as pork products such as farm made sausage) are sold cooperatively through the GIE which also sells locally made honey. To supplement their incomes Larzac farmers have also developed a network of *gites* where tourists can enjoy simple, but reasonable accommodations. Some of these *gites* offer Larzac products at their tables. During the tourist season the Jasse continues to offer locally made crafts and farm products.

During the Larzac struggle the plateau's population grew with the addition of militant squatters and new settlers. While there has been some turnover in the years following the victory, all available farms are now occupied. Those recent arrivals, who took no part in the struggle, are for the most part activist members of the *Confédération Paysanne*. As we have seen, although tactical differences sometimes occur between Larzac 'veterans' and some of these new inhabitants, the veterans generally support the political goals of the new arrivals and the new arrivals in turn support the continuing goals of the veterans. If anything, a new synthesis is emerging as more of the politically active *purs porcs* join the *Confédération*. This synthesis will increase the scope of the Larzac's commitment to its original goals but will not change them very much, if at all. The emergence of José Bové, who is both a veteran of the struggle and a militant of the

Confédération Paysanne, provides the Larzac with renewed prominence on the French national scene. Bové's leadership role is at present unchallenged on the plateau. He has in a real sense taken the place that Guy Tarlier occupied before his death as the master strategist and spokesperson for the movement, but he is also a major spokesperson for the *Confédération Paysanne* which, it should not be forgotten, is a national union with growing international ties.

But equally important to the Larzac, if less obvious to the outside, is the continued functioning of APAL with its present collective leadership, as well as the persistence of multiple forms of a rich associative life on the plateau with the doctrine of nonviolence a constant concern. In spite of superficial changes, the 'tradition of the new' has truly become the new tradition of the Larzac.

APPENDIX

The original "103" in 1991

Retired 42
Still active 38
Died 18
Moved away 5
TOTAL 103

Comparison data from 1971, 1981, 1991

	1971	1981	1991
Number of farms	77	63	61
Number of ewes and lambs	13,630	11,417	13,445
Milk production per year (in hectoliters)	9,707	17,170	23,403
Production by ewe per year	71	107	174
Number of meat sheep	0	350	3,245
Cultivated land (in hectares)	4,246	3,170	3,858
People engaged in agriculture	108	110	119
People engaged in non-agriculture	5	14	46

Number of GAECs

In 1971 there were only three GAECs on the Larzac. By 1991 there were nineteen, covering half the farmable land of the former extension area.

Source: *GLL*, July–August 1991

207

BIBLIOGRAPHY

Adams, R.N. and R.D. Fogelson
1977   The Anthropology of Power. New York: Academic Press.
Albert, C., M. Berlan, J. Caniou and M. Perrot
1989   Celles de la Terre: Agricultrice: l'invention politique d'un métier. Paris: Editions de L'Ecole des Hautes Etudes en Sciences Sociales.
Alphandéry, P., P. Bitoun and Y. Dupont
1989   Les Champs du Départ: Une France rurale sans paysans? Paris: Editions de la Découverte.
APAL
1980   La Blaquière. Village du Larzac. Millau: Arlypo.
1984   Maisons du Larzac. St. Georges de Luzençon: Imprimerie Causses et Cévennes.
Archetti, E. and E.S. Aass
1978   Peasant Studies, an Overview. In Perspectives in Rural Sociology. H. Newby, ed. New York: John Wiley and Sons.
Aron, R.
1989   Leçons sur l'Histoire. Paris: Editions de Fallois.
Aubert, D., Y. Léon et al.
1987   Agriculteurs en Difficulté. In Cahiers d'Economie et Sociologie Rurales 5. Paris: INRA.

Baillon, E.
1982   Larzac: Terre en marche. Millau: Arlypo.
Baillon, E. and D. Domeyne et al.
1980   Les Femmes du Larzac par Elles-mêmes. In Sorcières 20:133–150.
Bazin, G.
1986   Quelles Perspectives pour les Agricultures Montagnardes? Example du massif central et des Alpes du sud. Grignon: Station d'Economie et de Sociologie Rurales de Grignon.
Beau, G.
1974   Vie ou Mort du Larzac. Paris: Solar.
Bergmann, D. and P. Baudin
1989   Politique d'Avenir pour l'Europe Agricole. Paris: INRA/Economica.
Bloch, Marc
1966   French Rural History. Berkeley: University of California Press.
Bloch, Maurice
1975   Political Language and Oratory in Traditional Society. New York: Academic Press.
Bonnaud, A.
1991   L'Usage du Sol et les Outils de son Contrôle sur la Moitié Nord du Larzac. (Magistère Aménagement, Universités de Paris 1 et Paris VIII.) Montredon: CIR.

209

Bonnefous, P. and R. Martin
1984 Alors la Paix Viendra. Millau: Larzac Foundation.
Bouffanet, B. and E. Kuligowski
1973 Le Larzac Veut Vivre. Paris: Daniel Mauprey.
Boyer, H., P. Gardy and E. Hammel, eds.
1986 Le Larzac Revisité. In Amiras 14.
Brandes, P.D.
1971 The Rhetoric of Revolt. Englewood Cliffs: Prentice Hall.
Burmeister, H. and V. Tonnätt
1981 Il Importe Avant Tout de Lutter: Larzac. Montfermeil: Stenelec.

Chavagne, Y.
1988 Bernard Lambert: 30 ans de combat paysan. Quimperle: Les Editions La Gigitale.
Clifford, J.
1983 On Ethnographic Authority. In Representations 1:118–146.
1988 The Predicament of Culture. Cambridge: Harvard University Press.
Clifford, J. and G.E. Marcus
1986 Writing Culture: The Poetics and Politics of Ethnography. Berkeley: University of California Press.
Cohen, A.
1969 Political Anthropology: The Analysis of Symbolism of Power Relations. In Man (N.S.) 4:215–235.
1974 Two Dimensional Man. Berkeley: University of California Press.
1979 Political Symbolism. In Annual Review of Anthropology. Stanford: Stanford University Press.
1980 Drama and Politics in the Development of a London Carnival. In Man (N.S.) 15:65–87.
Colombel, D., ed.
1977 Résistance du Larzac. In Temps Modernes 371.
Comaroff, J.
1985 Body of Power, Spirit of Resistance: The Culture and History of a South African People. Chicago: University of Chicago Press.
Comité Larzac Paris
1981 Dix Ans de Dessins. Paris: Comité Larzac Paris.
1981 Rencontres Internationales pour La Paix, Larzac 17–23, August 1981. Recueil des débats. Paris: Comité Larzac Paris.
Crapanzano, V.
1977 The Writing of Ethnography. In Dialectical Anthropology 2:69–73.
Crisenoy, C. de
1988 La Politique Foncière des Années Quatre-vingt. In Economie et Sociologie Rurales. Paris: INRA.
Crisenoy, C. de and D. Boscheron
1982 Les Enjeux de la Politique Foncière. In Communications Présentées au Colloque National de l'Association des Ruralistes Français. Tours: INRA.

1986 Un Office Foncier en France: La société civile des terres du Larzac. Paris: INRA.

Danto, A.
1985 Narration and Knowledge. New York: Columbia University Press.
Deere, C.D. and A. de Jjanvry
1979 A Conceptual Framework for the Empirical Analysis of Peasants. *In* American Journal of Agricultural Economics 61:601–611.
Delannoi, G.
1990 Les Années Utopiques: 1968–1978. Paris: Editions la Découverte.
Dévelotte, C.
1979 Evolution du Contrôle Socio-Economique d'un Espace Rural: Le causse du Larzac. Montpellier: INRA.
Donegani, J.M. and G. Lescanne
1986 Catholicismes de France. Paris: Desclée, Bayard Presse.
Dwyer, K.
1977 The Dialogic of Anthropology. *In* Dialectical Anthropology 2:143–151.

Ellis, J.M.
1989 Against Deconstruction. Princeton: Princeton University Press.
Ennew, J., P. Hirst and K. Tribe
1977 Peasantry as an Economic Category. *In* Journal of Peasant Studies 4:295–322.

Fabian, J.
1983 Time and the Other: How Anthropology Makes its Object. New York: Columbia University Press.
Fédération Interdépartementale des Sentiers de Pays
1984 Tour Pédestre du Causse du Larzac. St. Affrique: F.I.S.P.
Feral, F. and D. Jourdan
1979 Modification et Réutilisation d'un Espace: L'extension du camp militaire du Larzac. Montpellier: M.S.
Fottorino, E.
1989 La France en Friche. Paris: Lieu Commun.
Frémion, Y.
1980 La Planète Larzac. Toulouse: Ponte Mirone.

Geertz, C.
1988 Works and Lives. The Anthropologist as Author. Stanford: Stanford University Press.
GLL
n.d. Dossier Etabli à l'Occasion de la Signature des Arrêtés de Cessibilité sur les Communes de La Roque Ste. Marguérite et La Cavalerie. *In* Dossier N.1 de *GLL*.
n.d. Une Spéculation Foncière à Caractère Politique est à l'Origine de la Décision d'Extension du Camp. Ses justifications sont fallacieuses. *In* Dossier N.2 de *GLL*.
1978 Marche sur Paris: 710 Km. *In* Dossier N.3 de *GLL*.

Guérin, G. and M. Vantses
1979 Paysannes: Paroles des Femmes du Larzac. Paris: Editions Albatros.

Hardy, Y. and E. Gabey
1974 Dossier L . . . Comme Larzac. Paris: Alain Moreau.
Hobsbawm, E.J. and T. Ranger
1983 The Invention of Tradition. Cambridge: Cambridge University Press.
Holohan, W.
1975 Jacquerie sur la Forteresse, Le Movement Paysan du Larzac (Oct. 1970–Août 1973). *In* Communautés du Sud. D. Fabre and J. Lacroix, eds. Paris: Union Générale d'Editions.

INRA
1988 Quotas Laitiers. *In* Cahiers d'Economie et Sociologie Rurales 7.

Jegouzo, G.
1984 Petite Paysannerie en France. Paris: INRA.

Lachaud, J.
1987 Les Institutions Agricoles. Paris: MA Editions.
Larzac Universités
1981 Montredon, Les Homps, St. Sauveur: Larzac Nord-Est. Millau: Larzac Universités.
Laur, F.
1929 Le Plateau du Larzac. Montpellier: Imprimerie de la Charité.
Le Bris, M.
1975 Les Fous du Larzac. Paris: Les Presses d'Aujourd'hui.
Lurie, A.
1989 A Dictionary for Deconstructors. *In* New York Review of Books 27:49–51.

Malcom, J.
1990 The Morality of Journalism. *In* New York Review of Books 37: 19–23.
Marcus, G.E.
1980 Rhetoric and the Ethnographic Genre in Anthropological Research. *In* Current Anthropology 21:507–510.
Marcus, G.E. and M.J. Fischer
1986 Anthropology as Cultural Critique. Chicago: University of Chicago Press.
Martin, D.
1987 Le Larzac: Utopies et realités. Paris: L'Harmattan.
Merquior, J.G.
1979 The Veil and the Mask. London: Routledge and Kegan Paul.
Mintz, S.
1973 A Note on the Definition of Peasants. *In* Journal of Peasant Studies 2:91–106.

Parkin, D.
  1984 Political Language. *In* Annual Review of Anthropology. Stanford: Stanford University Press.
Patre
  1986 Production Laitière Ovine. *In* Patre (special edition) 339.
Pilleboue *et al.*
  1972 Une Renaissance Rurale Menacée. *In* Revue de Géographie des Pyrénées et du Sud-Ouest 4:453–467.
Polier, N. and W. Roseberry
  1989 Tristes Tropes: Post-Modern Anthropologists Encounter the Other and Discover Themselves. *In* Economy and Society 18:245–264.
Popper, K.
  1957 The Poverty of Historicism. Boston: Beacon Press.

Rabinow, P.
  1977 Reflections on Fieldwork in Morocco. Berkeley: University of California Press.
  1986 Representations are Social Facts: Modernity and Post-Modernity In Anthropology. *In* Writing Culture. J. Clifford and G.E. Marcus, eds. Berkeley: University of California Press.
Rawlinson, R.
  1983 Larzac — A Victory for Nonviolence. *In* Nonviolence in Action Series. London: Quaker Peace and Service.
Rogers, S.C.
  1987 Good to Think: The Peasant in Contemporary France. *In* Anthropological Quarterly 60:56–63.
Roseberry, W.
  1983 From Peasant Studies to Proletarianization. *In* Studies in Comparative Development 18:69–89.
Rosenberg, H.
  1961 The Tradition of the New. New York: Grove Press.
Roth, P.A.
  1989 Ethnography Without Tears. *In* Current Anthropology 30:555–569.

Sahlins, M.
  1985 Islands of History. Chicago: University of Chicago Press.
Said, E.
  1983 Opponents, Audiences, Constituencies, and Community. *In* The Politics of Interpretation. W.J.T. Mitchell, ed. Chicago: University of Chicago Press.
Shanin, T.
  1980 The Conceptual Reappearance of Peasantry in Anglo-Saxon Social Science. *In* Soviet and Western Authors. E. Gellner, ed. London: Duckworth.

1983 Defining Peasants: Conceptualizations and Deconceptualizations: Old and New in a Marxist Debate. *In* Sociological Review 30:407–432.

1987 Peasantry as Concept. *Introduction to* Peasants and Peasant Society. T. Shanin, ed. London: Basil Blackwell.

Silverman, S.
1979 The Peasant Concept in Anthropology. *In* Journal of Peasant Studies 1:49–69.

Spiro, M.
1986 Cultural Relativism and the Future of Anthropology. *In* Cultural Anthropology 1:259–286.

Tedlock, D.
1979 The Analogical Tradition and the Emergence of a Dialogical Tradition. *In* Journal of Anthropological Research 35:387–400.

Tilly, C.
1986 The Contentious French. Cambridge: The Belknap Press of Harvard University Press.

Tirel, J.C.
1987 Intensification Hier? Extensification Demain? Paris: INRA.

Turner, V.
1966 The Ritual Process: Structure and Anti-Structure. Ithaca: Cornell University Press.

Weber, E.
1976 Peasants into Frenchmen: Modernization of Rural France: 1870–1914. Stanford: Stanford University Press.

Wolf, E.
1955 Types of Latin American Peasantry. A Preliminary Discussion. *In* American Anthropologist 57:452–471.

1966 Peasants. Englewood Cliffs: Prentice Hall.

Wright, G.
1964 Rural Revolution in France: Peasantry in the Twentieth Century. Stanford: Stanford University Press.

INDEX